San Francisco Museum of Art

Pioneer Museum and
Haggin Galleries

Oakland Art Museum

E. B. Crocker Art Gallery

Portland Art Museum

Charles and Emma Frye
Art Museum

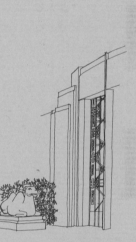

Seattle Art Museum

Vancou

Art Gallery of Greater Victoria

Phoenix Art Museum

Honolulu Academy of Arts

I thought and thought
of what you'd like best
And finally decided on—
Art in the West!

I hope you'll enjoy it—
It looked so like you.
Merry Christmas dear Rie,
As always, Love, Sue.

Merry Christmas 1966—

Susan

ART TREASURES in the WEST

A Sunset Book

ART TREASURES

by WILLIAM DAVENPORT and the Sunset Editors

in the WEST

Supervising Editor: Jack McDowell

Book Design and Layout: William Gibson
Architectural Renderings: Jim M'Guinness

Regional Art Consultants

SOUTHERN CALIFORNIA: Robert Wark, Henry E. Huntington Art Gallery
Henry J. Seldis, Art Editor, *Los Angeles Times*
NORTHERN CALIFORNIA: Thomas C. Howe, California Palace of the Legion of Honor
PACIFIC NORTHWEST: Richard E. Fuller, Seattle Art Museum
INTER-MOUNTAIN STATES: F. M. Hinkhouse, Phoenix Art Museum
HAWAII: Robert P. Griffing, Jr., Honolulu Academy of Arts

LANE MAGAZINE & BOOK COMPANY · MENLO PARK, CALIFORNIA

MUSEUM DIRECTORS AND CURATORS

We wish to acknowledge the fine cooperation and assistance received from the museums, art centers, and galleries throughout the Far West, at every step of development of this book. With infinite patience, directors and curators provided information, advice, and illustrative material, supervised the choice of works of art, checked proof on their specific museums, and replied to numerous questionnaires. Though their suggestions were the prime guidance in determining what works of art were the greatest treasures, neither they nor any of the special consultants are responsible for any errors that may have crept into this book.

SOUTHERN CALIFORNIA

RALPH ALTMAN, Director, Museum and Laboratories of Ethnic Arts and Technology, University of California at Los Angeles

WALTER AMES, President, Putnam Foundation (Timken Gallery), San Diego

WARREN BEACH, Director, Fine Arts Gallery of San Diego, San Diego

DONALD J. BREWER, Director, La Jolla Museum of Art, La Jolla

BRUCE BRYAN, Assistant Director, Southwest Museum, Los Angeles

NICOLAI CIKOVSKY, JR., Chairman of the Art Department, Pomona College Gallery, Pomona College, Claremont

KENNETH DONAHUE, Director, Los Angeles County Museum of Art, Los Angeles

BURTON B. FREDERICKSEN, Curator, J. Paul Getty Museum of Art, Malibu

Contents

Special Supplement

FINE ART in the FAR WEST

Old as prehistory, new as tomorrow's preview, art in the Western United States begins with scratches on a wall, as in the Fire Valley caves of Nevada or the Indian Picture Labyrinth of California's Chidalgo Canyon, and continues with later manifestations in the avant-garde galleries of Los Angeles' La Cienega Boulevard.

Almost as old as the impulse to create art is the instinct to prize and collect it. The golden ages of civilization are those epochs which have produced great art and treasured it, and a nation's culture is usually equated with the extent of its involvement with the fine arts. America's involvement has become very great. A *Fortune Magazine* survey estimates that Americans are spending as much as five billion dollars a year on the arts, more than they spend on spectator sports. A maturing nation, blessed with the greatest quantity of material riches in history, is concerning itself with the quality of existence. Sociologists speak of a cultural explosion. The pursuit of happiness has become the pursuit of art.

The most spectacular detonations in the art boom have taken place in the Western United States, as though bearing out the prophecy of William Butler Yeats: "Here of all places in America I seem to hear the coming footsteps of the muses." New art museums and new wings to old museums have been built or are abuilding in Los Angeles, San Francisco, Oakland, Phoenix, Pasadena, Sacramento, San Diego, Honolulu, Seattle, and Victoria, British Columbia. Attendance is soaring. The new Los Angeles County Museum of Art

counted two million visitors in the first eighteen months of its existence and is now a major tourist attraction of Southern California. Three thousand people a day flocked to the great Matisse show that opened the new Dickson Art Center at the University of California at Los Angeles in the spring of 1966. At the same time in San Francisco a hundred specially trained docents were guiding record crowds through the new wing of the M. H. De Young Memorial Museum and its huge Brundage Collection of Asian Art.

Fine art in the West ...a rich blend of several cultures

The intensity of art activity in the West may have something to do with an effort to catch up with an older tradition east of the Mississippi. Indigenously speaking, however, the West has always been far richer in art than the Eastern seaboard. Something about the equable climate must have been more conducive to creative expression here than the bitter extremes of eastern weather. In any event the Pueblo Indians have left us art and architecture far in advance of anything accomplished by those tribes that migrated farther east. The Hopi village of Orabai, Arizona, dating from A.D. 1200, oldest continuously inhabited community in the United States, still inspires Richard Neutra and other modern architects with its concept of enlightened city planning.

Nothing in the native art of the East can match the intrinsic beauty of the Zuni and Hopi pottery, of Navajo weaving and sand paintings with their inspired abstract designs, the envy of many a contemporary artist. Nor are these arts dead. The spark of Southwest Indian vitality has never been snuffed out. The embers have been rekindled today and with impressive results, as you will see at the Museum of Northern Arizona in Flagstaff, and in Phoenix at the Heard Museum and in Read Mullen's Gallery of Western Art.

As for the indigenous art of the Pacific Northwest, explorers from the East could not believe their eyes when they saw it. The great cedar houses, the boldly carved and painted totem poles were so unlike anything in their experience that they could not believe "mere Indians" had done them. The evidence is still there, however, awaiting you in Portland, Seattle, Vancouver, and Victoria where you may ponder another of art's mysteries: the affinity between the stunning ceremonial masks of the Haida and Tlingit Indians with those of the Japanese Noh plays. This serves as a reminder that the first settlers

ART MUSEUMS ARE LIVELY CENTERS of activity for anyone who visits them, and the museums in the West are a rich repository for world-famous paintings and sculpture. At the Henry E. Huntington Art Museum, San Marino, California.

CULTURAL AMBASSADOR FROM HOLLAND is what J. Paul Getty calls the splendid Rembrandt portrait of merchant Maarten Looten, *which he bought in 1938, gave to Los Angeles County Museum of Art. Painted in 1632, picture was Rembrandt's first commission in Amsterdam.*

who entered the New World twenty thousand years ago came from Asia, bringing the seeds of Oriental sensibility to the West.

European art came to the West with the Spanish padres. They brought not the spare limnings of puritan New England but the full-blown opulence of the Spanish baroque. The sculpture in stone and gilded wood will delight you at the California and Arizona missions. So will the 18th-century paintings. At the Mission San Gabriel Arcángel, for example, you will see a portrait of the Virgin that so impressed a mob of hostile Indians that they threw down their bows and arrows and brought gifts to the Queen of Heaven.

The opening of the Golden West, the Gold Rush, the mineral wealth of Arizona, Nevada, Idaho, the furs and timber of the Northwest, the transcontinental railroad produced huge fortunes. Great collectors appeared on the Western scene: Huntingtons and Crockers, Stanfords and Spreckels, Hills and Hearsts. Off they went on grand art tours of Europe, returning with enough art to start a dozen museums. Mrs. Phoebe Hearst financed the Reisner Expedition to Egypt for the University of California with the result that more than 17,000 examples of Egyptian art may now be seen in Berkeley. Acting anonymously, Mrs. Leland Stanford outbid the Boston Museum of Fine Arts for the Cesnola Collection of Cypriot sculpture which you will see today in the Stanford Museum. At San Marino, with the help of Sir Joseph Duveen, Henry Huntington established a collection of British art which the English cross an ocean and a continent to visit. The Fullers in Washington, the Cookes in Hawaii turned westward to the exotic East and brought back with them the Chinese and Japanese treasures that await you in Honolulu and Seattle.

The Donald Harringtons collected impressionist paintings in Phoenix. In Santa Barbara, Wright Ludington formed a collection of classical sculpture that became the nucleus for the Santa Barbara Museum of Art. The Spreckels family gave San Francisco a collection of French art and built the Palace of the Legion of Honor in which to house it. Farther south, huge grants of money and paintings by Earle Grant, James Copley, the Appleton Bridges, and the Putnam Sisters provided San Diego with its splendid Fine Arts Gallery. The

Our art heritage speaks out with many familiar voices

time-honored tradition of getting and giving art continues in the West with such headline-making collectors as Norton Simon and J. Paul Getty.

As the treasures accumulate and are bequeathed to the public, enthusiasm for the arts grows. With it come new bases for comparison and a corresponding improvement in public taste. To guide that taste Western museum directors are currently separating the wheat from the chaff and consigning art of doubtful quality and provenance to the basement. Children's art classes and full-fledged art schools are flourishing in our major museums from Honolulu to Houston, and a whole new generation of artists and gallery goers is being formed with fine examples of world art before their eyes, from the classical antiquities of Assyria and Egypt to the tangled barbs of our own times.

Schools and industry continue to enrich our art treasures

Universities and colleges of the West have played a signal role, not only in training artists and art historians, but in bringing the best of art to the attention of an ever widening public. From the University of Arizona's important modern collection to the University of British Columbia's Northwest Indian Art, the exhibits are as varied as the scenery from Tucson to Vancouver. College art departments have collected not only art but artists. Professor Alfred Neumeyer, for example, built up a superb print collection at Mills College and brought in some of the leading artists of our times as teachers, among them Lyonel Feininger, Fernand Léger, Max Beckmann, and Laszlo Moholy-Nagy. The inspired flame of the Bauhaus was rekindled in California.

The University of California rescued Hans Hofmann from Nazi Germany and brought this influential artist and teacher to Berkeley, where he began his American career. Diego Rivera was commissioned to paint murals at the San Francisco Art Institute and Stock Exchange Club. These works survive while more controversial ones in New York's Rockefeller Center have been destroyed. Orozco and Rico Lebrun did frescoes at Pomona College. Meanwhile, up in the Northwest, Amédée Ozenfant and Alexander Archipenko were teaching at the University of Washington, while the University of Hawaii imported Jean Charlot as a member of its art faculty, and, as visiting professors, such lights as Josef Albers, the venerable father of op art, and Max Ernst, greatest of the surrealist painters.

More recently, Western industrial firms, like the Renaissance banking families of Florence, have taken to buying and commissioning art to enhance their corporate image. At a recent exhibition, *American Business and the Arts*, the San Francisco Museum of Art showed 86 works loaned for the occasion by 71 corporations. Not to be outdone, the local chapter of the International Longshoremen's and Warehousemen's Union rescued Beniamino Bufano's beleaguered statue of Saint Francis and paid to have it properly installed in San Francisco. In Honolulu these art-minded longshoremen commissioned a two-story mural by a well-known Mexican artist with the revolutionary name of Pablo O'Higgins. Meanwhile, Los Angeles actor-collector Vincent Price was stocking the warehouses of Sears Roebuck with works by Picasso, Chagall, Braque, and Andrew Wyeth, and F. W. Woolworth went into the art business with the announced intention of making it possible for nearly everyone to become an art collector.

Libraries, banks, and other public institutions follow suit; their lobbies are sometimes indistinguishable from art galleries. Public participation is the keynote of the culture boom. Says F. M. Hinkhouse, of the perennially new Phoenix Art Museum: "Rich and diverse collections used to be reserved for the pleasure of kings and the nobility. Now they are available to everyone. The Phoenix Museum is the public's domain." In neighboring Utah, where people in remote communities now receive pictures by the nation's first art airlift, these sentiments are echoed in the slogan of the Salt Lake Art Center: Art is for you, not just the few.

In the West, art is everywhere being brought to the people

Catering to this aroused public interest, Western art museums are a far cry from the dusty tombs that once they were. They have become community centers, throbbing with activity, with brilliant international exhibitions, with group and one-man shows, art classes, lectures, movies, concerts, dance recitals, discussion groups, craft demonstrations, receptions, and parties. Almost all of them have book and gift shops where you can buy reproductions of your favorite paintings. Many of them have art rental galleries where you may rent an original painting or sculpture for a nominal fee and have the pleasure of living with it in your own home. If it wears well and you want to keep it, the rental fees apply to the purchase price; it's like installment buying without an interest charge. The museum volunteers its services, the money goes directly to the artist. A happy arrangement for all, art rental is becoming increasingly popular. The Crocker Art Gallery in Sacramento, for example, rents 2800 paintings a month. The Los Angeles County Museum of Art offers its members the works of 80 artists from Clinton Adams to Jack Zajac with rental fees as low as five dollars a month.

Art museums are fast becoming exciting and active art centers

Such service exemplifies that sense of responsibility which all Western museums feel to the public today. And excitement runs high in the West as contemporary exhibits are staged by the major museums in each state. From Vancouver to Yuma, the public art galleries are engaged in a perpetual hunt for local talent. Annual jury shows keep the public informed on the best work currently being produced by the painters and sculptors of the West. The living artist has seldom had a wider audience.

Regional art blooms in this favorable climate, and often attains international importance. It was a group of San Francisco painters, showing at the Oakland Art Museum and the San Francisco Museum of Art, who first revolted against the academic tyranny of abstract expressionism, even when they themselves had enjoyed success in that stimulating and emancipating idiom. In spite of disapproval in certain quarters, they continued their visual explorations and created a vigorous new figurative school.

With the development of this San Francisco school, the establishment of a second national art capital in Los Angeles, and the persistence of strong regional styles in Arizona, the Northwest, and Hawaii, it is now apparent that a significant decentralization has taken place and that important art activity in America is no longer confined to the left bank of the Hudson River.

The art museums of the West have played a vital role in bringing this about. They continue to play that role with increasing public support. More and more people are joining their local museums as members, enjoying the excitement of an active part in the art boom. The great thing about the new Los Angeles County Museum of Art,

MASTERY OF BRUSHWORK AND COLOR shows in every inch of Mother and Child by French Impressionist Auguste Renoir. His object was to find tints that would make flesh live and vibrate. Models were Coco, the artist's son, and the boy's nurse, Gabrielle. (California Palace of the Legion of Honor.)

said its former director Richard Brown, is that it is supported by more than a handful of great fortunes. "There are more than 30,000 dues-paying members—school children, dentists, bankers, bakers, bus drivers, carpenters; the whole city helped to buy what you see in the museum."

Art remains one of the most rewarding of public spectacles

The whole city—and it is not only the city of Los Angeles either. Not since the Renaissance rivalries of Italian city states has art been such a matter of civic pride. The laying of a museum cornerstone in Los Angeles sparks an affirmative vote on a lively bond issue to add a new wing to a major museum in San Francisco. Not to be outdone—and to liven even more the cultural atmosphere—the citizens of Oakland approve an even larger issue for a huge, new museum complex.

This healthy rivalry does not prevent the Western museums from pooling their resources in cooperative shows. A case in point is The Artist's Environment: West Coast, an exhibition presented in 1963 by the UCLA Galleries and Oakland Art Museum in collaboration with the Amon Carter Museum of Fort Worth, Texas, a show that underlined the vigor, originality, and variety of new Western art.

Aware of the cultural coming of age that all this implies, the editors of *Sunset* Books have felt the need of a pictorial album that would call the reader's attention to outstanding works of art in the public collections of the Western United States. We also wanted to provide visitors with an informal guide to Western art museums. Unless otherwise noted, all are open to the public free of charge. Art remains not only one of the most rewarding of public spectacles, but one of the least expensive.

Hundreds of treasures have been chosen from hundreds of thousands of paintings and sculptures produced by almost every race and nation in the world, and the choice has ranged over thousands of years in the history of art. It is hoped that this selection, which was made with the expert advice of Western museum directors, curators, and art professors, will lead you to visit the museums to see the original works of art that are reproduced in these pages as well as the other treasures that make up the rich heritage of fine art in the West. It is also hoped that the book will stimulate you to choose some favorites of your own. For in the last analysis, whether an art museum is treasure house or tomb depends on you.

ART TREASURES
in the
WEST

Southern California

Northern California

Pacific Northwest

Inter-Mountain States

Hawaii

Southern California

THE OFFERINGS ARE ENCYCLOPEDIC

Time was when art in Southern California had to fight for wall space among the mammals and fossils of the Los Angeles County Museum. Today it has not only a many-pavilioned temple of its own on glamorous Wilshire Boulevard, but more than 90 other public and commercial shrines from San Diego to Santa Barbara.

Since most of these galleries stage at least one new show a month, you can choose from more than a thousand exhibitions a year without leaving Southern California. The offerings are encyclopedic, covering every aspect of art from primitive pictographs to soup cans and plastic hamburgers. In between are the glories that were Greece and Rome, the marvels of Asia, the plastic pieties of the Middle Ages, the splendors of the Renaissance, the luxury of the Sun King's court, the stately elegance—and Tom Jones vulgarity—of 18th-century England, the bright-shining radiance of impressionism, the subconscious fantasies of surrealism, the subjective effusions of abstract expressionism, and much other evidence of the creative aspiration of the human race.

If that aspiration is currently enjoying one of its most untrammeled moments in Southern California, it was not always thus. Fifty years ago an academic pall stretched from ocean to desert. The old masters,

MOST FAMOUS PICTURE IN THE FAR WEST.
The Blue Boy, *painted by Thomas Gainsborough about 1770, reflects in its pose and colors the artist's admiration for Flanders' Van Dyck. The model was Jonathan Buttall, a friend of the painter.*
(Henry E. Huntington Art Gallery.)

21

many of them imitations sold by crooked dealers to naive collectors, were painstakingly copied. The laws of perspective laid down in the Renaissance were still in force. As for imitating nature, that was permitted, but the art symbols of the Southwest were eucalyptus trees and the purple sage. As in the development of California itself, pioneers were needed.

In 1923, a group calling themselves The Independent Artists of Los Angeles rushed in to fill the vacuum. Their leader was a man named Stanton Macdonald-Wright, who, in his own words, had fled to California from the proving ground of Paris.

NEW ERA IN SOUTHERN CALIFORNIA

Even cubism was too representational for Wright. In the 1923 Los Angeles exhibition he showed an abstract painting and accompanied it with a manifesto in the catalog. It was a declaration of artistic independence and a plea for public tolerance:

"The puerile repetition of the surface aspects of the old masters has ceased to interest intelligent men. The modern artist must strive to express his own age. He cannot be expected to project himself backward five hundred years and drag forth the corpse of an art inspired and nourished by a period environment, a greater art, if you will, but a corpse nonetheless . . . Let our final work affect you as it will, but at least let your final opinion not be the result of a preconceived antagonism."

That statement rang up the curtain on a new era in the art of Southern California, an era in which artists dared to experiment, and the public, though sometimes mystified, was apt to be more permissive than prejudiced. At that same epoch-making show, an artist named Max Reno exhibited a picture of a skeleton playing a cello with a nude woman as the bow. This pre-surrealist fantasy raised a lot of eyebrows, but even the most outraged had to admit that Reno's *Dying Vienna* was more interesting than the eucalyptus trees.

Other expatriates, other Europeans appeared in Southern California. The Danish surrealist Knud Merrild arrived, having been told that America would be the future art center of the world. His experiments included pouring and dripping paint onto a wet surface. He

"I CAN'T STAND ANOTHER ONE," *seems to be the reaction of the young lady escorting her younger sister around the annual all-city show at Barnsdall Park in Los Angeles. A prime center of activity, the show attracts painters, sculptors, viewers.*

CALIFORNIA INCENSE CEDARS *and classic sculpture flank entrances to Henry E. Huntington Library, adjacent to the Art Gallery, both at San Marino. The statue of Neptune once adorned the Hofburg Palace in Vienna.*

did it before Jackson Pollock. So did Hans Hofmann, who taught at the University of California summer session at Berkeley in 1930 and at Los Angeles' Chouinard Art Institute the following spring. In 1930 the fiery Orozco came from Mexico and painted the dynamic *Prometheus* fresco in Frary Hall at Pomona College. Thirty years later, on another wall of the same building, Rico Lebrun painted his famous *Genesis* and Howard Warshaw was at work on the walls of the University of California's new campus at Santa Barbara.

Between times experimental art had become so respectable that the United States Government, subsidizing artists during the dark days of the depression, appointed Stanton Macdonald-Wright as Southern California head of the WPA art program. His chief assistant was a pioneer of cool hard-edge abstraction, Lorser Feitelson.

These men—Macdonald-Wright is 76 as this book goes to press, Feitelson, 68—have witnessed a Southern California artistic revolution in which they played major roles.

The art museums of Southern California have also played a big part, not only in collecting and conserving of the old but also in the encouragement of the new. Modern exhibitions share the calendar

WHERE TO READ WHAT THE CRITICS WRITE

To keep up with the latest developments in the world of art, pick up a copy of *Art Calendar*, published quarterly by the Art Museum Council of the Los Angeles County Museum of Art, 5905 Wilshire Boulevard, Los Angeles 90036. Single copies, at the museum's book shop, are 50 cents; a year's subscription, $1.75 for the four issues. The calendar endeavors to list all public art exhibitions and events scheduled in museums, professional galleries, and other art institutions in Southern California.

Art exhibitions in the Southland, and especially in the Los Angeles area, are well reviewed in the *Los Angeles Times* by Henry J. Seldis. On Sundays this paper also lists the new art exhibitions of the week; there are seldom less than 25. *Artforum*, an illustrated monthly available at most newsstands, will also help to keep you abreast of the rapidly-changing art scene in this area. Its Los Angeles reviewers, nimble of leg and brain, cover hundreds of exhibitions. The battery of critics includes John Coplans, William Wilson, Nancy Marmer, Curt Oplinger, H. J. Weeks, Fidel Danieli and others. You may not agree with what they say, but they say it very well, and they'll keep you posted on the latest upheavals and goings-on in the Western art world.

with permanent collections of old masters, and the encouragement of contemporary artists is regarded as a community responsibility.

Experiments continue. Some artists' media now include electromagnets, movie projectors, electric eyes, and air compressors. Cybernetic sculptures threaten to have nervous breakdowns; and the art lover, striving to keep up with the hectic fashion changes of modern art, sometimes suffers from fatigue of the optic and aural nerves, vertigo, and sore feet. This is part of gallery-goers' syndrome. If you come down with it you have only to visit San Juan Capistrano. Here you can walk through the mission's silent, arcaded cloister, linger by the fountain of the sacred garden in the shadow of its perforated *campanario*, or stand in meditation in the Father Serra Chapel before the gilded altar whose radiance recalls the golden assurances of the past. This baroque *reredos* from Barcelona is one of the early art treasures of the West, more comforting perhaps to the human spirit than the violent expressionism of a harsher and more puzzled day.

LIKE A LATE GOTHIC NIGHTMARE, Christ Taken Captive, *by Hieronymous Bosch, is haunted by violence and brutality. (Fine Arts Gallery of San Diego.)*

San Diego and Coast North

More mementos of Spanish grandeur await you at San Diego, first of the mission towns. Here in the southwestern corner of the United States the year-round palms and sapphire skies resemble those of the Costa Brava, and you will find the Spanish note sustained in the Panama Pacific Exposition buildings of Balboa Park. Designed by Bertram Goodhue, they were built in 1915 to celebrate the opening of the Panama Canal. Although they were meant to be temporary, they were so beautiful that San Diegans have preserved this Iberian fantasy, with its Alcazar Garden and typically Spanish Plaza de Panama. On the north side of this plaza stands one of America's most attractive small museums.

CULTURAL LINK WITH SPAIN

THE FINE ARTS GALLERY OF SAN DIEGO. *Plaza de Panama, Balboa Park, San Diego. Hours 10* A.M. *to 5* P.M. *Tuesday–Saturday; 12:30 to 5* P.M. *Sunday; closed Monday. Spanish and Italian old masters; Goya's Marques de Sofraga.*

Given to the city by Mr. and Mrs. Appleton S. Bridges, the fireproof, earthquakeproof Fine Arts Gallery of San Diego was designed by local architects Templeton Johnson and Robert W. Snyder, and opened to the public in 1926. To harmonize with the Panama-Pacific style and to emphasize San Diego's cultural link with Spain, the architects chose the plateresque style of the Spanish Renaissance. The term derives from *platero*, the Spanish word for silversmith, and the ornamental style re-creates the elaborate embossing and intricate delicacy of the silversmith's art. Like Spain itself, the facade of the Fine Arts Gallery is a study in dramatic contrast. The richly decorated door and windows, with their fretwork of fruits, floral arabesques, and scallop shells, are relieved by the welcome severity of the plain ungarnished wall. The combination recalls early mission architecture.

The entrance door was inspired by the great doorway of Cervantes' alma mater, the University of Salamanca, but the sculptural relief at San Diego is more deeply incised. The arms of Spain and the seals of the United States, California, and San Diego are carved above this portal which is dominated by statues of great artists of the Spanish Renaissance: Ribera, Velasquez, Murillo, Zurbaran, El Greco.

Inside the gallery, thanks to the benefactions of three remarkable San Diego sisters, Anne, Amy, and Irene Putnam, you will find works by all these painters in the appropriate setting of an imitation Spanish palace. The Putnam sisters were among the West's most assiduous and most mysterious collectors. Daughters of a real estate and hardware tycoon, they were reared in seclusion in an Italian-style villa surrounded by a forged iron fence ten feet high. Constantly supervised, their lives recall the father-dominated fate of Elizabeth Barrett Browning. They were permitted to visit the museum only after hours and were driven there in a curtained car by a domineering chauffeur who doubled as a chaperon. For these cloistered sisters, art became almost a substitute for life. With the aid of an old family friend, Dr. Reginald Poland, who was also the director of the Fine Arts Gallery, they provided San Diego with one of the richest treasuries of old master paintings on the West Coast.

A WEALTH OF OLD MASTERS

Scholarly and energetic, Dr. Poland had a way of making national headlines with his acquisitions for the Fine Arts Gallery. In 1939, backed by the indispensable sisters, he bought Goya's portrait of *El Marques de Sofraga,* now generally acknowledged to be one of the finest male portraits by Goya in the United States. The picture had remained in the family of the Marquis for 200 years and had never been publicly exhibited. Its acquisition from the Spanish family by way of the Knoedler Gallery in New York was one of the most important old master purchases of the year.

Dr. Poland followed up this coup in 1940 by purchasing a portrait by Giovanni Bellini. Though the Fine Arts Gallery catalogs this picture as a portrait of Gentile Bellini, art expert N. S. Trivas claims that the sitter was not the painter's brother but the Venetian diplomat Paolo Morosini. This delicate problem of art scholarship will not detract from your pleasure in this brilliant and vital portrait, done nearly 500 years ago against the luminous sky of Venice.

A FAVORITE MODEL OF VELASQUEZ, The Infanta Margarita *of Spain was the
subject in a dozen of his paintings. The sparkling, brilliantly brushed likeness, which is
in the Fine Arts Gallery of San Diego, appears to be a study for a full-length
portrait in Vienna; it reflects Velasquez' joy in painting a most charming little princess.*

GRAND CANAL WITH THE RIALTO BRIDGE *is recorded by Francesco Guardi, who sold many similar views as souvenirs to tourists. The Venetian, who lived from 1712 to 1793, was a master at outdoor reporting. (Fine Arts Gallery of San Diego.)*

Heroine of the International Art Year 1941 was Velasquez' beguiling portrait of the *Infanta Margarita* of Spain, a freely brushed, sparkling likeness of the most famous little princess in art. Once again the buyer was Dr. Poland. Once again the Putnam sisters were the donors. Installed in her new home in San Diego, the Infanta gazed out also from every art publication in the world.

These spectacular Spanish acquisitions merely hint at the wealth of San Diego's collection of old masters. You'll find Giotto, Correggio, Tintoretto, Hans Memling, and Rembrandt among the treasures here, along with Titian's great portrait of *Francesco Donato*, Doge of Venice. Eventually the collection became so important that the Fine Arts

Gallery ran out of wall and storage space. That situation was remedied in 1966 with the opening of the new west wing. This provides an art reference library, a sculpture court, and exhibition space for the Asiatic, modern European, and American collections in addition to the old masters. The old building is now used for loan exhibitions.

JEWEL CASE FOR THE ARTS

TIMKEN GALLERY. *Plaza de Panama, Balboa Park, San Diego. Hours 10 A.M. to 4:30 P.M. Tuesday–Saturday; 1:30 to 4:30 P.M. Sunday; closed Monday. Superlative collection of old masters.*

Just east of the Fine Arts Gallery of San Diego is another recent addition to the Southern California art scene. This is the small (five rooms) Timken Gallery. Financed through gifts of the Timken and Putnam families, the fine building of marble and bronze has been appropriately described as a jewel case for the arts. The jewels are some twenty old masters which the Putnam Foundation recently reclaimed from the National Gallery in Washington and New York's Metropolitan Museum of Art, where they had been on loan. These have been augmented by twenty other old master paintings, gifts of the late Misses Amy and Anne Putnam, from the Fine Arts Gallery of San Diego. The Putnam sisters' remarkable collection of icons is also on view.

Air-conditioned and perfectly lighted, the Timken Gallery has been designed, like the Frick Gallery in New York, for viewing pictures in an atmosphere of quiet meditation.

"It is one of the finest small museums I have ever seen," said John Walker of the National Gallery in Washington, who was present at the opening. "The paintings, purchased by the Board of Directors of the Putnam Foundation in the '50's and '60's, are great works of art. In selecting them, quality was the touchstone of judgment. I congratulate you on the discrimination shown. You have been wise. Some cities have built large museums, and then hoped that innumerable works of art of true excellence would miraculously appear. I am afraid they won't any longer. Money is not the problem. The problem is to find pictures to buy. I can't replace those which have come to San Diego. Paintings like these are virtually unavailable at any price."

WARM HUMANISM of Italian Renaissance graces
Madonna and Child With Goldfinch, symbol of the
Passion of Christ. Sensitive drawing and dreamy
aura suggest it may be early work of Sandro Botticelli.
(Los Angeles County Museum of Art.)

LUMINOSITY, piety, human sympathy characterize
this glowing Madonna and Child by the great Flemish
master of the 15th century, Roger Van der Weyden,
a Renaissance treasure, in the Arabella Huntington
Memorial at the Huntington Gallery.

Among the priceless forty are works by Titian, Veronese, Carlo Crivelli, Tintoretto, Roger van der Weyden, Corot, Cézanne. If you've seen Rembrandt's portrait of *Maarten Looten* in Los Angeles, you may be interested in comparing that work with the Timken's *Saint Bartholomew*, a more profound work painted by Rembrandt in 1657 in the depths of personal despair and at the height of his powers. Few portraits can match its tragic grandeur and introspective nobility. You may also want to linger before another masterpiece of character delineation: Ribera's portrait of *Galileo*, which has an expression fraught with the conflicting perplexities of science and religion. No such doubt clouds the pure visual joy of Juan Sanchez Cotan's wonderful still life, *Quince, Cabbage, Melon, and Cucumber*. In this early 17th-century painting you will discover what Charles Sterling of the Louvre called the prodigious magic of Sanchez Cotan, who suspends vegetables in a dark window and makes them shine and turn.

The Putnam Foundation, according to its president, Walter Ames, will continue to acquire important paintings as funds accumulate and paintings are available. The quality of the old masters here would be a challenge to any buyer. Mr. Ames' own favorites in the collection are *Parable of the Sower* by Pieter Breughel the Elder, *Death of the Virgin* by Petrus Christus, *Portrait of a Youth Holding an Arrow* by Boltraffio, *Virgin and Child with Saints John, Elizabeth, and Justina* by Veronese, and Rembrandt's *Saint Bartholomew*.

BLENDING CONTEMPORARY AND PRIMITIVE

LA JOLLA MUSEUM OF ART. *700 Prospect Street, La Jolla. Hours 12:30 to 4:30* P.M. *Tuesday–Sunday; 7 to 10* P.M. *Wednesday; closed Monday.*

If, after the old-masterly pleasures of Balboa Park, you yearn for more modern fare, you'll find it in picturesque La Jolla at the northwest edge of town. Founded in 1941 as the Art Center in La Jolla, the La Jolla Museum of Art occupies a much-remodeled private house at 700 Prospect Street overlooking the ocean. The metamorphosis from a mission style home to a modern museum is fascinating to contemplate. So is the view from the observation lounge. It is no idle boast that the La Jolla Museum has the whole Pacific Ocean on permanent loan.

AGILITY AND VITALITY characterize the remarkable etching by Francisco Goya titled Bull Fight. *Note how the weight and force of the entire picture is concentrated at the left by placement of people, bull, man. (Fine Arts Gallery of San Diego.)*

The accent at La Jolla is on contemporary American art and primitive African sculpture. The nearest thing to an old master in this museum is Berthe Morisot, who was the first lady of Impressionism. The museum stages important exhibitions of the work of California painters and sculptors, providing a good survey of all tendencies, from Thomas Bangs' cool abstract geometry to the finely polished photographic realism of Wayne Thiebaud.

Recent shows have included the work of Marc Chagall, Henry Moore, Morris Graves. In 1965 the show, The Reminiscent Object, featured paintings by William Michael Harnett, John Frederick Peto, and John Haberle, 19th-century American painters whose preoccupation with objects presaged the pop art of the '60's. "Parallels between such work and that of the present day," wrote San Francisco critic Alfred Frankenstein, "confer a sense of historic continuity on the recent painting and reveal new, contemporary meanings in the old. To throw such bridges from past to present is one of the most important things an exhibition can accomplish."

The building of such bridges seems to be characteristic of the La Jolla Museum of Art. Concerts, film festivals, art classes, an art rental gallery, a leading artist in residence (most recently, Chicago-born George Cohen) are part of the La Jolla program. Active support by a wealthy and art-minded community is helping to achieve the director's aim to build a museum of the first rank.

PROMINENT PROFILE OF DANTE, at the Fine Arts Gallery of San Diego, is by
Ridolfo Ghirlandaio—a friend of Raphael—who painted in Florence two centuries after
Dante died. Artist was the son of Domenico Ghirlandaio, famous fresco painter.

BEFORE LEAVING LA JOLLA take a look at architect Lloyd Ruoco's Institute of Geophysics and Planetary Physics, just above the laboratory pier of the Scripps Institute of Oceanography. On the sea terrace of the prize-winning building you'll see a small garden dominated by Donal Hord's sculpture, *Spring Stirring*. Carved in black diorite in 1948, this massive cloaked figure seems to be emerging from sleep. The planes of the polished face reflect the sun of California as the wind stirs identical ripples in the surrounding grass.

THE ACTIVELY QUIET REFUGE

LONG BEACH MUSEUM OF ART. *2300 East Ocean Boulevard, Long Beach. Hours 10 A.M. to 5 P.M. Tuesday–Friday; 1 to 5 P.M. Saturday, Sunday; closed Monday.*

Also on the coast you'll find one of the youngest of the West's art museums and one of the most active. Overlooking the Pacific, the Long Beach Museum of Art occupies the former summer residence of Elizabeth Millbank Anderson. The lady built this brick and lava stone mansion in 1912 as a quiet refuge from the noise of New York. She should see it now, swarming with 28,000 house guests a year. A persistent local legend claims that Fatty Arbuckle once lived here, a contention that has been categorically denied in print by the museum staff. In any event the City of Long Beach purchased this solid seaside relic in 1950. After extensive interior remodeling, it opened as a Municipal Art Center in 1951 and became the Long Beach Museum of Art in 1957.

Its permanent collection includes contemporary paintings and graphics given to the young museum by Dr. Ludwig Uri, and a collection of African sculpture, gift of Dr. and Mrs. John Strom. The museum is building up a strong collection of the contemporary art of the West. This is augmented each year by gifts and purchases from the annual Arts of Southern California exhibitions. Number 15 in this series was devoted to California marine paintings and had a rousing success, despite the ever-present competition of the Pacific Ocean outside. These Southern California regional shows are nationally circulated and have brought the work of local artists to the attention of the public from Maine to Florida and from Pennsylvania to Hawaii.

The Long Beach Museum also sponsors a lively series of concert and film programs, an art rental service, lectures, and panel discussions.

SPRING STIRRING, a massive yet sensitive figure by San Diego's Donal Hord, basks in the sunshine high above the Pacific Ocean in garden of Scripps Institute of Oceanography at La Jolla.

Strange and interesting forms have recently risen on campus at the California State College at Long Beach, northwest of the Long Beach Museum of Art. If you approach the campus on Seventh Street you will see a series of nineteen monoliths and megaliths that may remind you of a concrete version of Stonehenge. These are the work of Dutch sculptor J. J. Beljon, who erected them here in 1965 as an *Homage to Simon Rodia*. This tribute to Rodia (whose strange towers rise in the Watts district of Los Angeles—see page 60) near the campus entrance sets the tone for further work created here in connection with the International Sculpture Symposium, sponsored by the college in 1965.

Nine sculptors of varying talents and temperaments were invited to the symposium, giving the art students of LBSC a remarkable opportunity to watch and assist the artists at work. Seventy industrial firms supplied the visiting sculptors with material. The nine were Kenjiro Azuma of Japan, J. J. Beljon of the Netherlands, André Bloc of France (famous as the creator of habitable sculpture), Kosso Eloul of Israel, Piotr Kowalski of Poland, Rita Letendre (a muralist) and Robert Murray of Canada, Gabriel Kohn and Claire Falkenstein of the United States. The results of their creative labors await you on the campus: highly individual and experimental constructions of steel pipe, fused glass, aluminum, concrete, laminated redwood, translucent polyester, stainless steel, and bronze. If some of it looks like

TWO VERSIONS OF THE LOVE GODDESS meet in the J. Paul Getty Museum at Malibu: Tintoretto's Toilette of Venus, c. 1575, and Venus With Dolphin, a Roman copy of 3rd-century B.C. Greek original, which once belonged to Cardinal Mazarin.

old radar equipment, never mind. Think of how much life and interest are brought to the campus by these punctuation marks. Try not to miss this latest link in the chain reaction of Southern California's art explosion. You can pick up a mimeographed guide, as an aid to studying the sculpture, from the art department.

GREEK MARBLES AT MALIBU

J. PAUL GETTY MUSEUM. *17985 Pacific Coast Highway, Malibu. Hours 2 to 4 P.M. Wednesday and Saturday by appointment.*

A special treat awaits you at Malibu, where J. Paul Getty has transformed his Malibu ranch house into an art museum. Visit is by guided tour with groups limited in number. You should telephone in advance to say you are coming.

As soon as you drive into the grounds you'll be glad you came. Mr. Getty's house, set among lemon and orange groves at the top of a pine and cypress-crowned hill, has an intimate charm and so does his collection, which he chose for his own pleasure over a period of twenty years. Marble lions guard the fountain-cooled entrance patio, beyond which you step into a gallery of marble sculpture that suggests the antique luxury of Hadrian's Villa. The dominant statue in the collection came from that Versailles of the ancient world, and was quite probably commissioned by the art-loving Emperor Hadrian himself. It is the famous Lansdowne *Hercules*, a Roman copy of the Greek original by Scopas. Purchased in England from the Lansdowne family for $30,000, the Hercules is a fine figure of a man, carrying a club in his left hand and a trophy in his right—the skin of the Nemean lion which he strangled with his bare hands as one of his twelve legendary labors. He is surrounded by various congenial companions: among them *Venus*, goddess of love, in a variety of poses; *Diana* with her stag and hound; and *Alexander the Great*, looking as though he had just received the disappointing news that there were no more lands to conquer. With these and other effigies Mr. Getty has re-created the classic world in microcosm high above the rolling surf at Malibu.

Does Mr. Getty, now in London, miss his marble companions? "The knowledge that countless thousands of people can see and enjoy the beauty of the things I collected over the years is ample justification for not having them with me for my own personal pleasure."

One of the beauties of the collection is Tintoretto's *Venus*, an opulent Renaissance reincarnation of the Greek goddess which you will enjoy comparing with her marble precursors.

In one room of Mr. Getty's house, ladies may be moved to kleptomania by the sight of some of the most exquisite Louis XV furniture this side of Versailles. And all will stand astonished at the unexpected sight of Louis XIV in the familiar portrait by Hyacinthe Rigaud. Preening himself like a peacock, the Sun King stands in coronation robes of satin and ermine, and wears elevator shoes, the better to show off his Bourbon legs; he looks perfectly at home in Mr. Getty's villa. But how did he get here from the sacrosanct walls of the Louvre or from his own palace at Versailles where the art world is accustomed to seeing him?

This is a third version of the Rigaud portrait, says Mr. Getty, painted for the Tuileries Palace in Paris, and removed thence by Charles X, last of the Bourbon monarchs, when he went into exile in 1830. (The other two pictures are still there in the King's palaces.) The picture was subsequently inherited by the Count of Chambord, tail end of the French Bourbon line, who died in the Austrian castle of Frohsdorf in 1883. Half a century later, on July 22, 1938, the count's heirs sent Louis XIV, or at least his portrait, to the auction block at Sotheby's in London. There His Majesty was knocked down to the highest bidder, Mr. J. Paul Getty, for a mere $725.

ON THE COAST you'll find a number of active community art galleries between San Diego and Los Angeles. Laguna Beach and Balboa are on State Highway 1. To reach the University of California at Irvine stay on U.S. Highway 101, which veers inland at Capistrano Beach.

UNIVERSITY OF CALIFORNIA, IRVINE. *Art Gallery, Third Floor, Fine Arts Building, Irvine (ten miles northwest of Laguna Beach). Hours 12 to 5 P.M. Tuesday–Sunday; 12 to 9 P.M. Wednesday. Very active exhibitions program featuring work of California, New York, and international artists.*

LAGUNA BEACH ART ASSOCIATION. *307 Cliff Drive, Laguna Beach. Hours 12 to 5 P.M. daily. Interesting monthly exhibits. Work in all media by Orange County artists and designers. Annual Christmas sale and auction.*

PAVILION GALLERY–FINE ARTS PATRONS OF NEWPORT HARBOR. *400 Main Street, Balboa. Hours 1 to 5 P.M. Wednesday–Sunday. Modern painting and sculpture. Special exhibitions for children.*

BRILLIANT PORTRAIT OF Lieutenant Legrand was painted by Baron Gros in 1809 in memory of 19-year-old officer killed in Napoleon's wars. Melancholy expression of youth, soft light add romantic aura to picture. (Los Angeles County Museum of Art.)

VINCENT VAN GOGH PAINTED at least six portraits of Roulin, a postman, though the "revolutionary" subject was supposedly not suited to academic portraiture. The ink and crayon sketch shows blunt, expressionistic strokes typical of the artist. (Los Angeles County Museum of Art.)

A BOLD POSTMAN *and a cold kiss*

MAN AND WOMAN KISSING, by Norwegian expressionist Edvard Munch, has impassioned line like Van Gogh portrait, presents distorted actuality far removed from classical or romantic art. The woodcut shows one of the most unromantic kisses on record. (Los Angeles County Museum of Art.)

ART COMES TO LIFE
when people come to art

HENRY MOORE

KIDS ARE DELIGHTED by abstract forms of Henry Moore sculpture at a big show in the La Jolla Art Museum. "Do Not Touch" signs are long a thing of the past.

RAPT ATTENTION and the world might just as well be falling down outside the museum. When that certain rapport is attained between a work of art and a viewer, time stands still, and nothing else exists.

IDEAL SPOT for browsing, the Ludington Court at Santa Barbara Museum of Art is full of classical vases and statues. Modern afficionados sometimes provide as big an eyeful as the exhibits themselves.

SOUTHERN CALIFORNIA   45

GRAPHIC ARTS *tradition —*
it's as new as today

DRAMATIC ETCHING by
Rembrandt shows Faust in His Study,
Watching a Magic Disk. *(Grunwald*
Graphic Arts Foundation, UCLA.)

THE RABBIT, a 1945 lithograph
by Rico Lebrun, combines
drawing with bitter social
commentary on war. There is superb
strength in every line.
(Fine Arts Gallery of San Diego.)

SAMSON AND THE LION, in a magnificent wood engraving by Albrecht Dürer.
Often called the German Leonardo, Dürer (1471-1528) worked in Nuremberg, traveled
widely, introduced many forms and new ideas of Italian Renaissance to northern
Europe. (Fine Arts Gallery of San Diego.)

Los Angeles Area

Once regarded as a cultural wasteland of crackpots and lotus-eaters, Los Angeles has recently blossomed out as the second art capital of America. One of the city's two municipal art galleries is in the City Hall. Twenty-five stories up, it may be said to symbolize the current status of art in this community.

Within the last decade, a surge of interest in the arts has created a 33-million dollar music center, bigger and acoustically better than its New York counterpart, and the 20-million dollar Los Angeles County Museum of Art, largest museum to be built in America since the National Gallery went up in Washington in 1941.

Focus of interest for such avid collectors as Norton Simon, who made headlines in every newspaper in Europe and America by paying $2,234,400 for a Rembrandt portrait, the new museum can draw on the resources of the greatest concentration of privately owned art west of the Mississippi. Of 122 pieces shown at an exhibition of painting and sculpture of the New York School, 49 were loaned by the art patrons of Los Angeles.

The new museum opened its doors on March 31, 1965. Before the year was out it had clicked in 1,700,000 visitors, the kind of attendance figure one usually associates with baseball or the movies. Art is competing with the artful Dodgers as the chief attraction of Los Angeles and its environs.

Aiding and abetting this interest are some sixty private art galleries in Los Angeles. Some of them have sprung up overnight, some will fade by tomorrow, a few have been here for more than a generation. Among the hardy perennials are Dalzell Hatfield, Frank Perls, Alexander Cowie, and Earl Stendahl.

Stendahl is perhaps the hardiest of all. The history of his gallery, now located at 7055 Hillside Avenue in Hollywood, reflects the evolution of art in Los Angeles. Stendahl started out in the '20's by opening a candy store on Wilshire Boulevard. Some of his friends and customers were painters—he hung their pictures on the walls of his shop. Before long the canvas was crowding out the candy.

Branching out, Stendahl introduced Los Angeles to the works of

Kandinsky, Feininger, and Josef Albers, precursor of op art and the hard-edge school. He also encouraged Los Angeles artists like Macdonald-Wright, Lorser Feitelson, and Helen Lundeberg, and helped them during the dark days of the depression. Today Stendahl deals in the very old and the very new, showing in the contrast between his contemporaries and his pre-Columbian and Iranian sculpture the mysterious affinities of ancient and modern art.

Alexander Cowie, who operated a gallery for many years in the Biltmore Hotel, still shows important representational works in a major gallery at 634 South Westmoreland Avenue.

Dalzell Hatfield, who died in 1964, was another pioneer dealer who spent some forty years guiding the desires of Los Angeles collectors and, not incidentally, supporting local painters. His widow, Ruth, now runs the Dalzell Hatfield Gallery in the Ambassador Hotel. Another influential dealer is Frank Perls. He's been in the art business at various locations since 1939, importing European paintings of museum quality. At his new gallery at 9777 Wilshire Boulevard he now shows old masters like Miro and Matisse, the avant-garde of yesterday, and new masters like Dubuffet, an old master of tomorrow. Don't miss either place.

WINDOW SHOPPING ON LA CIENEGA BOULEVARD is fun, especially on Monday nights. Most galleries stay open till ten or eleven, welcome strolling art patrons, regale browsers with everything from prehistoric art to pop off the easel.

50　SOUTHERN CALIFORNIA

TOURING THE LOS ANGELES GALLERIES

A downhill stroll southward from 968 N. La Cienega to 515 will take you past or into no less than 28 art galleries. Jay-walking seems to be the order of the day and Monday night. Most galleries open at 10 or 11 A.M., close at 5 or 6 P.M. Here's a brief directory:

968	Ceeje.	724	Heritage.
941	Sabersky.	723	Ferus.
910	Ankrum.	718	Feingarten Sculpture Galleries.
904	Adolph Loewi.	710	Martin Janis.
902	Adele Bednarz.	702	Felix Landau.
900	Carter.	669	Rolf Nelson.
847	Oscar Meyer.	667	Ryder.
825	Los Angeles Art Association.	665	Esther Robles.
816	Feingarten Galleries of Painting.	635½	Galerie Gregg Juarez.
		635	Kramer.
814	Nicholas Wilder.	629	Ernest Raboff.
807	David Stuart.	521	Terry de Lapp.
765	Paideia.	521	O. P. Reed.
748½	Rex Evans.	515	Feigen-Palmer.

Inveterate gallery crawlers will also want to investigate the Comara Gallery, just a step from La Cienega at 8475 Melrose Place.

The Dwan Gallery at 10846 Lindbrook Drive in Westwood features the *tableaux* of Edward Kienholz. These "frozen happenings" are like stage sets from the realistic theater, complete with props and figures. As moral as sermons, they appear to be in the great tradition of anecdotal art.

In *The Birthday*, for example, Kienholz' woman in labor suffers every conceivable agony, including, in her open bag, a couldn't-make-it note from her husband. Thus one of the "farthest-out" of Los Angeles artists brings back one of the oldest props of sentimental 19th-century painting: anecdote.

You should also check the Beverly Hills galleries. Frank Perls at 9777 Wilshire Boulevard and Paul Kantor, 348 North Camden Drive, are dealers of international importance, specializing in major modern masters. The P.N. Matisse Gallery, a few steps from Kantor at number 356, has outstanding examples of 20th-century painting, sculpture, drawing, and prints. Over at 445 North Rodeo, Harry A. Franklin has one of the best galleries of primitive art in town.

It was pioneers like these who changed the sunset-in-the-pine-grove tastes of Angelenos to such an extent that even the City Council now looks at art with new eyes. Ten years ago this group, to avoid controversy, forbade the use of public funds for the decoration of public buildings. Now they have accepted a recommendation of the Municipal Art Commission that at least one percent of the cost of such buildings be designated for sculpture, murals, or other art forms to relieve the monotony of new civic construction.

Private universities like the University of Southern California, and public ones like the University of California at Los Angeles, play a big role, not only in the teaching of art history and techniques but in bringing the work of artists in all media to the attention of the public. The latter spends half a million dollars a year on the plastic and performing arts, attracts 300,000 visitors annually to various shows on its sprawling campus.

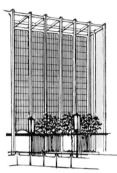

GREAT PAVILIONS OF ART

LOS ANGELES COUNTY MUSEUM OF ART. *5905 Wilshire Boulevard, Los Angeles. Hours 10 A.M. to 5 P.M. Tuesday–Sunday; closed Monday. Cafeteria in Bing Center.*

Newest and grandest of the city's cultural shrines is the already world-famous Los Angeles County Museum of Art, completed in 1965 on Wilshire Boulevard's Miracle Mile. It took six months to transfer the permanent collection from the old museum, built in 1913 in Exposition Park ten miles away. A hundred thousand items, valued at $30,000,000 had to be crated, labeled, moved, unpacked, and reinstalled in the process. In size the transferred treasures ranged from a bronze Etruscan statuette nine inches high to a towering seven-foot marble statue of Pallas Athena, both part of the William Randolph Hearst bequest that gave Los Angeles some of the most important classical sculpture in the United States.

To house such treasures properly, civic-minded Angelenos contributed $12,000,000 for the construction of their new museum. The county provided the eight-million dollar site in Hancock Park, famed for its La Brea Tar Pits. Here, just behind the museum, you will see a sobering, surrealist sight no museum can duplicate: the fossilized remains of antediluvian animals who, driven by thirst,

ART DOES NOT RENDER THE VISIBLE; rather it makes visible. This was the credo of Paul Klee, evident in his colorful Two Heads *from the Pasadena Art Museum.*

met death as they sank helplessly into these pools of pitch. Nothing in Dante's *Inferno* can equal the scene. To see this charnel house of mastodons is to peer into the long night before the dawn of human history. Listen as you stand here. The viscous tar still plops and bubbles as though biding its time.

The pavilions of art rise proudly above this sinister bog on a floating concrete raft foundation, three feet thick. There are three buildings, two of them named in honor of some of the museum's leading benefactors: Los Angeles realtor Leo S. Bing, and banker Howard Ahmanson. Designed by architect William L. Pereira and Associates, these steel frame buildings, which are faced with marble and cast stone, stand on a terrace above an ornamental pool on whose jet black and silver-rippled surface they appear to float.

In the center of the terrace is the Norton Simon Sculpture Court. An outdoor plaza designed for the display of monumental works, it rivals and even surpasses the famed sculpture garden of New York's Museum of Modern Art. The spacious court is dominated by Norbert Kricke's soaring space sculpture, a dynamic composition in welded stainless steel that suggests the flight of some splendid bird. The plaza also boasts a major work by Henry Moore, and Renoir's *Venus Victrix*, who holds out her apple of discord as though she were welcoming you to this newest of Western museums.

The Sculpture Court is a standing invitation to Los Angeles collectors to lend and give statues that will show off to advantage in this attractive setting. At the moment you will find more people than sculpture on the terrace. It has become one of the favorite meeting places of Angelenos from school kids to society matrons.

A WEALTH OF RARE TREASURES

The Los Angeles County Museum's permanent art collection is housed in the Ahmanson Gallery, a four-story building constructed around a central atrium designed to illuminate all floors. Quite apart from their contents, the galleries with their wall-to-wall carpeting and velvet-covered walls make this a most comfortable museum of art, easy on the feet and eyes. If you do get tired you can sink into the ultramodern furniture of Eero Saarinen and Mies van der Rohe.

The lowest or basement level contains the classical, medieval, and Oriental collections. Among the rare treasures here are a gilded statuette of the Egyptian god Osiris, dating from 1500 B.C.; a 6th-century B.C. Etruscan warrior; a 2nd-century Roman sarcophagus whose animated sculpture will give you a fascinating glimpse of life in ancient times as well as a good idea of the source material that inspired Raphael and other artists of the Renaissance when, a thousand years after the imperial city's fall, they re-created the dazzling grandeur that was Rome.

You'll have glimpses of this reborn splendor on the plaza level, where walls are adorned with pictures by Botticelli and other old masters, acquired by the Norton Simon Foundation from the famous collection of Duveen. This floor of the museum displays art from the Renaissance through the 18th century. One of the great attractions is Rembrandt's luminous portrait of *Maarten Looten* which J. Paul Getty acquired for $65,000 in Holland in 1938. In the light of recent Rembrandt prices, this portrait—Rembrandt's second commission, painted when the artist was 26—is now regarded as a very real bargain.

Don't leave the plaza level without studying its most impressive piece of sculpture: an unknown German Swabian's *Descent from the Cross*. In this masterpiece the life-size figures of polychrome wood have been imbued with the spirit of an anonymous genius. Contrast

TO BUY OR NOT TO BUY: that is the question under consideration by a couple pondering an abstract ceramic wall panel. You can reflect at leisure, take it or leave it, at La Cienega's open house. (See page 51.)

LOS ANGELES 55

LEONARDO DA VINCI'S INFLUENCE is evident in Madonna and Child With An Angel *by Lorenzo di Credi, Leonardo's fellow pupil. Flawless technical skill is typical of Florentine Renaissance. (J. Paul Getty Museum.)*

between the broken body of Christ and the sturdy Swabian peasant who lifts him tenderly from the cross is profoundly moving.

Nineteenth and 20th-century painting and sculpture are exhibited on the third level of the Ahmanson Gallery. Here you will find Cézanne's vibrant *Still Life with Cherries and Peaches*, a masterpiece of analytical form and glowing color; Pissarro's *Place du Théâtre Français*, suffused with the silvery light of Paris; Degas' *Bellelli Sisters*, a powerful double portrait which Modern Art Curator Maurice Tuchman considers the outstanding treasure of the whole collection.

On this level you can also trace part of the evolution of that incomparable modern master, Pablo Picasso. Note his *Woman With a Blue Veil*, painted in 1923 during his classic phase.

WHEELS, FUNNELS, AND JUNK

If you have a taste for assemblage you are sure to like Kurt Schwitters' *Construction for a Noble Lady*, an arresting arrangement of wheels, funnels, and other debris composed way back in 1919. The lowly "found objects" are organized into an esthetic experience, exploiting the texture of old wood and metal and an exceedingly subtle palette of mossy greens, sand color, and old rose. A more recent avant-garde eye-catcher on this floor is John Chamberlain's welded junk sculpture *Sweet William*, a concoction of crushed automobile parts that has all the morbid fascination of a motorcycle accident. Whether you like it or not, you will have to admit that nothing could be more contemporary.

The top floor of the Ahmanson Gallery is devoted to the graphic and decorative arts. The latter—antique furniture, silver, porcelain and the like—are lavishly displayed as in a department store. The prints and drawings cover five centuries from Albrecht Dürer to Stuart Davis. Here the first choice of Ebria Feinblatt, curator of prints and drawings, is *Architectural Capriccio*, a large pen and sepia wash by Francesco Guardi. Meticulously observed and rapidly sketched, it offers a lovely glimpse of his native Venice. At once grand and intimate, it doesn't hesitate to mix the ducal pride of the Piazetta with a pride of ducks in the Grand Canal.

If you want a graphic lesson in the origins of modern art, you should study the geometric forms and dynamic interacting planes and colors of one of its boldest innovators, Wassily Kandinsky. The print collection of the Los Angeles Museum offers a fine opportunity with the rare and handsome color lithograph of 1923, *Composition With Chessboard–Orange*. The longer you look at this geometric poem, precise as the ticking of a watch, the more fascinating it becomes. The museum has supplied a caption for the lithograph, eloquently summing up Kandinsky's aim as well as his accomplishment: "He worked from an inner world, as poet and mystic, searching through geometric signs and symbols for almost a visual equivalent of music or harmony. He was the first purely abstract painter in modern history."

A prolonged study of this composition will reward anyone who is interested in understanding the art of our times. Kandinsky helped emancipate that art from traditional dependence on objects observed in nature. He communicates a spiritual reality by means of non-figurative symbols and expresses his inner feelings in a new plastic language which is, perhaps, the nearest approach in the visual arts to music.

LOS ANGELES MEDICI

Many are the collectors and donors who have enriched Los Angeles with their treasures: William Randolph Hearst, Mr. and Mrs. George Gard De Silva, Judge and Mrs. Lucius Peyton Green, Mr. and Mrs. William Preston Harrison, J. Paul Getty, Mr. and Mrs. Norton Simon, to name a few.

In addition to this time-honored practice of giving art, private industry has now joined the art parade by having it made. Like the Medici of Florence, the bankers of Los Angeles have begun commissioning works of art to embellish their surroundings. Lurcat tapestries have been commanded from France, Henry Moore sculpture has been ordered from England. The metal flowers of Harry Bertoia bloom on Wilshire Boulevard. Jack Zajac's bronzes grace loan association lobbies, and copper fountains splash in the shade of banks. You'll find a notable example of the latter at the California Federal Plaza Building (5670 Wilshire Boulevard), where Claire Falkenstein's *Sculptured Water* delights the eye with its web of copper tubes, translucent glass, and silver spray, refreshing as a breaking wave.

FALKENSTEIN'S FANTASY on Wilshire Boulevard, Sculptured Water, *cools the plaza of California Federal Building, typifies Los Angeles' lively interest in commissioning art to beautify the city. Banks, loan associations, and insurance companies now fill their lobbies with art works, as well as commissioning painting and sculpture.*

PRIDE WILL BE ENGENDERED

The center of the three galleries flanking the Sculpture Court of the Los Angeles County Museum of Art provides a spacious and flexible setting for such major temporary exhibitions as Art Treasures of Japan and 7,000 Years of Iranian Art. The triad is completed with the Leo S. Bing Center, containing a 600-seat auditorium, a children's art work-shop and gallery, an art research library, and a cafeteria where you can eat on a terrace overlooking the pool and watch the antics of a Calder water mobile, slapped around by the jets of a fountain.

The Los Angeles County Museum of Art is raising $12,000,000 as an acquisitions fund, in order to realize the aim set down by its former director, Richard F. Brown: "... that more and more people will make discoveries about art more easily, earlier in life, and under such pleasant circumstances that they will return often to add to their accumulated treasure of visual delight and deeper understanding of nature, history, and man. Pride will be engendered: first in our cultural heritage, then in an ability to have and use im-portant manifestations of this heritage."

Pride has been engendered in Los Angeles, and the ability to have

LOS ANGELES   59

art and share it is one of the city's greatest assets. Gone are the days when great West Coast collections like the Arensberg went to East Coast museums for want of local space and interest. Among the many Los Angeles art patrons whose collections now have a local museum worthy to receive and display them are Norton Simon, Gifford Phillips, David Bright, Edward G. Robinson, Sidney Brody, William Goetz, Frederick Weisman, Leonard Asher, Stanley Freeman, and Taft Schreiber who recently bought Brancusi's marvelous *Bird in Flight*.

When the time comes for more major gifts from California's collectors, the Los Angeles County Museum of Art can provide both space and the ultimate in protection: closed circuit television that keeps a watchful eye on every art object in the galleries, and an equally modern alarm system.

THE FANTASTIC WATTS TOWERS

If you want to see Los Angeles' chief monument to the tradition of assemblage you must go to Watts, specifically to 1765 East 107th Street, to view the celebrated Watts Towers, hand-wrought by an immigrant Italian tile-setter named Simon Rodia. Rodia, who obviously loved his craft, assembled more than 75,000 seashells and other mosaic pieces for this astonishing project. Ignoring the neighbors, who thought he was crazy, he spent 33 years erecting three fantastic hundred-foot spires in his own back yard. Slowly from the monotonous plain of Watts rose airy creations of iron and wire, iced with concrete, decked out like the temples of Siam with seashells, bits of crockery, fragments of colored glass. Reminiscent of the exuberant fantasies of Gaudi, these spires proclaim once more those abiding cultural affinities between Spain and California, though Rodia could not have known the work of his spiritual Catalonian brother, except perhaps through photographs. You should see the towers, if possible, on a smogless day when the sun burnishes each gleaming chip of glass and crockery and the intricate tracery of the construction fractures the blue sky into a thousand glowing jewels.

The Watts Towers Committee, aided by *Los Angeles Times* Art Critic Henry J. Seldis, waged a long and successful battle to save the work of Rodia from the demolition squad, and the towers are now a historic monument. Visiting hours are from 11 A.M. to sunset.

OASIS IN WATTS was created by Italian tile setter Simon Rodia in gratitude to his adopted country. The Los Angeles hundred-foot towers are now protected as a historic monument.

TOURISTS GAPE in wonder at the brilliant mosaic work of Rodia. Visitors from everywhere proclaim the towers a masterpiece of imaginative assemblage. A small admission charge pays for maintenance, provides a souvenir booklet. (See page 60.)

LOS ANGELES COLLEGIATE CIRCUIT

UNIVERSITY OF CALIFORNIA AT LOS ANGELES ART GALLERIES. *405 Hilgard Avenue, Los Angeles. Hours 12:30 to 5 P.M. Monday–Friday; 1:30 to 5 P.M. Sunday; closed Saturday.*

The Art Galleries of UCLA are handsomely installed in the new (1966) Dickson Art Center on the Westwood campus. The permanent collection includes a brilliant Matisse of the late "cut-out" period, unique on the West Coast, also works by Picasso, Kirchner, Lehmbruck, Lipschitz, as well as older masters in the Willits J. Hole and James Kennedy Collections.

The Print Room (Grunwald Graphic Arts Foundation) has a large collection of 19th and 20th century prints, notably in the German Expressionist field. Through a gift of Norton Simon, it is also particularly rich in Matisse graphics. The UCLA Galleries have originated many retrospective or didactic exhibitions over the last decade, and continue to offer some of the most stimulating exhibitions of art to be seen on the West Coast.

Visitors to the UCLA Galleries should not miss the nearby Museum and Laboratories of Ethnic Arts and Technology. Don't let the formidable title scare you off. For here, because of the recent (1965) acquisition of the Wellcome Collection of Art and Ethnology, you will find masterpieces of primitive sculpture. Knowingly arranged and documented, these treasures from the South Pacific Islands, Africa and pre-Columbian America exert an appeal beyond the apprehension of reason. They probe to the dark realms of the unconscious, beyond the wisdom of the brain to the wisdom of the blood. After you've looked at these haunting images, the classic calm of Lehmbruck and the convulsive contortions of Lipschitz may seem bland and tame.

UNIVERSITY OF SOUTHERN CALIFORNIA FISHER GALLERY. *University Park, Los Angeles. Hours 12 to 5 P.M. Monday–Friday. University parking is available off Hoover Street between Exposition and Jefferson Boulevards.*

The University of Southern California's attractive Fisher Gallery on Exposition Boulevard west of the clock tower displays jade from the Quinn Collection, pictures from the Elizabeth Holmes Fisher Collection, and paintings from the recently acquired (1965) collection of Dr. Armand Hammer.

Dr. Hammer, who spent forty years gathering this collection, gave it to USC because, according to him, "it would be enjoyed by the largest possible cross section of American life if its home were in a great university located in the most populous section of the most populous state in the Union."

Rich in Flemish and Dutch portraits and in those realistic scenes of daily life known as *genre* painting, the Hammer Collection will regale your eyes with topers, fishwives, lusty peasants, and rambunctious kids fighting in the schoolyard, as seen by such masters as Jan Steen and Pieter Breughel the Younger. For a glimpse of high life in the Low Countries you must turn to the silk-and-satin clad burghers of Pieter de Hooch and Anthonie Palamedesz. Rubens is represented by a flamboyantly baroque *Nativity*, a flamboyantly fat *Venus* (in both of which his pupils had a large hand), and a superlative woodcut of *Susanna and the Elders*, in which the lady, not only

BARNSDALL PARK'S COMMUNITY SPIRIT

Art is blossoming in the olive groves of L.A.'s delightful Barnsdall Park, 4800 Hollywood Boulevard, where you can visit Frank Lloyd Wright's Hollyhock House, a 1920 creation of Mayan aspect and solidity. Los Angeles preserves it as a historic monument while its more famous contemporary, the Imperial Hotel in Tokyo, molders under the day-to-day threat of demolition.

Attached to Hollyhock House is the second of the city's Municipal Art Galleries, a spacious, well-lighted exhibition hall, which is usually vibrating with all the colors of the spectrum painted by the artists of Los Angeles, professional and amateur. The children's work, uninhibited in all media, is wonderful to behold. A happy community spirit prevails. Everybody involved in the Barnsdall exhibits seems to be a painter, a sculptor, or at the very least a critic.

You'll have an especially lively time at Barnsdall Park if you time your visit to coincide with the Annual Outdoor Art Festival in July. At this time the once staid and peaceful precincts of Olive Hill become a veritable midway of art exhibits, craft demonstrations, puppet shows, folk singing, dancing, and jazz. If you've always yearned to wield the brush, here's your chance. One feature of the festival is a free-for-all, do-it-yourself mural. Fifty feet long, its proportions would give pause to Michelangelo. But this is a community project. Everybody can contribute his mite of agony and ecstasy. The latter is dominant at Barnsdall Park.

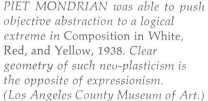

PIET MONDRIAN was able to push objective abstraction to a logical extreme in Composition in White, Red, and Yellow, 1938. *Clear geometry of such neo-plasticism is the opposite of expressionism. (Los Angeles County Museum of Art.)*

surprised but actually manhandled by two aging lechers, is fainting dead away.

The Fisher Gallery also offers a survey of American landscape painting all the way from Winslow Homer's *Maine Coast* to Albert Bierstadt's *A Stream in the Rockies*.

Among the British pictures at the Fisher Gallery is Thomas Hudson's portrait of *Peg Woffington*. Peg has an Irish gleam in her eye. Daughter of a Dublin bricklayer, this beautiful colleen helped her mother take in washing until her histrionic talents were discovered by a traveling tightrope walker. Peg got her start hanging head-down from the tightrope. Eventually she became the chief ornament of the 18th-century theatre, an actress of such fiery Irish temperament that she once drove a rival from the stage and stabbed her. "A weak fortress, besieged by every rake in London," bewitching Peg had many admirers—and she still does, here on the peaceful and quiet walls of the Fisher Gallery at USC.

GALLERY GOERS wishing to complete the collegiate circuit of Los Angeles should check the exhibitions schedule of Occidental College's Gallery in Thorne Hall at 1600 Campus Road; the Otis Art Institute of Los Angeles, 2401 Wilshire Boulevard; Cerritos College Gallery, 1110 E. Alondra Boulevard; Art Gallery of Mount St. Mary's College, 815 Adams Boulevard; and the Los Angeles Valley College Gallery at 5800 Fulton Avenue, Van Nuys. Immaculate Heart College is an important center of modern art activity.

EXCURSIONS CLOSE TO LOS ANGELES

Within easy driving distance of Los Angeles proper you'll find half a dozen smaller museums and galleries whose art treasures range from the bronze horses of Bryaxis (4th-century B.C. Athenian sculptor) to the bucking broncos of our own Frederick Remington. There are some fine Remingtons along with the work of another American, Charles Russell, at the William S. Hart Park at 24151 Newhall Avenue in Newhall. The famous movie actor's mansion (take the little bus to the top of the hill) is now an informal museum, filled with frontier weapons, Indian artifacts, and other fascinating bits of Western Americana, so take the children. In addition to the Remington bronzes there's plenty of real livestock around: horses, ducks, goats, even peacocks. The park is open every day but Monday.

Here are several galleries worth investigating close to Los Angeles:

PALOS VERDES COMMUNITY ARTS ASSOCIATION. *2400 Via Campesina, Palos Verdes Estates. Hours 1 to 4 P.M. Monday–Friday; 3 to 5 P.M. Saturday, Sunday. Paintings, graphics, sculpture, stained glass, folk art. New exhibition each month.*

DOWNEY MUSEUM OF ART. *Furman Park, 10419 South Rives Avenue, Downey. Hours 1 to 5 P.M. Tuesday–Sunday. Monthly exhibitions featuring one-man and group shows in various media, mostly by California artists.*

CHARLES W. BOWERS MEMORIAL MUSEUM. *2002 North Main Street, Santa Ana. Hours 10 A.M. to 4:30 P.M. Tuesday–Saturday; 1 to 5 P.M. Sunday; 7 to 9 P.M. Thursday. Interesting new shows each month with an American and Mexican accent: paintings, photographs, architecture, early American duck decoys, old-fashioned toys.*

SANTA MONICA ART GALLERY. *1343 Sixth Street, Santa Monica. Hours 9 A.M. to 9 P.M. Monday–Friday; 9 A.M. to 5:30 P.M. Saturday. Interesting program of monthly exhibitions. Many American painters show here, including Women Painters of the West.*

OPULENT CANVAS *of* Virgin and Child with Saints John, Elizabeth, and Justina, *by Veronese (his real name was Paolo Caliari), follows tradition by showing Elizabeth, the mother of St. John, as an old woman. But Justina, a patron saint of Venice, is portrayed as a fashionable, 16th-century Venetian beauty. The masterpiece, by the 16th-century master (1528–1588), is from the Timken Gallery.*

*JOSEPH DRAWS WATER from the well, while Mary watches over infant Christ
in an architectural engraving by Albrecht Dürer. Note Dürer's initials on the signboard
at top of the building. (Los Angeles County Museum of Art.)*

REWARDING THE ART LOVER

SOUTHWEST MUSEUM. *234 Museum Drive, Highland Park, Los Angeles. Hours 1 to 5 P.M. Tuesday–Sunday; closed Monday.*

The Southwest Museum, founded in 1907 and built in 1913, is strikingly situated on a hilltop dominating Highland Park. Access is by tunnel and elevator built into the core of the hill, or by road up to the parking lot. At the foot of the hill is an interesting adjunct to the museum: the Casa de Adobe, authentic replica of a Spanish colonial *hacienda*.

Although the Southwest Museum is basically an ethnological museum devoted to the anthropology handcrafts, and history of the American Indian, it will reward the art lover with many artifacts that transcend any limitations of folklore. There is a superlative Zapotec funerary urn from Oaxaca, for example, a piece of ceramic sculpture that will stand comparison with the best of pre-Columbian art. There are some impressive wood carvings of Makah Indian figures in a boat, and there is a small collection of fish and animal sculpture carved in gray steatite by the Indians of the Southern California coast and the Channel Islands.

ACTIVITY EAST

Two important inland galleries should not be overlooked:

PEPPERS ART CENTER–UNIVERSITY OF REDLANDS. *1200 East Colton, Redlands. Hours 1 to 5 P.M. Tuesday–Friday; 2 to 5 P.M. Saturday, Sunday; closed Monday.*

EDWARD-DEAN MUSEUM OF DECORATIVE ARTS. *9401 Oak Glen Road, Beaumont. Hours 1 to 4:30 P.M. Tuesday, Thursday, Saturday. Closed in August.*

The Peppers Art Center at Redlands presents monthly shows of work in all media, selected and organized by the University Art Department. There are many important loan exhibitions throughout the year. The museum at Beaumont, as the name implies, emphasizes antiques, 18th-century furniture, and other examples of the decorative arts, but there is also a collection of oil paintings and watercolors from the Renaissance to the present day.

POLICY—DYNAMIC EXHIBITIONS

PASADENA ART MUSEUM. *46 North Los Robles Avenue, Pasadena. Hours 10* A.M. *to 5* P.M. *Wednesday–Saturday; 10* A.M. *to 9* P.M. *Tuesday; 2 to 5* P.M. *Sunday; closed Monday. German Expressionist painting.*

Rivaling the Rose Bowl as a landmark, the Pasadena Art Museum was built in 1924-25 as Grace Nicholson's Chinese treasure house. Dying in 1948, Miss Nicholson deeded her gallery to Pasadena. A bronze plaque commemorates this generosity: "Her Vision Made This Beauty Possible for All." Who can resist this Oriental fantasy with its multiple ski-jump roofs of green tile, its Pekinese ceramic dogs pretending to be lions, and its bronze finials slicing the blue sky of Southern California? But if all this quaint chinoiserie leads you to expect a treasure trove of traditional Oriental art, you're in for somewhat of a shock.

The museum's central patio, graced with bamboo and a Chinese gingko tree, is a tranquil court of contemplation until the kids take over on Saturday mornings. Then look out. You might end up in the ornamental pool or be drafted into an impromptu ballet suddenly improvised on the theme of the falling gingko leaves. The atmosphere at Pasadena is permissive. You can emulate the children, if you've a mind to, and climb all over the statuary. If it has movable parts, go ahead and manipulate them. No one will say a word.

The tiled galleries opening off the central patio contain no Chinese treasures, but are more apt to display experimental paintings designed to atomize the optic nerve. They have been known to provoke angry stupefaction and attacks of vertigo.

All this reflects the spirit of Pasadena's energetic director, Walter Hopps. A native Californian, Hopps has carried on with the dynamic exhibitions policy established by his predecessor Thomas Leavitt, who has since become director of the Santa Barbara Museum. At Pasadena in 1963 Leavitt organized a major retrospective show of the work of Marcel Duchamp, a legendary, iconoclastic, prophetic figure in the history of modern art, so ahead of his time that contemporary artists are just catching up with him. Mr. Hopps installed the show with great style. Its 114 items included the famous *Nude Descending a Staircase* that scandalized our grandfathers at the New York Armory Show in 1913 and provoked a laconic bit of art criticism from Theodore Roosevelt.

CHILDREN INTERPRET *the two-dimensional feeling of a painting into living, three-dimensional movement. The Pasadena Art Museum is more than a repository for fine art; it is a veritable beehive of activity, most of it provided by the youngsters.*

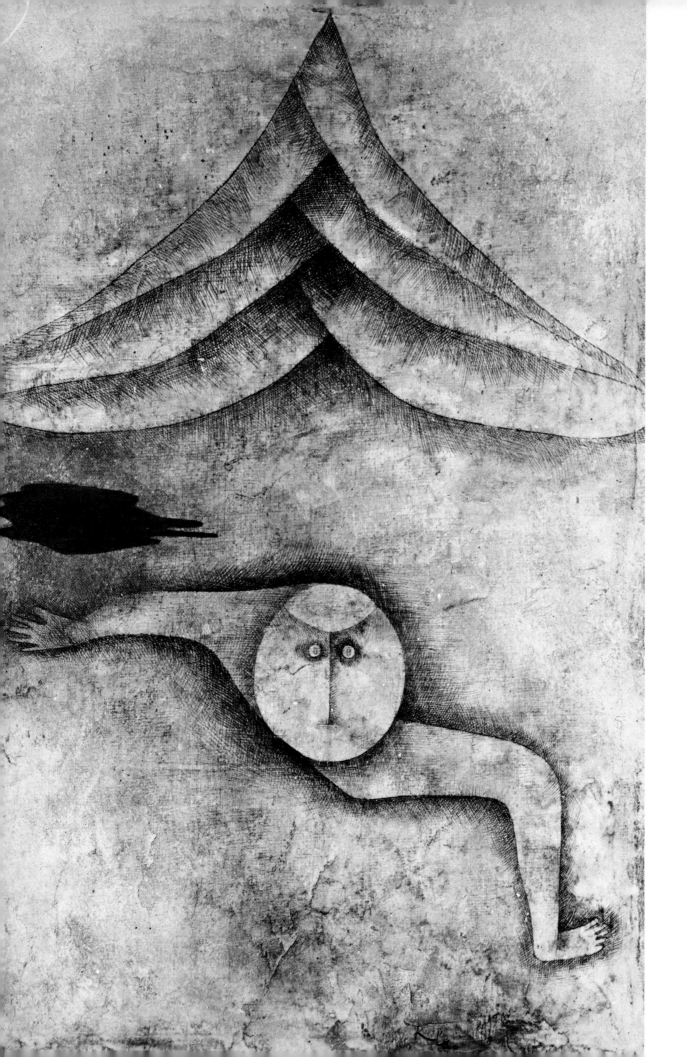

"Looks like an explosion in a shingle factory," said Teddy.

Several Roosevelts later, Marcel Duchamp turned up at his Pasadena opening. Most people had believed him dead, but there he was, a legend in the flesh, the distinguished foxy grandpa of pop and op, a hearty youngster of 77. By general critical consensus the show was a great success, Duchamp the seminal influence of our times. The art world buzzed with excitement; the critics, perhaps revealing a certain mental instability, "raved." Why had no one thought of such an exhibition before? What was the matter with New York's Museum of Modern Art? The Whitney? The Guggenheim? Pasadena had brought off the art event of the year. Levitated by Leavitt, the place has been hopping ever since.

In 1965, at the invitation of the U.S. Information Agency, the Pasadena Art Museum organized the United States Exhibition at the Eighth Biennial of Modern Art in Sao Paulo, Brazil. As Comisárrio,

THERE'S LIFE IN Marcel Duchamp yet, as the grand old master of assemblage describes a fine point of his famous bicycle wheel to Walter Hopps at the Pasadena Art Museum. Born in 1887, Duchamp is still very much alive.

LIKE A SWIMMER, Paul Klee's figure in Refuge, facing page, peers deep into the eyes of the viewer. (Pasadena Art Museum.)

EDGAR DEGAS was interested in the development of photography when he painted the masterful portrait of Bellelli Sisters in 1862, but the structured realism of painting surpassed any daguerreotype. (Los Angeles County Museum of Art.)

Hopps chose seven artists to represent the country, including three from Southern California: Larry Bell, Billy Al Bengston, and Robert Irwin, all more or less masters of that impersonal mechanistic technique which critic Irving Sandler calls cool art. When certain critics of Hopps' choices were baffled by a static, empty quality in some of this work, he blandly confounded their confusion by replying that these pictures established a new kind of non-active activity.

There's nothing non-active, however, about the activity at the Pasadena Art Museum. Its adult and junior art workshops are among the most dynamic in the nation. Classes are given in art, music, and dance, and most groups combine all three in one. If you want to see something dynamic, watch one of the kids imitating the rhythms of a Kandinsky painting. Every facility of the museum is used to provide the ideal atmosphere for achieving Pasadena's educational goal of experiencing the excitement of visual invention, the profound personal involvement possible in the fine arts.

ALWAYS FRESH—ALWAYS CHALLENGING

The Pasadena Art Museum's permanent collection is strong in German Expressionist painting and in the graphic arts. Its small but selective collection of pre-Columbian sculpture is of superb quality. A most important attraction is the Galka E. Scheyer Collection of works by Feininger, Jawlensky, Kandinsky, and Paul Klee. Madame Scheyer was the American agent for this important group which Feininger suggested calling "The Four." With nostalgic recollections of Munich and The Blue Rider Group (Kandinsky, Franz Marc, Münter, Kubin, and four other painters who took their name from a 1903 Kandinsky painting, *Der Blaue Reiter*) Galka Scheyer named *her* group the Blue Four, and the label stuck. The collection includes more than forty paintings and prints by Paul Klee, the most important American ensemble of this modern Swiss master's outside of the Guggenheim Museum, in New York.

TEN YEARS after Bellelli Sisters, *Degas embarked on his famous series of dancers. Pastel of* Ballet Girl Resting *is drawn with such perception you can share her fatigue. (Santa Barbara Museum of Art.)*

As suggested by the Duchamp show, Pasadena's exhibitions program is actively directed toward fulfilling the museum's avowed aim to provide something always fresh and challenging to the eye. The museum, for which greatly expanded facilities are planned in Carmelita Park, is also a showcase for local accomplishment. More than eighty of Southern California's artists have exhibited here in the past decade. The museum also sponsors the California Triennial Exhibition of Design, a major show of outstanding work by contemporary California artists in all media.

GREATEST WORK...GREATEST MASTER

HENRY E. HUNTINGTON ART GALLERY. *1151 Oxford Road, San Marino. Hours 1 to 4:30 P.M. Tuesday–Sunday; closed Monday. Closed entire month of October for annual renovation of gallery, library, and gardens.*

The prototype of California art collectors and benefactors was Henry Edwards Huntington (1850-1927). He has left his own memorial eleven miles west of Los Angeles in the garden suburb of San Marino. This is the celebrated Huntington Library and Art Gallery, home of California's oldest and most famous junior citizen, *The Blue Boy*, by Gainsborough.

Henry Huntington was the hard-working nephew, collaborator, and principal heir of Collis P. Huntington, the biggest of California's Big Four (the other three were Stanford, Crocker, Hopkins). Much ink, often mixed with vitriol, has flowed on the subject of the Huntingtons, on the business acumen of Collis, on the aspirations of his wife Arabella, who, after the death of Collis in 1900, became more and more dependent on the advice of the famous and shrewd art dealer, Sir Joseph Duveen.

In 1913, when Arabella became Mrs. Huntington twice-over by marrying her nephew Henry, this dependence had become so marked that Duveen made all the wedding arrangements right down to the bridal bouquet. With the fine hand of Duveen encouraging their Duveenly inspired craving for art, not to mention their inexhaustible resources, the Huntingtons acquired not only Gainsborough's *The Blue Boy* ("The greatest work of England's greatest master," said Duveen), but also enough other distinguished companion pieces to

TURNER'S LOVE of light, air, space found ideal subject in The Grand Canal, *bathed in golden atmosphere of Venice. (Henry E. Huntington Gallery.)*

establish the Huntington Collection as the most important ensemble of 18th-century British art in the United States.

The marble home of Henry Huntington, built in the Georgian style in 1910, is now the Huntington Art Gallery. A few yards to the northeast is the famous library with its Gutenberg Bible, original Shakespeare quartos, and its great collection of *incunabula* (books printed before 1501) and manuscripts, richest in the country outside of the Library of Congress.

BRONZES AND BRITISH WATERCOLOURS

The grounds surrounding these buildings cover 200 acres. Landscaped by William Hertrich in collaboration with Mr. Huntington, they are a botanical idyll of noble vistas: tree-shaded, sculpture-studded lawns, ferny bowers, palmy glades, rose arbors, pergolas, a ten-acre desert garden spiked with more than 25,000 specimens of cacti and succulents, a cool romantic canyon ablaze with a thousand varieties of camellia.

Favorite of most visitors is the Japanese tea garden. In 1913, to welcome eastern Arabella to the marble halls of her new western domain, Huntington had Hertrich transplant this entire garden, teahouse, pagoda, moon bridge, and all from neighboring Pasadena to the San Marino estate.

Mrs. Huntington didn't like the garden. She preferred tapestries, paintings, and *objets d'art* from the Italian and Flemish Renaissance. These treasures await you in the Arabella D. Huntington Memorial Wing of the gallery, along with beautiful examples of Sevres porcelain, French furniture, and French sculpture.

The Huntington Art Gallery has the intimate charm of a private house. Mr. Huntington wanted his British portraits to feel at home. So he provided them with the furnishings of their own epoch, an elegant decor that will enhance your pleasure as it enhances their aristocratic distinction. Gainsborough's *The Blue Boy* and Reynolds' majestic *Mrs. Siddons as the Tragic Muse* have been placed with love in this perfect setting. One can almost sense the presence of the departed collector who lived with the pictures in this house.

The much-publicized presence of *The Blue Boy* should not be permitted to obscure the other treasures of the Huntington: the other

HOW BLUE BOY CAME TO CALIFORNIA

Knowing that Henry E. Huntington was eager to acquire Gainsborough's famous *The Blue Boy* for his English collection, the art dealer Joseph Duveen bought it—on credit—from the Duke of Westminster in London in 1922. The duke was eager to sell. In addition to *The Blue Boy* Duveen also bought Gainsborough's *The Cottage Door* and Reynolds' portrait of *Sarah Siddons as the Tragic Muse.* The price for all three pictures was just a little more than the $600,000 which Duveen had told Huntington he would probably have to pay for *The Blue Boy* alone.

Duveen promised Westminster full payment in cash within a week. Then he went to his London office and phoned the Huntingtons who were in France.

"I have acquired *The Blue Boy,*" he announced. "It's yours for $620,000."

Huntington raised the cash within 48 hours.

When Duveen delivered *The Blue Boy* to the Huntingtons they were disappointed that it wasn't as blue as a reproduction they had seen of it. In fact it wasn't blue at all; it was green.

"The dust and grime of the ages," explained Duveen. "I'll have it cleaned."

When the restorer removed the layer of discolored varnish from the painting, the boy's murky green costume emerged a brilliant shade of azure, fresh as the day it left the painter's studio.

The Blue Boy made a farewell appearance at the National Gallery in London from January 4 to 24, 1922. Meanwhile steamship companies were vying for the honor—and publicity—of shipping him to America.

"Their interest," said Duveen, "was not disinterested. There was the small matter of the freight charge of one percent ad valorem."

The dealer saved his clients this $6,200 charge by sending the picture as an employee's hand luggage on the French Line. Encased in wood and steel, it cost $200 in excess baggage charges.

The Blue Boy arrived in New York on February 7, 1922. The American art world was agog. The Metropolitan Museum of Art wanted to exhibit the distinguished immigrant, but Duveen turned them down. He considered his own Fifth Avenue gallery, a copy of an 18th-century French palace, a far more appropriate setting than a mere museum.

The painting was exhibited at Duveen's from February 14 to March 7. Ten days later it was packed up again and began the last leg of its long journey to California by rail. Once again it had a personal escort. This time it was Sir Joseph Duveen himself. Both arrived in San Marino on Tuesday, March 21, 1922, along with *Mrs. Siddons* and *The Cottage Door.* Duveen had sold them to Huntington too at an undisclosed price, though his profit was probably not more than 100 percent.

ONE OF RAREST PICTURES *in America, Juan de Flandes' portrait of* Juana la
Loca *is a psychologically penetrating portrayal of the mad daughter of Isabella of Castile.*
A contemporary of Columbus, John of Flanders was employed by the Spanish
court from 1496 to 1504. (Sedgwick Collection: UC at Santa Barbara.)

superlative Gainsboroughs, the works of Sir Thomas Lawrence (many visitors prefer his *Pinkie* to *The Blue Boy*), the Constables, the Raeburns, and the Romneys. Nor are all the paintings from the British Isles. The collection includes a dozen paintings of that favorite Renaissance subject, the Madonna. Most notable is the *Madonna and Child* of Roger Van der Weyden, a 15th-century Flemish masterpiece that attracts appreciative visitors from as far away as the country of its origin.

There are superb bronzes by Giovanni da Bologna and outstanding works by the great French sculptor Houdon. See his endearing, lifelike portrait bust of his daughter, Sabine, one of the finest 18th-century marbles in the West. Another great favorite of this master is the splendid life-size bronze of *Diana the Huntress*.

In the department of British water colors and drawings, few museums can match the Huntington. Its 3,000 items include 60 Constable drawings, 24 Gainsboroughs, eleven Thomas Girtins, and a dozen wonderful Turners from the Gilbert Davis Collection. From the founder's collection come rare and beautiful examples of Blake's water color drawings for the poems of Milton. The *Paradise Lost* series is one of only two in America, the other being in the Boston

"YOU NAME IT...THEY'LL DIG IT"

On Los Angeles' La Cienega Boulevard, art is a matter of life and death —and sales. Any levity or irreverence in the presence of the merchandise is apt to be reproved by looks that would slay an army of Philistines. Not that there are many of that prosaic band around. "Our public is adventurous," says one La Cienega dealer. "In San Francisco they're cautious. Here they'll buy anything: action, pop, op; you name it, they'll dig it."

Best time to dig it is on Monday nights when a score of galleries stay open until ten o'clock or later and you're welcome to gawk and browse. Don't hesitate. Dealers like to have their galleries populated (on Monday nights some of them are *over*-populated) and they won't bother you with a sales pitch unless you want to buy. See Gallery Guide on page 51.

You can dine in the area, then stroll from gallery to gallery to see what's old, new, borrowed and blue in the yeasty world of modern art. Some canvases actually *are* blue, unrelieved fields of monochromatic color applied with a roller. This depersonalized painting is said to be conducive to the contemplative exercises of Zen. You may happen upon a vernissage (literally a "varnishing"), one of those openings at which the spirit of art is stimulated by the art of spirits. At one vernissage a lady got so confused she mistook a broom closet for a painting by Robert Rauschenberg. A word of advice: don't buy a picture after imbibing; come back and look at it again in the sober light of dawn. Not too early; on La Cienega Boulevard dawn breaks about an hour before noon.

La Cienega's art row, extending for five blocks south of Santa Monica Boulevard, is now thought to be more *avant-garde*, farther out than New York's 57th Street. Although there are Renaissance drawings, Luristan bronzes and other items of traditional appeal, the emphasis is on the new and experimental. You'll find the most recent fashions and some that are left over from last season. As of 1966 pop is on the wane, op has nearly exhausted itself along with the beholder's eye, and top is in the ascendant. This last refers to those bumpy canvases that duplicate the contours of topographical maps, usually with less relief, and, it must be admitted, less imagination. Accessories are in vogue: mirrors, for example, so you can observe your own reaction to the picture. Some of the sculpture is still made of junk. A lot of it moves. Some of it is wired for sound. A recent female torso startled gallery goers with a recorded message, presumably emanating from the "baby" inside. "Go soak your head," said this voice from the womb.

Another tendency evident in some of the galleries is a proclivity for erotic art. There have been police raids, and semantic battles rage as to what is and is not obscene. Pornography in art is at least as old as the frescoes of Pompeii. La Cienega Boulevard has yet to surpass those.

GENTLENESS AND GRACE are manifest by Jean-Antoine Houdon's Portrait of a Lady, *left, and Giovanni Bologna's* Crouching Venus. *The bust is marble, the statuette is bronze; both are from the Huntington Museum.*

Museum of Fine Arts. Mr. Huntington managed to get an entire set by buying them up separately in 1911 and 1914. They may not be on exhibition when you visit the gallery. So delicate is their coloring that they are sensitive to daylight, and, though frequently displayed in special exhibits, cannot remain on permanent view.

What was Huntington like, this paragon of Western collectors, who served on as many as sixty boards of directors at a single time, and who, upon retirement, spent millions on rare books, rare pictures, rare flowers, rare porcelains, even dipping into capital to satisfy his passion for beauty?

According to Estate Superintendent William Hertrich, he was a man who could work eighteen hours a day, and a thoroughgoing eccentric, "spending millions with his right hand, pinching pennies with his left." So economy-minded was Henry E. Huntington that, when the library was abuilding, he personally picked up the nails the carpenters dropped. Extravagant Arabella, who once in an antique shop forgot her handbag containing three million dollars worth of pearls, chided her husband for these petty economies.

"You pay $10,000 for a rare book," she said, "then walk the full length of this mansion to save pennies by switching off a light."

WISTERIA FACES MARTINEZ across the walk along the south wall of the Margaret Fowler Garden at Scripps College at Claremont. The well known Mexican artist Alfred Ramos Martinez began the bold work in 1945, but was never able to complete it, owing to his death in November of 1946. Scripps College has had on its faculty several artists of note, among them Millard Sheets, Henry Lee McFee, Roger Kuntz, Phil Dike, Paul Darrow, and Douglas McClellan.

84   SOUTHERN CALIFORNIA

"My dear," her husband replied, "if I didn't save the pennies I couldn't buy the book."

One wonders how many petty economies were necessary to finance the purchase of *The Blue Boy*. Duveen quoted the price at $620,000. It took Henry Huntington all of 48 hours to raise the pennies for that particular cash transaction.

Library, art gallery, and gardens have all been bequeathed to the public along with a liberal trust fund to maintain and expand them. "The reward of all the work I have ever done and the realization of much happiness," said the collector, referring to this extraordinary public bequest. The Huntington is worth a full day or more.

DAFFODILS AND MURALS AT CLAREMONT

RAND-LANG GALLERIES. *Scripps College, Claremont. Hours 2 to 5 P.M. daily.*

POMONA COLLEGE ART GALLERY. *Montgomery Art Center, Pomona College, Claremont. Hours 1 to 5 P.M. daily. Closed on college holidays.*

The olive and lime-tree shaded campus of Scripps College at Claremont seems like a cloistered corner of the Old World. Here you will find a striking fresco by Mexican artist Alfredo Martinez under the wisteria-festooned pergola of the Fowler Memorial Garden. Nearby are the spacious Rand-Lang Art Galleries, where the art department of Scripps College has frequent invitational exhibitions ranging in interest from the aboriginal art of New Guinea to the newest trends in contemporary painting and sculpture. A discovery here is the original sculpture of Jan de Swart, who has invented a process of casting metal into forms of wood. In the spring, when this lovely campus is golden with daffodils, see the annual Ceramics Invitational Show. It's been going on for 22 years and offers some of the most beautiful and imaginative pottery anywhere.

At neighboring Pomona College you can visit the attractive Pomona College Art Gallery which features a new exhibition every month. Its permanent collection ranges from the 14th to the 20th century, includes a dozen Renaissance and Baroque paintings from the Kress Foundation, a haunting surrealist Chirico, *Furniture in a Landscape*, and an important early Matisse, *Jetty at Collioure* (1906).

POWERFUL PARABLE of protest and aspiration, Orozco's Prometheus *fresco vitalizes a wall of Frary Hall at Pomona College in Claremont.*

But the big things at Pomona could hardly be confined within a gallery's walls. These are mural paintings by two modern masters, José Clemente Orozco and Rico Lebrun.

You'll find Rico Lebrun's huge *Genesis* on the interior wall of the south entrance portico of Frary Hall. Commissioned by Mr. and Mrs. Donald Winston as a gift to Pomona College, it was completed by the artist in 1960. The mural is 29 feet high, 25 feet wide. To give you an idea of its scale and the special problems of mural painting, note that the central figure of Noah is 12 feet tall, that of Job in the semicircular left lunette is 7 feet high and nearly 12 feet wide. If you are surprised to find Job in *Genesis*, remember that painters also have the right to poetic license.

Inside Frary Hall on the north wall of the dining room you will see Orozco's *Prometheus*, powerful representation of man's ancient rebellion against the gods, a subject most congenial to the incendiary temperament of Orozco. The fresco is magnificent. Painted in 1930 before the same artist's Dartmouth College frescoes, it has a massive unity and strength. Pomona's mural remains one of the Mexican master's strongest statements, one whose message is not vitiated by satirical and literary overtones.

*GENESIS, BY RICO LEBRUN, recalls Old Testament grandeur graphically in
mural at south entrance portico of Pomona College Frary Hall. The painter has added
long-suffering Job to story as a cry of protest.*

INFINITY IN A SINGLE FLOWER is the theme of the smoothly executed tempera picture, Lucid Solitude, *a recent painting in the tradition of magic realism by Kennard Harris. Note the strong tonal contrasts. (La Jolla Art Museum.)*

88   SOUTHERN CALIFORNIA

FLOWERS, FRUIT, and other things

NOSTALGIA for the past expressed through still-life
was the favorite theme of John Frederick Peto.
Things to Adore—My Studio Door, was painted in 1895.
(Santa Barbara Museum of Art.)

TEMPTING still life combines
Victorian opulence with a deep respect
for everyday objects. English
artist Samuel Marsden Brookes
painted it in his adopted
San Francisco in 1869.
(Oakland Art Museum: Gift
of Herbert Gray Hills Foundation.)

THREE GENTLEMEN *sit for a portrait*

AMERICAN ARTIST Benjamin West painted
Portrait of Stephen Carmick in 1759. Leaving the
colonies the following year, he became president
of England's Royal Academy, taught younger American
painters. (Santa Barbara Museum of Art.)

BOSTON-BORN John Singleton
Copley left America for London in
1744 with reputation already
established with such portraits as this
of General Joshua Winslow.
(Santa Barbara Museum of Art.)

COMMANDING PORTRAIT of Marques De Sofraga was painted by Goya c. 1795,
year of his appointment as Director of Painting in Spanish Academy. The picture
remained in the sitter's family a century and a half before its acquisition by the Fine
Arts Gallery of San Diego in 1938.

NOTORIOUS BEAUTY of 18th-century England, Emma Hamilton was the daughter of a blacksmith. She married Sir William Hamilton, became mistress of naval hero, Lord Nelson. Artist George Romney met her in 1781, painted many pictures of her, often in flimsier costumes than this one, Lady Hamilton in a Straw Hat. (*Henry E. Huntington Gallery.*)

A *SCANDALOUS* lady, an unhappy queen

TRAGIC QUEEN *Henrietta Maria, wife of Charles I of England, fled to her native France when king was beheaded in 1649. This portrait, showing the queen in rich dress, by Anthony Van Dyck is in Fine Arts Gallery of San Diego.*

BROODING *strength of American realism*

REALISTIC CELEBRATION of American life was the aim of regional painters like Charles Burchfield, who found inspiration in town and countryside of his native Middle West. (He was born in Ashtabula Harbor, Ohio in 1893.) Rainy Night, *from Fine Arts Gallery of San Diego, is a stark picture of a small town, alleviated by poetic mystery of brooding sky, reflected lights.*

THREE STUDIES *in personal style*

LONG HAIR *and skullcaps were the vogue for men in the 15th century. Sebastiano Mainardi's* Portrait of a Young Man *is dressed in the height of Italian Renaissance fashion. (Henry E. Huntington Gallery.)*

OLDER MEN *adopted the style. Giovanni Bellini's portrait of* Gentile Bellini *shows his brother stern-lipped, but gentle-eyed. Giovanni was known for his greater imagination; two of his pupils were Giorgione and Titian. (Fine Arts Gallery of San Diego.)*

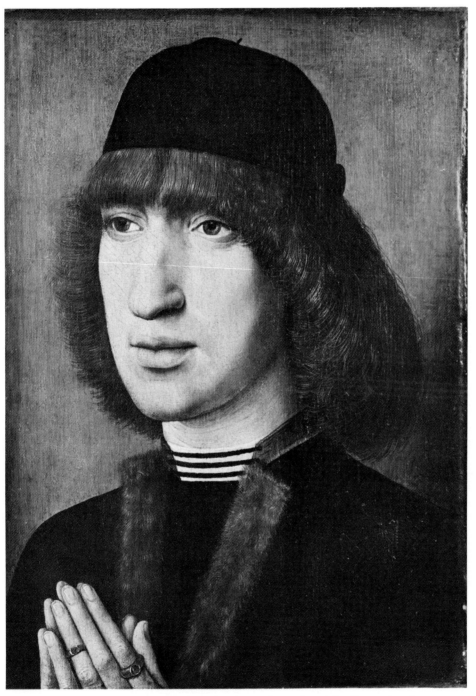

INTERNATIONAL STYLE spread to Flanders, where Hans Memling painted sensuous but pious Young Man With Folded Hands. *The masterpiece of portraiture, in the Fine Arts Gallery of San Diego, shows Italian influence.*

SOPHISTICATED ABSTRACT HEAD from the Congo was used as a mask in ceremonial funeral rites for chiefs and in the enthronement of village headmen.

PRIMITIVE SCULPTURE
at UCLA Ethnic Arts

EMOTION-CHARGED quality of Tsimshian (Northwest American Indian) sculpture haunts Janus-faced head. Note rawhide scalp, once garnished with fur. Base of neck is concave, with straps for tying the sculpture on a dancer's head.

ANOTHER TSIMSHIAN dance mask combines naturalistic carving with an assymetrical painted design in red and black. Bold and sensitive modeling is typical of Northwest American Indians.

THE LADY was lampooned by the best

OUTSIDE SENSE OF THE RIDICULOUS enlivens Thomas Rowlandson's drawing of famous 18th-century actress Sarah Siddons. (Henry E. Huntington Gallery.)

SIR JOSHUA REYNOLDS was more reverent, painted same Mrs. Siddons as the Tragic Muse *in 1784, signed his name on her skirt.* (Henry E. Huntington Gallery.)

102 SOUTHERN CALIFORNIA

SUCH SCENES
made him a painter

*GREEN MEADOWS of Suffolk were
inspiration of British artist John
Constable. "These scenes made me a
painter," he said.* View on the
Stour near Dedham *was painted in
1822, shows artist's love of
nature, mastery of composition.
(Henry E. Huntington Gallery.)*

PERILS *of Pallas Athena*

*GREEK GODDESS of wisdom glares up at workmen
who have trussed her in process of installing the classic
sculpture in the new Los Angeles County Museum
of Art. "Let's go," she seems to say.*

*ON THE RACK, she awaits next
episode in a career that began in 2nd
century A.D. when Roman sculptor
copied her from a 5th century B.C.
Greek original. The sphinx on her
helmet is a symbol of wisdom.*

THAT'S BETTER, THANK YOU, but the goddess still looks anxious, perhaps remembering centuries of burial in ruins of Ostia before she was excavated in 1797. William Randolph Hearst bought her, gave her to museum. A classical Amazon, she measures 7 feet 2 inches from sandals to helmet.

NATURALNESS *of nature in watercolor*

JOHN MARIN SAW NATURE as architecture, dynamic with pushing and pulling forces; Composition —Cape Split, Maine is in Santa Barbara Museum of Art.

DIGNITY, DISTORTION, and economy of line make Robert Gwathmey's Share
Croppers a memorable picture. Note how the strong dark and light tones emphasize
each other and strengthen the composition. Painted in 1941, it won top honors in
National Watercolor Exhibition. (Fine Arts Gallery of San Diego.)

ELONGATED GOTHIC FORMS of native Catalonia influenced The Frugal Repast,
an etching from Picasso's early Blue Period when he found models among the poor and
hungry of Paris. (Fine Arts Gallery of San Diego.)

108 SOUTHERN CALIFORNIA

PRODIGIOUS, *protean Pablo Picasso*

VIOLENT, CONVULSIVE *expressionism of* Weeping Woman With Handkerchief *was Picasso's response to Spanish Civil War. The oil painting in Los Angeles County Museum is part of his Guernica series.*

MONUMENTAL *sculptural cubism was another facet of Picasso.* Head of Woman, *1930 oil in UCLA Gallery, is one more example of distortion and reshaping of form. (Gift of Stanley N. Barbee.)*

BLEAK, SEVERE, PIOUS, A Franciscan Monk *reflects on the mystery of life and death in painting by Francisco de Zurbaran. Like many 17th-century Spanish artists, he painted altar pieces. (Santa Barbara Museum of Art.)*

THE MYSTIC monk and the Lamb of God

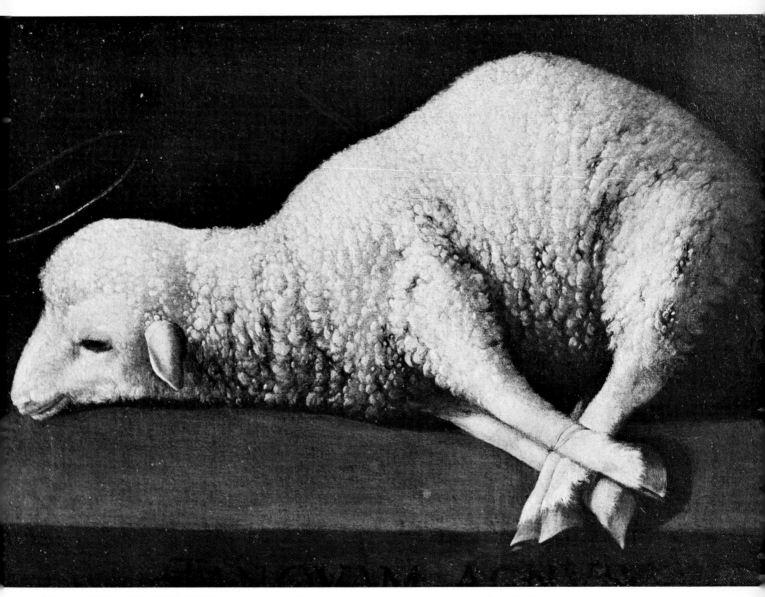

DRAMATICALLY RESTRICTED to essentials, Zurbaran's Agnus Dei portrays Lamb of God meekly awaiting slaughter, a sacrifice of atonement symbolizing crucifixion. The gentle and appealing work is in the Fine Arts Gallery of San Diego.

IN ROMANTIC *approach, Eugene Delacroix's*
Martyre de Saint Etienne *invests the stoning of Saint*
Stephen with the visual excitement of a battle
scene, adds elements of Near Eastern exoticism.
You can feel the excitement, sense
the drama and death.
(Santa Barbara Museum of Art.)

Santa Barbara

Relatively serene at the northern end of the Southern California spectrum is Santa Barbara. The art treasures of Santa Barbara begin with the noble classic facade of the Queen of Missions, designed by no less an architect than the great Vitruvius. Though this 1st-century B.C. Roman lived before anyone had ever dreamed of Santa Barbara or any other saint, the Spanish padres had access to an 18th-century translation of his book. When you visit the mission you'll probably approve of their choice. In 1786, nearly three decades before the Vitruvian facade was built, they lit an altar candle to dedicate the mission. That flame has never been allowed to die. It symbolizes the city's legacy from the Mediterranean World.

ASTROLOGY AND AMMUNITION

SANTA BARBARA MUSEUM OF ART. *1130 State Street, Santa Barbara. Hours 11 A.M. to 5 P.M. Tuesday–Saturday; 12 to 5 P.M. Sunday; closed Monday.*

You'll be conscious of the Latin inheritance when you enter the Ludington Court of the Santa Barbara Museum of Art. Here, just a step from busy State Street, you'll find yourself surrounded by relics of the antique world: a torso of Venus, a sinewy Hercules, a nymph and a satyr forever panting and forever young. On the loggia stands Castor or Pollux, one of the twin sons of Jupiter; you might be in the atrium of a Roman house.

This setting was contrived by Santa Barbara Collector Wright Ludington and Chicago architect David Adler when, in 1939, they began transforming what had once been an abandoned U.S. Post Office into an attractive art museum.

"We kept in mind," says Mr. Ludington, "the unusual parallel between California and the Mediterranean and the interest in classical art that adapts so well to this area. The Latin background of both, as well as the climate and vegetation, all add to the similarities."

A classical faith in the stars determined the opening date of the museum. Mr. Buell Hammett, first president of the board of trustees, was a believer in astrology. He had the new museum's horoscope

SURGE AND THUNDER of Homer's epic poem echo in the Ortega Dining Commons at the University of California at Santa Barbara, where artist-in-residence Howard Warshaw has covered

cast: June 5, 1941, at just 11:43 A.M., said the stars, under the sign of Gemini, those legendary twins, Castor and Pollux, defenders of Rome. The carpenters and plasterers were still at work when the star-decreed moment rolled around. Undaunted, Mr. Hammett, who combined a strong practical sense with his astral beliefs, had 2,000 Santa Barbara schoolchildren ushered into the building at precisely 11:43 on the morning of the fateful day.

It must have been auspicious, for the Santa Barbara Museum has prospered ever since, except for a brief lapse during World War II when the Home Guard stashed its ammunition in the museum safe. War's end saw the safe restored to more artistic purposes and the installation in the museum basement of Rico Lebrun as the first artist in residence. This appointment, typical of the imaginative policy of founding director Donald Bear, sparked a resurgence of interest in art that shows no sign of flagging in Santa Barbara.

"In a very real sense a community gets the art museum it deserves," says director Thomas B. Leavitt. He aims to expand the collections so that the museum will tell the whole story of man's creative expression. In pursuit of this goal he stages more than twenty exhibitions a year at the museum, as well as annually sending as many as seventy works of art from the collection to museums throughout the world.

In addition to its Greek and Roman antiquities, the Santa Barbara Museum offers the New World pleasures of the Preston Morton Collection of American Painting. Ranging from 1755 to the present, it provides a vivid survey of the history of American art. The earliest picture, and one of the rarest, is John Singleton Copley's portrait of

600 square feet with his Images from the Odyssey. *The heroic work is a grand and a graphic retelling of the ancient, classic story in acrylic polymer-based paint applied directly to a plaster wall.*

General Joshua Winslow, resplendent in his red coat and lace-trimmed satin vest. It was painted in 1755 when the Boston-born artist was only 18. After a great success in his native land, Copley left America two years before the Declaration of Independence, settled in London, and was elected a full member of the Royal Academy at the time Cornwallis was surrendering at Yorktown.

For a striking contrast with Copley's drawing room warrior, see the *Buffalo Hunter*, an Indian brave on horseback with bow full drawn. Bristling with action, this anonymous masterpiece has made Santa Barbara famous on the art circuit. For the *Buffalo Hunter* still rides the plains and has crossed the Rockies too, traveling from exhibition to exhibition.

Of interest is Rembrandt Peale's portrait of George Washington. Painted about 1795, it is a dignified and unpretentious performance by a painter, who, incidentally, opened the first fine arts gallery in America. For another dramatic contrast compare this classic portrait of Washington with Thomas Cole's dreamy landscape, *The Greeks' Departure for Troy*, a classic theme bathed in the light that never was on sea or land except at the dawn of the romantic age.

These are but four of some 400 paintings in this collection. From Adams and Avery to Zajac and Zornes, Santa Barbara has the strongest collection of American art on the West Coast.

In the European section there are excellent old master drawings, including a rare Watteau. You'll find a beautiful Degas drawing of a ballet girl resting, and a dramatic painting by the Spanish master Zurbaran, of a Franciscan monk holding a skull and, like Hamlet, pondering the mysteries of life and death.

Outstanding in the small Oriental collection is a graceful statue of Kwan Yin (Chinese goddess of mercy) from the Sung dynasty, A.D. 960-1127.

Two special attractions of the Santa Barbara Museum are the Henry Eichheim Collection of antique musical instruments, and the remarkable Schott Collection of Dolls. The latter traces the history of toys from ancient Egyptian times to our own. You may be surprised to learn that dolls could speak, sing, and even dance long before the 20th century. Many of the dolls are dressed in the height of fashion, thus presenting a history of costume through the ages— a rare treat for children, not to mention their parents.

SALVAGE FROM A FLOOD

UNIVERSITY OF CALIFORNIA AT SANTA BARBARA ART GALLERY. *Goleta. Hours 10 A.M. to 4 P.M. Monday–Saturday; 1 to 5 P.M. Sunday.*

About five miles north of Santa Barbara (take U.S. Highway 101) is one of the West's newest art galleries, the UCSB Art Gallery. On view is the Sedgwick Collection: a score of Italian, Dutch, Flemish, and German paintings of the Renaissance, some attributed to such masters as Carpaccio and Giovanni Bellini. This collection is the cream of a large ensemble collected by Robert S. Minturn and salvaged by his nephew Francis Minturn Sedgwick, who found the pictures floating around in his uncle's basement after a flood. The pictures have been admirably restored.

A most interesting item in the collection is a portrait of the mad Spanish princess, *Juana la Loca,* by Juan de Flandes. An exact contemporary of Columbus, John of Flanders, to use his English name, was a Flemish painter in the employ of Queen Isabella of Spain. He worked in Spain from 1496 until his death in 1519. Paintings by his hand are exceedingly rare. This striking and pathetic portrait of Isabella's daughter, Juana, who married Philip of Austria and produced the Holy Roman Emperor Charles V, is the chief treasure of the Santa Barbara campus. Note the psychological asymmetry of the sitter's face, half lucid, half lost, a study in split personality four hundred years before Freud.

The UCSB Gallery also houses the Sigmund Morgenroth Collection of Renaissance and Baroque Medals and Plaquettes. These are,

PITTSBURGH-BORN Mary Cassatt—who was praised by Degas—achieved renown as impressionist artist, loved to paint rosy-cheeked babies and their loving mothers like this pair in Los Angeles County Museum of Art.

SIGNORA MALATESTA shares medal with elephant (by Matteo de' Pasti, 1446), while Emperor John of Constantinople rides horseback on reverse side of his medal (by Pisanello, 1438). Both are from Morgenroth Collection, UCSB.

for the most part, commemorative medallions by Pisanello, Niccolo Fiorentino, and other masters, both major and minor. The collection has historic as well as artistic value. Among the subjects whose features are recorded here are Pope Julius II (the patron of Raphael and Michelangelo), the fiery priest Savonarola, and Mohammed II, conqueror of Constantinople in 1453. The Morgenroth Medals—there are nearly 500 of them—are like a miniature portrait gallery of the Renaissance.

The UCSB Gallery sponsors many exhibitions and art programs. Among the artists on the university faculty is Howard Warshaw. You can see his large mural, *Images from the Odyssey*, on the wall of the Ortega Dining Commons. Visitors may not eat at the cafeteria except as guests of students or faculty, but you're welcome to enter the dining room and feast your eyes on sacrificial sheep, Circe's swine, the oxen of the sun, and other meaty images of Warshaw's Odyssey in toil on high.

At the southern end of the magnificent San Joaquin Valley, Bakersfield sits astride the Kern River and occupies itself with oil and oil painting, cotton and culture, alfalfa and art. This center offers visitors as many as 25 art exhibitions a year, thanks to the presence of two flourishing galleries:

BAKERSFIELD COLLEGE GALLERY. *1801 Panorama Drive, Bakersfield. Hours 9 A.M. to 4 P.M. Monday–Friday; 7 to 9 P.M. Monday and Thursday. New exhibition every month sponsored by college art department, featuring local, national, and international work.*

BAKERSFIELD ART ASSOCIATION: THE CUNNINGHAM MEMORIAL GALLERY. *1930 R Street, Bakersfield. Hours 1:30 to 4:30 P.M. Tuesday–Sunday; closed Monday. Very active program includes frequent exhibitions, art festivals, adult and children's art classes. For guided tour, telephone ahead of time.*

OUTSIDE MUSEUM WALLS

Art in Southern California is by no means the exclusive property of museums. You'll find it in parks and post offices, in banks and churches, in court houses, on college campuses, even in cemeteries. Glendale's much-satirized Forest Lawn Memorial Park, for example, is chockablock with marble copies of Michelangelo's sculpture, exact replicas of medieval English churches (including the one at Stoke Poges where Gray wrote his famous *Elegy*), a stained-glass copy of Leonardo da Vinci's *Last Supper*, and an original 16th-century chapel, the Temple of Saint Sabina, brought here lock, stock, and *baldacchino* from Rome in 1929.

If you want to go way back into the dateless origins of Southern California art, you should visit the Indian Picture Carving Labyrinth of the Chidalgo Canyon near the Nevada border. Here in the awe-inspiring desert country you will find a mile-long maze of petroglyphs, crude rock carvings of human figures and such local animals as deer, bears, and longhorn sheep. There are also geometric designs, witness that abstract art is not exactly a novelty in Southern California.

To see what Indian artisans did under Spanish tutelage, visit the Mission of San Gabriel Arcángel on Mission Drive in San Gabriel, nine miles east of downtown Los Angeles. Here inside the buttressed walls which architect Father Cruzano designed on the model of the famous mosque-cathedral of his native Cordova, you will find the Stations of the Cross painted on sailcloth by Indian neophytes. In passing you can also see one of the earliest European art treasures of Southern California, a portrait of the Virgin painted on a banner. When the Spanish padres unfurled it before a mob of howling, hostile Indians on September 8, 1771, it had a miraculous effect. The Indians threw down their bows and arrows and offered gifts of beads and seeds to "the Beautiful Queen."

It is interesting to compare the primitive Indian paintings of the mission with the studied, retrospective view of history offered by the Edward Biberman mural, *The Founding of Los Angeles*, which adorns the walls of the Los Angeles Federal Office Building and Post Office. Among other mural decorations in Los Angeles and vicinity you'll find work by Dean Cornwell and Charles Kassler in Bertram Goodhue's imposing Los Angeles Public Library. In the Santa Monica Public Library see *Man's Twofold Development*, an interesting symbolic painting by California's Stanton Macdonald-Wright.

Don't forget that Los Angeles landmark, Simon Rodia's fantastic towers in Watts (see page 60). You can compare these with a more conventional obelisk north of Los Angeles in mountainous Griffith Park, celebrated for its wonderful views. Here, in front of the Planetarium, is the 40-foot Astronomers' Monument, topped by an astrolabe and embellished with figures of Copernicus, Galileo, Newton, and other stars.

SOLID *and durable expressionistic forms*

BRILLIANT COLOR, substantial form of Cézanne's
Still Life With Cherries and Peaches, *painted in 1883,*
exemplify the artist's success in making something
solid and durable from Impressionism.
(Los Angeles County Museum of Art.)

SIMILAR SCENES *with centuries between*

THREE CENTURIES separate Flemish Pieter Breughel (called The Elder) from American Albert Bierstadt, but the two have much in common. Both traveled in Italy and responded to the grandeur of the Alps. Crossing the Alps in 1554, Breughel was perhaps more impressed by them than by all the paintings he had seen in Renaissance Italy. Bierstadt, returning from his Italian journey in 1857, inspired to paint places which no other artist had rendered, found ideal landscapes in America's Rockies.

IN PARABLE OF THE SOWER by Breughel, painted about 1560, note the interesting manner in which the sower is incidental to painter's interest in landscape. (Timken Gallery.)

*YOSEMITE VALLEY, painted by Bierstadt in 1868. He
was more concerned with grandeur of the mountain
scenery than tiny fishermen, who merely emphasize
scale. Romantic pictures like this made Europeans
and Easterners eager to see the West. Exhibited in
Rome,* Yosemite Valley *drew record crowds.
(Oakland Art Museum: Gift of Marguerite Laird in
memory of her parents.)*

KALEIDOSCOPE OF COMPLEMENTARY COLORS is provided by a gallery goer lost in admiration of Thomas Bangs' Tweeters and IBM Tube. Both European and American fabric designers are now finding inspiration in the latest color experiments of op and pop art.

FORMS ON CANVAS *and in junk*

Kurt Schwitters, a German, and Wassilj Kandinsky, a Russian, were outstanding innovators. Despite the purposeful negative character of the Dada movement (see *Glossary*), leader Schwitters could not resist being constructive, even when using old wheels, funnels, and other "found objects" in his compositions. Kandinsky freed art from its dependence on externals, achieved effects close to music. Note the similarity of design between Schwitters' construction (1919) and the Kandinsky lithograph (1923). Both works are part of the collection of the Los Angeles County Museum of Art.

WITH LOVING care, Kurt Schwitters assembled debris for Construction for Noble Ladies, *arranged it with unerring taste into artful composition. (Los Angeles County Museum of Art.)*

DYNAMIC INTERACTION of planes, colors, geometric forms, makes Kandinsky lithograph, Composition With Chessboard-Orange, *exciting visual adventure. (Los Angeles County Museum of Art.)*

SOUTHERN CALIFORNIA **125**

AMERICA'S Ash Can School

AT THE END of the 19th century a group of American painters reacted against soft-focus impressionism by looking closely at the realism of commonplace subjects. They were Robert Henri (1865–1929), George Luks (1867–1933), John Sloan (1871–1951), William Glackens (1870–1938). Slums, saloons, and prize fights appealed to them as subject matter. Conservative art patrons referred to them as the Ash Can School. Henri, who preferred common people to aristocrats, was a figurehead of the group, but its spiritual godfather was Thomas Eakins (1844–1916), painter of American athletes.

THE WRESTLERS, by Thomas Eakins, shocked academicians. "Why paint gladiators," he said in answer, "when there's a gym around the corner." (Los Angeles County Museum of Art.)

GEORGE BELLOWS, *most vigorous of Ash Can painters, shows teeming life of New York slums in* Cliff Dwellers, *captures sultry atmosphere of summer night in crowded slum. Note clotheslines as compositional device, linking two sides of picture. (Los Angeles County Museum of Art.)*

BLEEKER STREET KID, *by George Luks, is dressed up like an angelic choir boy, but the starched collar emphasizes traits of a slum urchin, favorite model for painter's candid but sympathetic portraits. (Scripps College Art Galleries.)*

SOUTHERN CALIFORNIA 127

DRAMATIC LIGHTING *deepens introspection*

EARLY IN THE 17th century the Italian painter Caravaggio revolutionized art by the simple technique of illuminating his figures in a narrow beam of light. The idea spread north to Holland, east to Spain, sparked the sometimes theatrical movement known as Baroque. Among its masters were El Greco, Ribera, and Rembrandt. All used the magic of light to capture human personality, and deepen analysis. As shown here, St. Bartholomew's face seems illuminated from within, St. Peter's by some celestial spotlight. Galileo's lighting adds enigmatic mood.

PENETRATING portrait of Galileo, by Jusepe de Ribera, probes mind of the scientist whose discoveries clashed with church dogma. (Timken Gallery.)

PENITENT ST. PETER, by El Greco, gazes heavenward in mystic ecstasy. Picture was most popular at New York and San Francisco World's Fairs, 1939 and 1940. (Fine Arts Gallery of San Diego.)

REMBRANDT'S Saint Bartholomew, at left, emerges from deep shadow, holding symbol of his martyrdom—he was flayed alive. (Timken Gallery.)

129

MOTHER AND CHILD—*an ageless theme*

Every artist adds his own variations to the basic theme of mother and child. Though none had ever seen the Madonna, painters of the Middle Ages and Renaissance vied with each other in creating visions of maternal protection and heavenly majesty on which believers could feast their eyes in the dazzling House of God.

If Crivelli endows his Madonna with the gold and velvet trappings of royalty, Rembrandt, two centuries later, prefers a simpler iconography. He shows us not the Queen of Heaven but a timeless peasant woman and her family escaping from the persecution of Herod. Personally acquainted with similar tyranny, Ben Shahn fled his native Russia in 1906 as a boy of eight and achieved fame in America as a social realist painter of the 1930's.

MARY ENFOLDS JESUS in a homespun cloak as Joseph leads his family to safety in Rembrandt's great etching of 1654, Flight Into Egypt. *The contrast of light and dark, typical of Rembrandt, heightens drama of nocturnal escape and emphasizes isolation and unity of family. (Mills College Gallery.)*

GOTHIC PIETY, *Renaissance luxury blend in* Madonna and Child *painted about 1470 by Carlo Crivelli. The reflective mother tenderly encircles the baby, while every line of composition draws attention to his dreamy expression. (Fine Arts Gallery of San Diego.)*

FIERCELY PROTECTIVE, this mother shields her child from social injustice and every menace of an anxious age. The distorted hands of the mother and the infant's stunted feet add power and pathos to a classic theme. (Lullaby by Ben Shahn, Santa Barbara Museum of Art.)

STUDENT STUDIES in shade of stainless steel sculpture by Piotr Kowalski, whose specialty is exploding metal underwater. The graceful 30-feet high arcs are a form of habitable sculpture, ideal for a quiet hideaway. More often than not, they are used for study.

SCULPTURE *transforms a college campus*

IN THE SUMMER of 1965, thanks to the combined efforts of Art Professor Kenneth Glenn, his students, and nine internationally known artists, the placid campus of California State College at Long Beach was transformed into a showplace of modern sculpture. The college and local community raised funds to play host to the first International Sculpture Symposium to be held in America. Private industry put redwood, concrete, aluminum, stainless steel, and other materials at the disposal of visiting sculptors. One firm, North American Aviation, provided special equipment for shaping steel through controlled underwater detonations. These made less noise than the sculpture explosion now visible on campus.

HEAVY TIMBERS bound with steel straps mark southwest corner of campus, invite strollers, climbers, sitters, readers. One of the more interesting of the group, this subject was executed by a team of students during symposium. Its massive strength is main attraction.

SOUTHERN CALIFORNIA   133

ARE THEY...or aren't they...or are they?

SUSPECT PAINTINGS have been a problem ever since art began. So many spurious pictures have infiltrated the United States that the federal government has passed a law making it a crime if a person "with intent to defraud alters the appearance of an object to give it antiquity or parity or changes the source of authorship." Museum directors are constantly on guard against bogus works, even though fakes may have more appeal than authentic works by the very artist who has been aped.

NO QUESTION AS TO AUTHENTICITY of these girls. They are Emily Anderson and Pinkie, by Sir Thomas Lawrence, acquired through Sir Joseph Duveen by Henry E. Huntington. Turn pictures upside down to see how Lawrence's beautifully brushed, fluid background is plastic complement to figures.

IMPOSING PORTRAIT of Sedki Effendi is "definitely attributed to Sir Thomas
Lawrence" (according to the Fine Arts Gallery of San Diego), as well as "probably by
one of Lawrence's pupils" (according to Kenneth Garlick, foremost Lawrence expert).
There's never a dull moment in art.

THE BLUE FOUR
in Pasadena

AMONG THE PROUDEST possessions of the Pasadena Art Museum are works by the Blue Four (*Die Blaue Vier*), an important group of painters formed in Germany in 1924 by Wassilj Kandinsky, Lyonel Feininger, Paul Klee, and Alexei Jawlensky. They exhibited in Dresden and Wiesbaden, exerting a strong influence on the development of modern art. Their American agent, Galka Scheyer, introduced their work to the West Coast in 1926.

WATERCOLOR by Kandinsky, Severe in Sweet, is an austere geometry lesson.

GATE TO HADES, a watercolor and ink painted in 1921 by Paul Klee, "took line for a walk" in his own words, with witty and satiric effect.

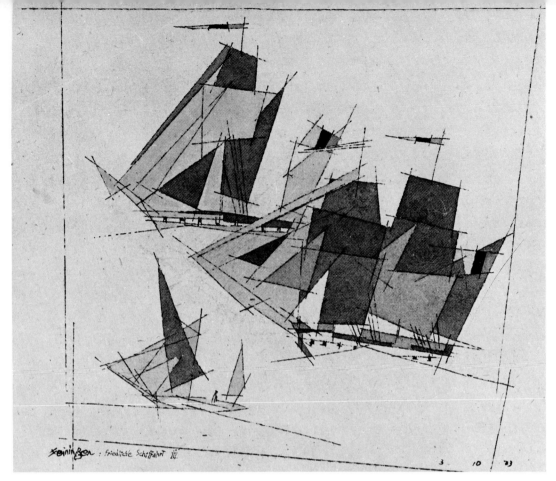

PEACEFUL VOYAGE III reveals Lyonel Feininger's unique combination of
architectural vision and fantasy, suggesting much with economy of line; the ships
almost move. Artist began career as a cartoonist in Paris.

MOST REALISTIC of Blue Four was
Jawlensky, in whom "love for art
burned like a holy fire." Influenced
by Van Gogh, Cézanne, Gauguin,
he became a powerful expressionist,
as witnessed by this boldly
painted Blonde, a major work done in
1911, before he joined the Four.

SOUTHERN CALIFORNIA 137

Northern California

NEW DIRECTIONS AND NEW POSSIBILITIES

The recorded art history of Northern California begins with a 16th-century shipwreck in Drake's Bay and continues with 20th-century "happenings" in San Francisco. In 1966 one of the latter attracted 9,000 people to the Longshoremen's Auditorium for three days of high jinks, leaning heavily on audience participation. There were strip teasers, obligingly rerobed by the police, a free-for-all trampoline, a female pelted with raw eggs, people dressed up in American flags, ear-splitting music on the bongo drums. Where was the art? On the walls and ceilings, projected there by means of pop and op art color slides, as in an old-fashioned magic lantern show.

The shipwreck was less contrived. It wasn't arranged, it really happened in 1595 to one of Cermeño's Spanish treasure galleons, the favorite victims of Sir Francis Drake. On the long voyage home from China to Mexico, this ship was driven onto the shoals by a violent tempest in the vicinity of Drake's Bay, north of San Francisco.

Among the silks and spices of the lost cargo were porcelains of the Chia Ching (1522-1566) and Wan Li (1573-1619) periods. The Spaniards, like most subsequent collectors, found those luminous colors and glazes hard to resist, especially the famed "Mohammedan blue" of the Chia Ching ware, a dark violet of great strength and intensity.

BARN OWLS, BY JOHN JAMES AUDUBON.
Such dramatic drawings of American birds earned
international renown for the artist. The color
aquatint is in the Achenbach Foundation for Graphic
Arts at the California Palace of the Legion of Honor.

FROM ANY POINT OF VIEW, San Francisco and the Bay Area offer feast for the eyes with five major art museums, active galleries, many new shows each month. The offerings range from pre-Columbian artifacts to cybernetic sculpture.

Some of the lost pieces were recovered centuries later and may now be seen at the California Historical Society in San Francisco. In point of time they are California's first Oriental collection, and they make an interesting comparison with the 6,000 piece Brundage collection of Oriental art which went on public view for the first time in a new wing of San Francisco's De Young Museum in 1966.

The physical beauty of San Francisco and the Bay Area, along with the gold rush prosperity of the city and the excitement of a burgeoning international port, made San Francisco a magnet for artists from all over the world. William Keith came here from Scotland, Samuel Marsden Brookes from England, Marius Dahlgren from Denmark, C. C. Nahl from Germany. You will find paintings of their adopted homeland in the Oakland Art Museum.

CHECKLIST OF SAN FRANCISCO GALLERIES

Three non-commercial art centers in San Francisco are worth visiting for their permanent and changing exhibitions. The California Historical Society, 2090 Jackson Street, is a treasure trove of California art and history, beginning with the Chinese porcelains salvaged from Cermeño's shipwreck in 1595.

The Society of California Pioneers, 456 McAllister Street, in the Civic Center, has a museum of California relics, a library, archives, and a gallery devoted to early California art. The Society's facilities are open to the public, free of charge, Monday through Friday from 10 A.M. to 4 P.M. You'll see California landscapes and portraits by Thomas Hill, C. C. Nahl, and others. The kids will love the first U.S. Mail coach of the Wells Fargo Overland Express. It is polished daily and looks as good as new.

Here is an alphabetical list of San Francisco's commercial galleries. Check the Sunday *Examiner and Chronicle* for current shows.

Arleigh	1812 Pacific Avenue
Artists' Cooperative	2224 Union Street
Berkeley	855 Sansome Street
Bolles	729 Sansome Street
Conacher	134 Maiden Lane
Dilexi	631 Clay
Galerie de Tours	559 Sutter
Gilbert	590 Sutter
Gump's	250 Post Street
Karamanduca	1843 Union
Labaudt	1407 Gough
Laky	Mustard Building, Ghirardelli Square
Lesser's	685 Sutter
Maxwell	551 Sutter
Museum West	900 North Point, Ghirardelli Square
Pantechnicon	1849 Union
Pearson	3489 Sacramento
Quay	521 Pacific, entrance at 2 Jerome Alley
Rabow	2130 Leavenworth
Stewart-Verde	539 Sutter
The Little Gallery	1980 Union
Triangle	578 Sutter
Vorpal	17 Adler
Willoughby-Toschi	521 Sutter
Williams	2059 Union Street
Winblad	1814 Union Street

San Francisco Bay Area

Art, ever the handmaiden of prosperity, arrived in post-gold rush San Francisco in the unexpected form of much-needed fire engines. What they lacked in water pressure they made up for in beauty, judging from a description in the contemporary newspaper *Alta California*. This paper was owned by a pioneer Mormon journalist named Sam Brannan, who also owned the fire engines and can thus claim to be San Francisco's first art collector:

"We yesterday obtained a peep at the new fire engine belonging to the Brannan Fire Association of this city, which arrived Saturday on the clipper *Bostonian* from Boston. On the left side of the box is a landscape painting, with horses, trees and a lake with a boating party; above it on the same side of the air chamber is an exquisite painting on copper, said to have been copied from an old English engraving, worth $60 in itself. We were not quite satisfied as to what the painting was intended to represent. There are four female figures in the foreground, dancing to the music of old Father Time, who sits playing upon a harp, his scythe lying at his feet and a shield beside him on an hour glass; beyond the dancers is a monument with carved busts upon it, wreathed with ivy; and above, on a cloud, in his golden chariot, sits Phoebus, reining the bold coursers of the sun. On the right side of the box is a beautifully correct view of Niagara Falls from the Canadian side; above, on the same side is a painting copied from a French picture and representing three females at the bath, one of whom is dallying with a swan upon the stream. To complete the beauty and symmetry of the engine there are four richly-painted fire buckets hanging upon the scroll work, one at each corner. The paintings upon them . . . are beautiful in conception and execution."

This was a start for San Francisco.

If subsequent collectors never got so much in a single haul as Sam Brannan's fire engine, they nevertheless accumulated enough art to fill several museums. Almost overnight San Francisco was termed the emporium of a new world. As early as 1853 Oriental art objects were being sold by importing merchants Tobin and Duncan in their San Francisco Chinese Sales Room, which contemporary lithographs show thronged with ladies in crinolines, gentlemen in stove pipe hats. In

BATHED IN ROMANTIC LIGHT, Albert Bierstadt's
Yosemite Valley *was painted in 1868. El Capitan*
rises in majesty on the right; on the left, The Sentinel
with Cathedral Spires and Cathedral Rock beyond.
The Merced River winds placidly across the valley
floor. The artist made sketches on location throughout
Yosemite, then he later painted the picture in
Rome, where people flocked to see it. Such landscapes
made California, as well as Albert Bierstadt, famous
around the world. (Oakland Art Museum.)

FAR FROM POMP and luxury of Versailles, Louis Le Nain painted stoic, stolid Peasants Before their House, stern as a silent reminder of reality. (Detail: Legion of Honor.)

1876 the first Japanese art store opened in the Palace Hotel, and Oriental art was the rage of Nob Hill.

In the meantime California's Big Four—Charles Crocker, Mark Hopkins, Leland Stanford, and Collis P. Huntington—linked the two oceans with a golden spike and began to buy up the old masters of Europe. The Hawaii-U.S. reciprocity treaty was signed in 1876, and San Francisco sugar refiner Claus Spreckels was on his way to making the fortune that would eventually build the California Palace of the Legion of Honor. The craze for owning art was amply nourished by the means to obtain it.

Like journalist-firechief Sam Brannan, one of the great collectors was a newspaperman. He was Michael Henry De Young, owner of the *San Francisco Chronicle*. The paper was just one of his holdings. Others included a theater and 80,000 lots of urban real estate. Since he had bought these for only eight dollars apiece, he sometimes gave one away as a door prize at the theater.

De Young had the voracious appetite of a born collector. "Most intelligent men and women go through life with fads," he said, "some for literature, some for art, some for gathering things. When I was a young man I acquired a fad for antiquities. I didn't want to dispose of them. I wanted to keep them. That is where I got the museum bug."

He began by accumulating several hundred stuffed birds. Then he went to an auction and bought a lot of Chinese carvings. To make room for the carvings he had to get rid of the birds. He offered them to the city of San Francisco. Birds belong in the park, they decided, and dumped the problem in the lap of the park commissioner. The park commissioner hooted; he had no place for De Young's feathered friends, especially since they were stuffed.

"I had to put them up at auction," said De Young. "The auctioneer returned me $56 for a collection that cost me $600. It burned a hole in my brain."

That hole in De Young's brain was the foundation of the Art Museum that now bears his name.

In 1893 De Young was named director general of the California Midwinter International Exposition in Golden Gate Park, which was then a barren waste of sand hills and thickly growing chaparral. De Young had already been California Commissioner to the World's Columbian Exposition in Chicago, and he knew how a world's fair should be run. The California fair was a success; it even made money. The grateful directors turned the net profit and the fair's Egyptian-style Fine Arts Pavilion over to De Young to use the building and the money for the benefit of San Francisco in whatever way he saw fit.

He had his heart set on a museum, but the park commissioner told him that a museum did not belong in the Park.

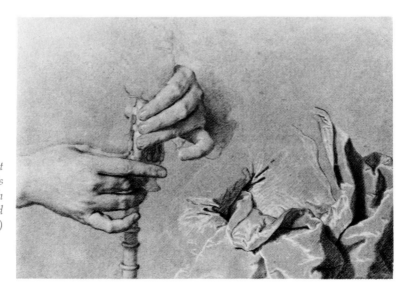

PEASANTS WERE of no interest to Hyacinthe Rigaud. Painter of Louis XIV was more concerned with exquisite details of hands and drapery. (Legion of Honor.)

GIRL WITH GREEN EYES, by Henri Matisse, gazes serenely at visitors to San Francisco Museum of Art. She caused a furor when first exposed in Paris in 1909.

146 NORTHERN CALIFORNIA

"Every great museum in the world is in a park," said De Young, and he reeled off a list from the Tuileries to the Tiergarten to prove his point. "The setting is important," he added prophetically, "I want a museum that people will go to."

"All right," said the commissioner. "Put your museum in the park." "I knew what I was about," said De Young.

THE CITY'S OLDEST ART MUSEUM

M. H. DE YOUNG MEMORIAL MUSEUM. *Golden Gate Park, San Francisco. Hours 10 A.M. to 5 P.M. daily. Encyclopedic collections of Western art, Avery Brundage collection of Asian Art. Japanese Tea Garden adjacent.*

The earliest acquisition of the De Young Museum is a 6,000-pound bronze vase by Gustave Doré that's twice as tall as you are. Called *The Vintage*, it is a sculptural saga of vine and wine involving battalions of cupids, satyrs, nymphs, and bacchantes, some of them in such a bibulous state that they seem to be falling off the vase. The artist never got around to paying for the casting of this vase, and the French foundry exhibited it hopefully at the Columbian Exposition in Chicago, but found no takers. They had better luck at the San Francisco Midwinter Fair, where De Young fell in love with the distressed property and bought it for $10,000. It would be worth that much melted into pennies.

This unique bargain (it is the only thing of its kind in the world) is a vestige of the mixed grab bag of art that the De Young Museum used to be in the days when people came to gape at Napoleon's bed and an alabaster model of the Taj Mahal. Such items have been stowed away under the guiding hands of such directors as Walter Heil and Jack McGregor, and the De Young's 200,000 square feet of floor space are now occupied by more authentic art treasures. The De Young welcomes more than a million visitors a year. Multiple visits are recommended; you cannot assimilate it all in a single day.

During your explorations you will find many masterpieces. From the golden age of Athens comes a black-figured amphora with nymphs, sirens, insatiable satyrs, and spirited horses, drawn with such style and verve that they may very well be by that anonymous 5th century B.C. genius known as the Antiope Painter. Another favorite from the antique world is an Egyptian ibis of bronze and wood, a sculpture at once stylized and deeply felt. Genoa's contribution to your pleasure is a canvas by Magnasco, *Soldiers Feasting*, painted in the 18th century but eminently modern in feeling. Flanders offers a great Rubens, *The Tribute Money*, a masterful composition aglow with the golden aura of that Naples-yellow which this painter used with such immediate and lasting effect.

Some of the best French works at the De Young are in the field of sculpture: a marvelous medieval *Madonna and Child* from Metz, infused with the simple faith of the 14th century; a self-portrait bust by Antoine Coysevox, equally articulate with the skepticism of a more rational age.

The Kress Collection offers some 40 paintings in three galleries in the north wing of the museum. They span the history of European art from the Middle Ages to the 18th century—from Fra Angelico to Tiepolo. Outstanding is the latter's *Triumph of Flora*, an exuberant allegory by this great decorative painter. Note El Greco's *Saint Francis Venerating the Crucifix*. It was chosen especially for the museum by the donor, Rush Kress, as a dramatic representation of the saint for whom San Francisco is named.

Prominent among the American painters at the De Young are Copley, Benjamin West, James Peale, Thomas Cole, and that prolific recorder of California life, Charles Christian Nahl. Here, however,

TEA AND FORTUNE COOKIES

You will approve Michael Henry De Young's choice of setting for his museum (Golden Gate Park), especially when you visit the adjoining Japanese Tea Garden with its moon bridge and many-tiered pagodas. It is beautiful at any season, but most of all in spring when the buildings seem to float on clouds of cherry blossoms. You can sip tea and munch on fortune cookies in the teahouse, then stroll along the garden paths to admire the ornamental pools and the huge bronze statue of Buddha, ensconced on a lotus flower. Cast in Tajima in 1790, he weighs a ton and a half, and is said to be the largest Buddha ever to leave Japan.

It's interesting to compare this massive and majestic figure with some of the other statuary in Golden Gate Park. An agreeable modern addition is the glistening ellipse of Robert Howard's Whale Fountain, which you will see opposite the De Young Museum, in front of the California Academy of Sciences. Watch out for wind-blown water.

JASMINE OR GREEN TEA? Kimono-clad waitresses take orders in San Francisco's Japanese Tea Garden adjacent to De Young Museum. The garden's bronze Buddha, a handsome gift of S. & G. Gump Co., is the largest in America.

you will find the last in a classic mood with a realistic triptych that must have raised Victorian eyebrows when it was painted in 1870. It is *The Rape of the Sabines* in three thrilling episodes—Abduction, Captivity, Invasion—a high-water mark in the history of anecdotal painting, and a popular favorite.

The Roscoe and Margaret Oakes Collection contains fine examples of Dutch, Flemish, French and English art of the 17th, 18th and early 19th centuries. The Dutch school is represented by two Rembrandts, Frans Hals' popular *Cavalier*, and a landscape by Aelbert Cuyp. Rubens and Van Dyck are the stars of the Flemish collection. Among the painters of the French school are Boucher, Poussin, Georges de la Tour, Nattier, Greuze, and David. Portraits by Sir Joshua Reynolds and Sir Henry Raeburn represent the British school.

Much of the De Young's French furniture was also given to the museum by the Oakes. There are three French salons, filled with the bronzes, *boiseries*, and *bibelots* of Louis XVI's time. See also the charming, painted bed-sitting room from a chalet in the Italian Alps, the 15th-century Spanish room with its richly carved ceiling, and the Wespien room, a beautifully installed German rococo interior from the 18th-century palace of Johann von Wespien, lord mayor of Aachen. Hit by bombs during World War II, it has been at least partially resurrected here on the shores of the Pacific.

The De Young Museum has long had a notable collection of Asiatic art. One of the popular favorites is the great stone *Hand of Buddha*, a striking example of Chinese sculpture of the Northern Ch'i Dynasty (A.D. 550-577). This beautifully-articulated hand is in the central court of the De Young's new west wing, which, opened to the public in June, 1966, houses the largest collection of Asian art in the American West and overlooks the Japanese Tea Garden.

A BRIDGE OF KNOWLEDGE

In 1959 Avery Brundage, art connoisseur and president of the International Committee for the Olympic Games, offered his collection of Oriental art to San Francisco if the city would provide it with a proper home. The public responded by voting a $2.7 million bond issue to build a new wing onto the De Young Museum, including the last word in facilities for the display, conservation, and restoration of Oriental art. Two floors of exhibition galleries provide 100,000 square feet to show the treasures. A dry room in the basement has three controllable climates to prevent excessive oxidation of the centuries-old bronzes. Another room with moist-air control protects wood and lacquer pieces from dry rot and warping.

Brundage has given San Francisco the fruit of 30 years of collecting. In donating it, he said it was his hope that San Francisco and the Bay Area would become one of the world's great centers for the study and appreciation of Oriental culture. There is no doubt that this hope has now been fulfilled. The 6,000 pieces in the Brundage Collection provide one of the world's largest collections of jade, the most representative display of Chinese bronzes in the West, one of the world's best ensembles of Khmer sculpture, and perhaps the greatest collection of Chinese ceramics in the United States.

Altogether, in the words of the donor, the collection builds a bridge of knowledge between the East and the West. Experts have tried to estimate the collection's value, but, since Asiatic governments have now clamped export restrictions on their national treasure, the pieces that Avery Brundage had the good fortune to collect at the right moment are not replaceable at any price.

The oldest Chinese artifact in the collection is a neolithic ceramic jar from Kansu Province, made about 2,500 years before the birth of

NEPALESE IDEAL of feminine beauty is realized in 18th-century image of goddess, White Tara, *masterpiece of repoussé work in which gilded copper is richly ornamented with patterns in relief made by hammering on reverse side of metal. (Avery Brundage Collection, De Young Museum. Photo courtesy Asia House Gallery, New York.)*

Christ. Other rare Chinese pieces are a beautifully preserved 11th-century bronze rhinoceros, and the first recorded gilded bronze statue of Buddha, created in 338 B.C.

From a T'ang Dynasty tomb (A.D. 618-907) comes a rare blue-glazed horse, typical of the lively naturalism of the sculpture produced in this golden age of Chinese sculpture. Older and more stylized are the Haniwa clay tomb figurines that guarded the graves of Japanese *samurai* as early as the 5th century. They have a haunted and haunting look, these simply modeled figures, like people risen from the dead. The helmeted *Haniwa Warrior* in the Brundage Collection is one of many fine examples.

For the more decorative side of Japanese art you can turn to the peonies and plum trees on the painted screens. In the Momoyama Period (1578-1615) the feudal barons vied with each other to brighten their castles with all the delights of nature lavishly painted on sliding doors and enormous screens, often against backgrounds of gleaming gold and silver. The Brundage Collection has 35 of these screens, ranging in subject matter from *Crows on a Snowy Branch* to scenes from the *Tale of Genji*, Lady Murasaki's exquisite novel of life in medieval Japan nearly a thousand years ago.

The Indian sculpture of the Brundage Collection reflects the multifarious forms and subject matter of the world's most fantastic mythology. Here you will find contemplative Buddhas side by side with whirling Sivas, ascetic Hindu saints with every rib showing, and voluptuous Parvatis. You'll meet all the Brahmanic gods, among them Ganesh with his elephant's head, Kali with her necklace of human skulls, Krishna in perpetual pursuit of milkmaids. Especially noteworthy is the standing Bodhisattva Maitreya, the Buddha of the Future, who will return to earth from paradise to save the world.

FROM ASIA TO PARIS

THE CALIFORNIA PALACE OF THE LEGION OF HONOR. *Lincoln Park, San Francisco. Hours 10 A.M. to 5 P.M. daily. French art and furniture, sculpture by Rodin.*

From the magic mythology of the Orient to the Cartesian logic of France is just a step in San Francisco. It is merely a question of changing parks. A bus or cab ride from the De Young and the Japanese Tea Garden to Lincoln Park at the north end of town is like going from Kyoto to Paris.

A replica of Pierre Rousseau's Palais de la Légion d'Honneur in Paris, the California Palace of the Legion of Honor is one of America's most beautiful museums. Its setting, overlooking the green pines of Lincoln Park and the vista of the Golden Gate, is without peer anywhere.

The French note is struck as soon as you drive around the circular terrace. Rodin's *Three Shades* stand there with the Golden Gate Bridge in the background. His famous *Thinker* sits in the court of honor beyond the arch of the Ionic entrance portico. To pass through that arch is to enter the atmosphere of 18th-century France, the classic calm of which is punctuated by the rugged and powerful mass of Rodin's sculpture. Behind *The Thinker,* the six Corinthian columns of the entrance are crowned by a simple pediment inscribed, as in Paris, "*Honneur Et Patrie.*"

It was Mr. and Mrs. Adolph Spreckels who gave this superb memorial to the City of San Francisco in 1924 as a museum of art dedicated to the memory of California soldiers who fell in the first World War. A dedicated Francophile, Mrs. Spreckels was also a personal friend of Auguste Rodin. With the sculptor's help she chose the 40 Rodin bronzes which constitute one of the Legion's outstanding collections.

A SAINT, A SACRIFICE, A SCANDAL

Inside the museum you will see some of Rodin's greatest pieces. Outstanding are the larger-than-life size *Saint John the Baptist* and the dramatic, distorted *Burghers of Calais*, Rodin's 19th century version of those 14th century heroes who volunteered to sacrifice their lives when King Edward III of England offered to spare the beleaguered town if six leading citizens were delivered to him barefoot, bareheaded, and with ropes around their necks. Although the figures at the Legion are a miniature replica of the life-sized group still in France, they have lost little of their monumentality, none of their emotional power.

Don't miss the beautifully articulated male figure called *The Age of Bronze*. In 1877, when the plaster cast of this statue was first shown at an exhibition in Brussels, it was called *The Vanquished*. It was so lifelike that Rodin was accused of having molded it directly on a living model! Vehemently denying the accusation, the then little-known sculptor had the plaster statue shipped to Paris and exhibited under its present name. Again the hue and cry went up: He had molded it on a living person! Rodin demanded an investigation. Belgian friends came forward as eye witnesses to the honesty of the work, but the Purchasing Commission of the French Museums declined to buy the suspect statue. Because of all the noise the public flocked to see Rodin's *Age of Bronze*. Scandal had made the sculptor famous, and famous he has been ever since.

FRENCH FRIVOLITY, AMERICAN AUSTERITY

The garden courts and attractively appointed galleries of the Palace of the Legion of Honor invite the leisurely inspection of a famous collection of French antiques. Most of the furniture—and it includes some of the finest pieces in America—came from the New York house of Collis and Arabella Huntington. That landmark, long since replaced by Tiffany's, was inherited by the Huntingtons' son Archer, who gave his parents' furniture to the museum. You will see it now in a series of handsomely installed French rooms, authentic to the last detail, and but a step backward in time.

This congenial setting is a perfect complement for the Legion's French paintings. Don't miss Largillière's portrait of the *Marquis de*

DESPITE WIG and fancy clothes,
The Marquis of Montespan *emerges*
as a strong-willed character in
revealing portrait by Nicolas de
Largillière. Husband of Louis
XIV's mistress, the Marquis detested
artificiality of Versailles, defied
the king. (Legion of Honor.)

Montespan, husband of a mistress of Louis XIV. Largillière's *Marquis* is a strong and hot-tempered character, but this is more than the portrait of a man: with its extravagant peruke and its plethora of taffeta and lace, the portrait sums up the luxury and elegance of that vainglorious charade that was life at the court of Versailles.

That charade becomes sensual with Vigée-Lebrun's *Bacchante* and Nattier's intimate portrait of the *Duchess of Chateauroux as Thalia*, the Comic Muse, and downright cute in Carle Van Loo's amusing panels of children representing the arts of painting, music, sculpture, and architecture. These were commissioned by Madame de Pompadour and came to California by a devious route. Having been stolen by the Nazis from the Rothschild collection, they were found during World War II in the Austrian salt mines of Alt-Aussee by Thomas Carr Howe, deputy chief of monuments for the U.S. Army and director of the Palace of the Legion of Honor. When the Rothschilds consigned the restored pictures to a New York dealer, Howe bought them for the museum, where they await the visitor.

STEAM HEAT is just what is needed on a cool San Francisco day. Chabas' famous September Morn, on loan to Palace of Legion of Honor, seems in need of a little warmth, as she waits for return trip to New York.

You'll find a striking contrast to the frivolities of the French court in the rough and uncouth atmosphere of Louis Le Nain's *Peasants Before Their House*. These were the people of France who would soon be clamoring for bread and blood. They stare out at you with the dull inquiry of the undernourished mixed with a smouldering resentment that would burst into flame with the revolution. Le Nain's prophetic realism went unheeded. Pictures like this were not shown at Versailles because they were too true.

The Legion's collection of French painting continues into the 19th century with Corot's tranquil *View of Rome*; Renoir's monumental but lightly brushed *Mother and Child*, a spontaneous and affectionate observation of the artist's son Coco and his nurse Gabrielle; Pissarro's light-flooded *Harbor of Dieppe*; and Daubigny's limpid *River Scene*, enough to make you pack a hamper for a picnic on the banks of the Seine. And if you want to discover the quiet charm of a little-known French genre painter, see the *Portrait of the Artist's Son* by Louis Boilly, an introspective picture of an appealing, imaginative child, painted with talent and love.

Do not let the predominance of French art in this museum make you neglect the paintings of other schools. The Legion has a dazzling

*LAUGHING HER HEAD OFF, Rufino Tamayo's
Laughing Woman, painted in 1950, combines hot color,
Zapotec primitivism, and modern
expressionism. (Crocker Art Gallery.)*

*ANOTHER BY TAMAYO, shows artist's love for humor and bright color.
Fumador (The Smoker) is from Arizona State University. Like Orozco, Rivera, and
Siqueiros, Tamayo is a Mexican artist well represented in the West.*

Guardi, *The Church of Santa Maria della Salute at Venice*, and many paintings by Spanish, Flemish, Dutch, and German masters.

Outstanding among the last is a magnificent picture by Lucas Cranach the Elder, depicting *A Lady of the Saxon Court as Judith*. The Protestant conscience of the German Reformation has penetrated the mind of this determined and stylishly dressed lady who has just cut off the head of Holofernes. The picture is a great favorite with painters. As you study it, you will see why. Every shape is sharply defined and the contrast of forms is extraordinary. Notice especially the almost musical repetition of circular forms and how they are punctuated by the thrust of the vertical sword. There is no decoration for its own sake. Every detail—the hat, the headband, the choker, necklace, bodice, sleeves, and stomacher—contributes to the dynamic composition. And all is painted with the visual clarity of the hard-edge school but with greater warmth. For in addition to its plastic virtues, the Cranach painting palpitates with inner life. Judith, with all her elegance, emerges as a female of sufficient resolve to have seduced and murdered the enemy of her people, and the severed

ACHENBACH FOUNDATION FOR GRAPHIC ARTS

The Achenbach Foundation—a department of the California Palace of the Legion of Honor—has the largest collection of graphic arts in the American West. It was founded in 1950 by Mr. and Mrs. Moore S. Achenbach, who expressed the desire to build up the collection to include the best drawings and prints of old and modern masters. A generous acquisitions fund was provided by the donors, and the collection of some 80,000 items is annually augmented by 300 purchases. Under the guiding hand of its scholarly director, E. Gunter Troche, the Achenbach Collection is now third in the U.S., ranking just behind those of the Metropolitan Museum of Art and the Boston Museum of Fine Arts in importance. Recent acquisitions, reflecting the wide scope of the collection, include one of the finest prints in existence of Rembrandt's great drypoint etching, *The Three Crosses*; a twelve-color lithograph by Marc Chagall on a fourfold screen, number 22 in a limited edition of 100 signed by the artist; and four handsome color lithographs by Sam Francis. The Foundation has its own staff, arranges frequent exhibitions, and the prints can be seen on appointment by telephoning the museum.

NERVOUS FATHER drags kids
away from 19th-century sculpture
show, with remark that all sculptors
are rogues. The 1847 lithograph
is by Honoré Daumier. (Achenbach
Foundation for Graphic Arts.)

head with its glassy eye and mouth agape is an unforgettable study
of death and sensuality.

Beside this masterpiece the *Duchess of Chateauroux* is nothing but
fun and games. Even Rembrandt's *Rabbi* seems pale by comparison
with Cranach, and so does red-jacketed English *Lord Seaham as a
Boy*, which may or may not be by Sir Thomas Lawrence, but which
is such a popular favorite with visitors that it has been called the
Legion's answer to *The Blue Boy*.

The museum's American art ranges from John Singleton Copley
to Ben Shahn. You will probably enjoy comparing Copleys portrait of *Joshua Henshaw* with his *General Jonathan Winslow* which
is at the Santa Barbara Museum of Art. In the Henshaw portrait,
painted in the early 1770's, Copley has dispensed with all ornamental
detail, except for the red drapery on the left, in order to emphasize
the aggressive, no-nonsense character of his subject, whose pursed
lips proclaim the Puritan patriot and whose expression almost seems
to condemn the vanity of posing.

For other glimpses of American life see the two excellent genre
portraits by Thomas Waterman Wood, evidence that the dignity of

WIT AND VERVE of Fragonard shine through rare self-portrait in California Palace of the Legion of Honor. Much admired by French court, he recorded its frivolity and elegance. Losing courtly patrons in 1789, he died in poverty in Paris in 1806.

the Negro race is not a recent discovery; Ben Shahn's *Ohio Magic*, a poetic rendering of the commonplace; and Walter Stuempfig's fine, luminous *West Wildwood*, in which the painter shows us a storm-threatened house on stilts at ebbtide.

The Achenbach Foundation for Graphic Arts, largest print collection in the West, is also housed in the Palace of the Legion of Honor —see page 158 for details on this fine collection.

WILD BEASTS IN THE WAR MEMORIAL

SAN FRANCISCO MUSEUM OF ART. *Civic Center, McAllister Street at Van Ness Avenue, San Francisco. Hours 10 A.M. to 10 P.M. Tuesday–Friday; 10 A.M. to 5 P.M. Saturday; 1 to 5 P.M. Sunday; closed Monday. Modern European and American art.*

Founded in 1921, the San Francisco Museum of Art was the first museum of contemporary art in the West. It currently occupies galleries on the fourth floor of San Francisco's massive granite War Memorial Veterans Building. The contrast between the gray exterior of this edifice and the blaze of color when you get off the elevator is enough to make you reach for your sun glasses. Matisse and other "wild beasts" of modern art are responsible for the colors, along with a newer generation of painters whose optical experiments are presented in as many as 30 exhibits a year.

Stars of the permanent collection are Braque, Matisse, Picasso, Léger, Utrillo, Derain: the roster of famous Paris masters. You'll probably be tempted to linger long before the sumptuous Braque still life, *Le Gueridon*. A gift of William W. Crocker, this cubist masterpiece is a picture any museum would envy.

Don't miss the very early *Paris Street Scene* by Picasso, painted when this giant of modern art was a boy of 19, newly arrived in Paris from his native Catalonia. Among the soft contours of this nostalgic scene, only the human figure on the left suggests the violent distortions which were to come. Having studied this work of Picasso's youth, you can now leap 54 years in a matter of inches to a product of his genial old age, *Les Femmes d'Alger*.

Among the American paintings in the fine collection is Jackson Pollock's *Guardian of the Secret*. Painted in 1943 and first exhibited in Peggy Guggenheim's Art of This Century gallery in New York, it was brought to San Francisco two years later. With its cabalistic signs, as personal as handwriting, and its web of freely scrawled interlacing lines, it remains one of the important monuments of abstract art.

Probably the museum's greatest treasures are half a dozen paintings and drawings by Matisse. These include the masterpiece of 1909, *The Girl with the Green Eyes*. See also the masterful sketch of Sarah Stein and the sad and noble painting which was the finished product. In addition to their plastic virtues, these have a special biographical interest. Sarah and Michael Stein of San Francisco (their house is still standing at 3169 Washington Street) were the first American collectors of Matisse. Gertrude Stein followed her brother's lead and became interested in the Paris painters. The Michael Steins moved to Paris in 1903, became devoted supporters and friends of Matisse, who was then in his thirties, and were the first to bring his work to the United States when they returned to San Francisco after the fire of 1906. The *Portrait of Sarah Stein* was a gift to the museum from one of its trustees, Mrs. Walter A. Haas, a friend of the Stein family.

ALONG THE NORTH COAST

From San Simeon to Big Sur, from Monterey to Mendocino, the coast of Northern California is so grandly spectacular that the portable easel now vies with the fishing rod as vacation equipment. At Big Sur, La Verne Allen represents some 50 local artists in her Big Sur Coast Gallery. open from 10 A.M. to 4 P.M. every day but Monday. At Carmel, one of America's most famous art colonies, you will enjoy a stroll among the shops and galleries of Dolores Street where the Carmel Art Gallery, owned by the artists themselves, shows paintings and sculpture by some 200 members of the Carmel Art Association. The American Federation of Arts Art Gallery is one of the best in town. Carmel has a score of other galleries where you will find everything from souvenir watercolors to the most avant-garde work from Los Angeles, New York, and Paris.

At Santa Cruz, famous for its nearby Big Basin State Park, you will find paintings and sculpture, both abstract and figurative, at the Castle Gallery, 1320 East Cliff Drive.

Mendocino, a town with more New England flavor than any other settlement west of Vermont, has long been a favorite haunt of artists. After you have explored its quaint Victorian streets and watched the community fishing activity at picturesque Point Cove, you will enjoy seeing the work of local painters at Sankey's Gallery, 271 Evergreen Street.

That San Francisco was ready and eager for such a program has been evident for 30 years. Visitors poured into the museum's big Cézanne retrospective of 1937 at a rate of a thousand a day. Annual attendance at the museum approached the quarter-million mark in 1965. Between times the San Francisco Museum of Art has kept the public informed on 20th-century art with major exhibitions of the work of Kandinsky, Klee, Braque, Picasso, Rouault, Léger, Miró, Matisse, Jackson Pollock (his first West Coast showing was here in 1945), Hans Hofmann, Henry Moore, Mark Rothko.

The museum continues to present "new discoveries, new evaluations, new possibilities, and new directions born out of new technology." A recent exhibition of Colorists 1950-1965, for example, provided a dazzling retinal report on the experimental ways in which 33 contemporary artists are exploiting the plastic energy of color and the kinetic effect of color and shape relationships.

All this not only washes and rinses the public eye but also stimulates artists, especially those painters of the Bay Area who have created not one but two San Francisco schools of painting. The first, back in the '40's, was abstract expressionism. The second school was figurative. It included the representational paintings of artists like Richard Diebenkorn and David Park, who had been through the abstract mill, so to speak, and had seen degeneration into a formula. In a sense, they used abstract expressionism as a kind of training ground for a new and revealing exploration of nature, a rigorous new definition of natural form. Scene of the annual exhibits of the San Francisco Art Institute, the San Francisco Museum of Art continues to remain constantly attuned to such changes in the development of art.

AN AGITATED PLACE

SAN FRANCISCO ART INSTITUTE. *800 Chestnut Street, San Francisco. Hours 10* A.M. *to 4* P.M. *daily. Closed Sunday. Diego Rivera mural.*

Oldest art school west of the Mississippi, the San Francisco Art Institute was founded in 1871 and has been functioning under various names continuously ever since. It is essentially a community of artists with a faculty of eminent painters, sculptors, printmakers, and photographers, and more than 700 students. The present building was designed by Bakewell and Browne, of Coit Tower fame, and features an Italian campanile and a Renaissance courtyard where you can usually see an exhibition of avant-garde sculpture. Some of California's most distinguished artists teach or have taught here, among them Richard Diebenkorn, David Park, Elmer Bischoff, and Nathan Oliveira. Their work is often exhibited at the Institute. The Institute also maintains an "Art Bank," a continually renewed collection of painting, sculpture, prints, and drawings, all done by its members.

Gurdon Woods, a former director of the college of the San Francisco Art Institute, has described it as "a loose federation of autocratic individuals who alternately antagonize and pacify each other, depress and stimulate each other, and continually challenge each other. An agitated place, but one where something important can happen."

THIS WAS SAN FRANCISCO BAY in 1887 as seen from Goat Island, now Yerba Buena, by Danish-born artist Marius Dahlgren. (Oakland Art Museum: The Kahn Collection.)

WILLIAM KEITH'S DARK NOVEMBER *offers poetic*
glimpse of California valley mildly threatened by
storm cloud on right. Painting shows painter's interest
in Barbizon School. A native of Scotland, Keith
came to San Francisco in 1858, became most honored
California artist of his time. (Oakland Art Museum:
Gift of Keith Art Association.)
His painting A Western Canyon, *showing*
Weber Pass, can be seen in the main
conference room of Sunset Magazine, *in Menlo Park.*

BAY AREA   165

Important things have been happening ever since World War II, when the fires of abstract expressionism were kindled here by such faculty members as Mark Rothko and Clyfford Still, the latter a messianic painter and teacher who emphasized individual vision and meaningful new forms and who often delighted his students by discussing the dynamics of baseball. The ferment persists though the Still is gone, and you will do well to look in at the lively, frequently changing exhibits at the San Francisco Art Institute.

THE MAKING OF A MURAL

Back in the '30's the ferment was supplied by an agitating agent from south of the border. This was Mexico's Diego Rivera. In 1926 Rivera was invited to the Institute, then known as the California School of Fine Arts, to paint a mural. The proferred fee, donated by William Gerstle, president of the San Francisco Art Commission, was $1,500 for a 120-square-foot fresco. When Rivera finally got to San Francisco in 1930, he took one look at the assigned wall, said it was too small, and proceeded to paint a 1,200-square-foot mural, ten times the size of the commission, for the same fee.

The title of the Institute fresco is, appropriately enough, *The Making of a Fresco*. It shows a group of artists and architects, many of them recognizable San Francisco personalities of the day, busy at work on a wall. In the center of the scaffold with his back turned squarely on the audience is Rivera himself. His stocky figure is unmistakable; it's one of the most unusual self-portraits on record.

Rivera's work in San Francisco was not confined to the Art Institute. In spite of violent opposition on the part of certain conservative members who thought Rivera might undermine the foundations of capitalism, he did a mural for the San Francisco Stock Exchange Club. Capitalism and the club survived. So does the mural, but you will have to join the club to see it, or get a member to take you in. There's nothing subversive in the mural; its central figure is one of California's heroines of the '20's: Queen of the Courts Helen Wills Moody.

In 1930 Rivera was given a show at the California Palace of the Legion of Honor. He had become thoroughly respectable. Back in his native land he was less so. He was suspected, unjustly, of complicity in the murder of Trotsky, and was glad to return in 1940 to San

EVERYONE LOOKS. Diego Rivera mural in San Francisco Art Institute holds its own with abstract sculpture exhibit below. Fascinated by his own profession, Rivera depicted artist and plasterers in act of creating fresco, painted himself in center, seated broadly on the scaffolding, with back to audience.

PRIMARY COLORS, GEOMETRIC PLANES push and pull in Heraldic Call,
*painted by Hans Hofmann in 1963 at age of 83. Picture is one of 45 left by painter to
University of California, Berkeley, where he taught.*

168 NORTHERN CALIFORNIA

Francisco, where he was invited to the Golden Gate Exposition to participate in a show called Art in Action and Art in Use. For this he painted a huge movable fresco, covering an area of 1,700 square feet. Though thousands flocked to Treasure Island to see the completed work, it was put in storage for 20 years until a suitable space could be created to accommodate it. In 1961 it finally found a home in the lobby of the theater of the City College of San Francisco, 50 Phelan Avenue, where you may view it during school hours. This is said to be the best Rivera fresco in the United States, reputedly more interesting plastically than the one in the Detroit Art Institute. Rivera had a field day with his theme, which is almost as grandiose as the mural itself: The unity of the Indian civilization and plastic arts of Mexico and the creative mechanical expression of the United States.

A huge symbolic adumbration, half Indian totem, half American machine, divides the fresco into two parts, Mexico to the left, the United States to the right. Against a background of Popocatepetl and Treasure Island are scores of characters from naked Indians to periwigged diplomats. You'll have a lot of fun identifying persons and events. Fulton is there with his steamboat, and so are those champions of liberty, John Brown and Simon Bolivar. You will recognize Charlie Chaplin, Rivera's favorite actor, in a number of places. This time the artist has not turned his back on the spectator, but shows himself full-face gaily holding hands with actress Paulette Goddard. Also present, left of center, is Rivera's wife and fellow artist, Frida Kahlo, dressed as an Indian for the occasion.

STEEL FROM THE CENTRAL PACIFIC

LELAND STANFORD JUNIOR MUSEUM. *Stanford University, Palo Alto, California. Hours 1 to 10 P.M. daily. Classical antiquities; Leventritt Collection of Asian Art.*

One of the most venerable of university art museums is the Leland Stanford Junior Museum, on the palm-studded campus of Stanford University at Palo Alto. Founded in 1891 by Senator and Mrs. Leland Stanford, it was named, like the university, in honor of their only child. The boy had already developed a taste for collecting when he died of typhoid fever just before his 16th birthday. Leland Junior's curios became the nucleus of the university collections, soon

*REFRESHING NEW FORM on Stanford campus, Aristides Demetrios' White
Memorial Fountain cools plaza in front of bookstore. Sculptor is famous for bronze
embodiments of wind, water, flame. Students call this one The Claw.*

augmented by many gifts from Mrs. Stanford. It was she who acquired most of the museum's Egyptian and Oriental material. And Jane Stanford was the unknown Westerner who outbid the Boston Museum of Fine Arts for the rich plum of the Cesnola Collection of classical sculpture from Cyprus.

The central part of the Stanford museum, constructed in 1892, is the first steel-reinforced concrete building in the United States. The steel reinforcing was supplied by surplus rails from Leland Stanford's Central Pacific Railroad. In the museum you will see the famous golden spike with which Stanford linked the Central and Union Pacific rails at Promontory Point, Utah, in 1869.

The main building of the museum withstood the whiplash of the San Francisco earthquake that reduced most of the Stanford campus to rubble just before dawn on April 18, 1906. The brick and stucco wings of the museum were pulverized. The debris was stored in the basement in a chaotic state for many years.

A RESTFUL, PLEASANT PLACE

"We are the phoenix of museums," says Director Lorenz Eitner.

You will doubtless agree as soon as you pass through the bronze doors and visit the renovated galleries, designed to set off paintings, jade, porcelains, and bronzes to maximum advantage. This is a restful museum, a pleasant place to browse and choose your favorites from the art treasures of many epochs.

In the Egyptian section the range of choice extends from a seated, bearded Pharaoh (1400 B.C.) to the votive sculpture of a sacred cat, a mysterious black tabby of the 26th dynasty, 2500 years old. Of the 5,000 items purchased by Mrs. Stanford in the Cesnola Collection, the Cypriot bulls from the bronze age are outstanding, and so is a small, clay Cyprian horse, an especially appealing figure.

You will notice that the Chinese and Japanese sculptors had a more sophisticated approach to animals. Among the museum's most beautiful objects are the horses and riders of the Chinese Six Dynasties period (A.D. 220-589) and a superb glazed pottery horse of the T'ang Dynasty (A.D. 618-906), one of some 300 Far Eastern treasures in the Leventritt Collection. A serene and enigmatic Siamese bronze head of Buddha is another exceptional piece from the Leventritt group. Among the many Japanese items, don't miss the sly Kyoto-ware fox, dressed up as a Buddhist monk and wearing a look of piety that would fool anyone but another fox.

A curiosity in the Stanford Museum's collection of European paintings is Cornelius Van Dalem's *Landscape with Adam and Eve*. A rare example of this 16th century Flemish master's work (there are only three other Van Dalems in the public collections of the world), it shows our first parents as cave dwellers after the fall. Vestiges of Eden still cling to this peaceful scene in which Eve nurses Abel, while Adam, holding little Cain by the hand, returns home with a bunch of carrots under his arm. This is the first family's evening meal. It is historically accurate, says Stanford Art Professor John La Plante, for, according to *Genesis*, and most Bible scholars, the human race remained vegetarian until the time of Noah's Ark.

ART IN AN INDUSTRIAL SETTING

On the San Francisco Peninsula you might take a look at the painting and sculpture at Syntex Laboratories Inc. and the Syntex Research Center in Stanford Industrial Park at Palo Alto. Pioneers in steroid and hormone research, Syntex is one of many industrial firms that have shown an interest in buying and displaying works of art. The well-landscaped grounds, with pools and fountains, are an ideal setting for planned additions to the company's collection of sculpture. At this writing, their collection is concentrated in the Administration Building. In the courtyard of this building you will find Henry Moore's thin-necked *Seated Woman*, a striking bronze cast in 1961. She makes an interesting comparison with the *Standing Woman* by the modern Greek sculptor Christos Kapralos, located on the second floor balcony. In the reception area on the first floor, Kenneth Armitage's bronze statue, *Standing Man*, completes a trio of modern sculpture.

Two Mexican painters are the stars of the growing collection: Enrique Climent and David Alfaro Siqueiros. Climent's *La Caravela*, strongly influenced by synthetic cubism and primitive Mexican art, hangs at the end of the hall of the second floor. The Siqueiros you will find in the lobby of Research Building No. 1. The emotional violence and political bias one expects in this fiery Mexican's work is notably absent in this painting, *The Treasure of the Jungle*. It depicts the gathering of the barbasco root, a basic ingredient in the production of steroids.

THOMAS WATERMAN WOOD CAPTURED DIGNITY of Moses the Baltimore
News Vendor *in 1858. Picture was acclaimed in the 1964 show, Portrayal of Negro in
American Painting, at Bowdoin College, Maine. (Legion of Honor.)*

NO OTHER SCULPTOR of the 19th century had such deep knowledge of anatomy as did Rodin. In The Kiss *he combined it with pathos to sublime effect.*

174 NORTHERN CALIFORNIA

HARMONY *of the human form*

ASCETIC FIGURE of John the Baptist reveals sculptor's awareness of tragic human destiny. (All three Rodin works from Legion of Honor.)

MICHELANGELO would have recognized his heir in The Age of Bronze, *a triumph of action and tension in repose worthy of his own superhuman vision.*

TWO WOMEN... *by two women*

CUBISM INSPIRED MARGARET PETERSON, one of the leading modern artists of the West Coast, now painting in British Columbia. Two Women, painted in Berkeley in 1938, hangs in the Oakland Art Museum. (Gift of friends of the artist.)

SOFT, PASTEL COLORS are almost luminous in the California sunshine, as Marie Laurencin's Lés Déguises is taken outdoors, the better to photograph its delicate hues and tints. Associated with Braque, Picasso, Apollinaire, Laurencin developed an original style, painted The Disguised Ladies *in 1926. (Haggin Galleries.)*

BURIED treasure of American history

EMANUEL LEUTZE'S historic canvas, Washington Rallying the Troops at Monmouth, *was recently excavated from basement of Hearst Gymnasium at Berkeley, is proud addition to new University of California Art Museum. Best known for* Washington Crossing the Delaware, *German-born Leutze specialized in scenes from American history, here re-creates a stirring battle scene.*

STRONG FORM, VAST SPACE, contained power of **Figure** on a Porch, *by Richard Diebenkorn, are typical of this artist who turned from abstract to figurative art in 1955. Diebenkorn helped to create a vigorous new Bay Area school launched by Oakland Art Museum in 1957 exhibition. (Oakland Art Museum: Anonymous gift through American Federation of Arts.)*

180   NORTHERN CALIFORNIA

CALIFORNIA'S *new directions in art*

*DAVID PARK broke away from
abstract painting in 1950, refound the
human figure, portrayed it with
linear economy as in* Rehearsal.
*(Oakland Art Museum:
Anonymous gift through American
Federation of Arts.)*

*LYRICIST OF BAY AREA realists, Elmer Bischoff
achieves poetic harmony of colors and shapes in his
solidly composed* Figure in Landscape.
*(Oakland Art Museum: Gift of Women's Board of the
Oakland Museum Association.)*

THE FEMININE *touch of the French*

MOST PROLIFIC PAINTER *of women, Auguste Renoir captured their coquetry in the softly brushed* La Coiffure—The Hairdo. *(Haggin Galleries.)*

SWISH OF SKIRTS *is almost audible in masterful etching by Degas,* Mary Cassatt at the Louvre, *from Mills College Art Gallery.*

WHITE SHOULDERS, BLACK DRESS were made to order for Edouard Manet, who painted directly from the model, based his brilliant technique on contrast of light and shadow. At The Milliner's, painted in 1879, shows an elegant French woman about to try on a hat. Influenced by Goya, Manet was a bridge between realism and impressionism. (Legion of Honor.)

SENSE OF EXPECTANCY and impending drama was consciously created by Italian surrealist Giorgio di Chirico in his Vexations of the Thinker. *(San Francisco Museum of Art.)*

DREAMS *of the present, dreams of the past*

THE STAGE WAS ALREADY SET for surrealism in the 18th century, when Giovanni Panini painted nostalgic Roman Ruins, peopled their space with ghosts of the past. (Crocker Gallery.)

MOST POPULAR PICTURE at the De Young Museum, The Russian Bride *shows a pretty girl being dressed for her wedding. Painted in 1889 by Konstantin Makowski, the 9 by 12 foot, larger-than-life work was a gift of M. H. De Young to the museum he founded.*

UNHAPPY ENDING is graphically depicted by Fragonard in an anecdotal etching, The Armoire, *whose door has just been opened by furious parents of the girl who weeps at left. (Achenbach Foundation for Graphic Arts.)*

OLD-FASHIONED anecdote is ever-popular

AMERICAN ANECDOTALIST Toby Rosenthal painted The Cardinal's Portrait
in Munich in 1896. Dilemma of artist monk whose august model has fallen asleep still
delights visitors to California Palace of the Legion of Honor, as does contrast
between sleeper and spiritual image on monk's canvas. One sympathizes with the
sitter; it must have been a difficult pose to maintain. The realistic Renaissance
trappings are characteristic of late Victorian taste.

MASTERS of fantasy from the Achenbach Foundation

SPANISH SURREALIST Joan Miro followed dictates of thought free from reason's control in witty lithograph, Little Girl In the Wood.

LOVERS FLY with the greatest of ease in Marc Chagall's four-panel screen, a nostalgic glimpse of Paris in spring. Lithograph is one of several thousand works in Achenbach Foundation collection at Legion of Honor (see page 158).

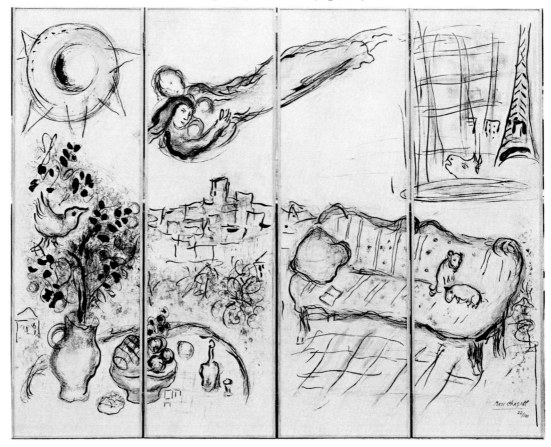

FOUR FANTASTIC ANIMALS populate this lithograph by Max Ernst, a founder of Dada who became enduring surrealist. His lively imagination invented pseudo-organic forms, incongruous juxtapositions, plastic re-creations of visions from world of dreams, recorded in fastidious drawing.

190   NORTHERN CALIFORNIA

A LIVELY SUNDAY
in a mining camp

SUNDAY MORNING IN THE MINES, by
Charles C. Nahl, is a famous California genre painting.
Born in Germany, trained in France, where he
painted battle scenes, Nahl arrived in California in
1850 at height of the Gold Rush. He discovered
no gold but found perfect subject matter for his art.
(Crocker Art Gallery.)

The East Bay

Newest building developments in the Bay Area art world are taking place not in San Francisco but across the bay in Oakland and Berkeley. In both cities a long tradition of concern for art and regard for artists is now literally concretizing itself in two ultramodern museums. These developments are a source of great satisfaction to residents of the East Bay, who have long resented the notion prevalent in San Francisco that culture stops short the moment you pay your east-bound toll on the Bay Bridge. To help set this little matter straight, Oaklanders went to the polls in 1961 and voted overwhelmingly for a $6,000,000 bond issue to finance their museum.

OAKLAND'S SPECIAL PROVINCE

OAKLAND ART MUSEUM. *Tenth and Fallon Streets, Oakland. Main entrance at Tenth Street. Hours 10 A.M. to 5 P.M. daily. 19th and 20th century painters. New museum opening in spring of 1968. Archives of California art.*

Founded in 1916, the Oakland Art Museum began to attract national attention in 1952 when its policies of collecting and exhibiting were given new vigor through the appointment of a dynamic young director, Paul Mills. Sizing up the situation in the Bay Area, already well provided with three major museums, Mills decided that the most neglected and most challenging field open to Oakland was that of California art. Focusing his attention on this area, he launched the Archives of California Art. It was a little acorn to begin with but by virtue of tireless collecting and collating of source material and soliciting of public and private support, it has grown to the dimensions of a California oak. The Oakland Art Museum has accumulated some 15,000 California paintings in the last decade; and this collection, painstakingly documented by Mills, his staff, and volunteer researchers, has made the museum a sort of state gallery of art.

The expansion continues. So does the museum's concern for living artists. For, according to Mills, "We want to relate the new sense of discovery of older American art to the current explorations in contemporary American art."

The Bay Area Figurative Painting Exhibition, organized at the Oakland Museum in 1957, was consonant with this aim. It was one of those epoch-making shows which attracted national attention by establishing a new direction in art, the widely admired Bay Area New Figurative School. It was led by David Park, Richard Diebenkorn, Elmer Bischoff, and other painters, many of whom had worked successfully in the abstract idiom, but who saw it degenerating into an academic formula and felt the need of fresh visual inspiration. This they found all around them in the charged atmosphere and solid forms of the California landscape and in the human figure, which had all but disappeared from modern painting.

California history has become the special province of Oakland, and the variety of visual experience is fascinating. Bear hunts, horse racing, gold mining, cattle rustling, life in San Francisco's Chinatown, the earthquake and fire of 1906: these are a few of the subjects immortalized here by California's painters.

But most of all you'll enjoy viewing the grandiose landscapes and seascapes of California, and comparing various artists' versions of the same scene: Yosemite Valley, for example, as seen by Thomas Hill, William Keith, and Albert Bierstadt. By the time these artists got through with their loving delineations of El Capitan, the Sentinel,

LONGING is appropriate title for eloquent watercolor by Winslow Homer, painted in 1865 after artist's stint as pictorial reporter in the Civil War. (Mills College Art Gallery.)

and Cathedral Rock, there was no need for a California tourist bureau. Bierstadt's *Yosemite Valley* series, of which Oakland has one of the best examples in existence, made this beauty spot famous throughout Europe. Painted in 1873, the pictures were exhibited in London, Paris, Vienna, Moscow, and Saint Petersburg. William Keith's landscapes were almost as popular. You can see a fine collection of them in the Keith Gallery which the Oakland Art Museum maintains in the Oakland Public Library, 125 Fourteenth Street.

As for the *new* Oakland Museum (scheduled for completion in spring of 1968) its like has not been seen since the Hanging Gardens of Babylon. Designed by Kevin Roche of Eero Saarinen Associates, it is a three-tiered complex of interlocking pavilions, providing separate but related quarters for Oakland's museums of art, history, and natural science, all under the supervision of Director James M. Brown III. The topmost tier in this grand cultural stairway is devoted to art. The roof of one gallery is the entrance garden and terrace of another, affording wonderful vistas of indigenous California trees, shrubs,

POWERFUL AS ITS SUBJECT is Albert Bierstadt's striking animal study of Bull, done in 1863. The painting was exhibited in Italy along with other pictures depicting the Western frontier. (Oakland Art Museum.)

and vines. Every effort has been made to bring the outside inside.

The interior appointments, including lavish use of carpeting, create an atmosphere of warmth and comfort. A major innovation is the art observatory which enables a seated audience to view original works and compare them with related color slides at the same time.

"In every aspect of the design," says Director Brown, "the quality of the visitor's experience has been the first consideration. You will not be overwhelmed with vast staircases and intimidating halls. Rather, the architects have planned a delightful place in which to spend a day."

BOLD, BRILLIANT, AND CHALLENGING

UNIVERSITY OF CALIFORNIA ART MUSEUM. *University of California, Berkeley. Until completion of the new University Art Museum, scheduled to open in 1968, temporary exhibitions of art are held at the following places on campus: University Art Gallery, hours noon to 6 P.M. daily; Student Union Lobby (graphics, oils, and watercolors by Bay Area artists), hours 8 A.M. to midnight Monday–Saturday; noon to midnight Sunday; Worth Ryder Gallery, Kroeber Hall, hours 12:30 to 4 P.M. Tuesday–Saturday, 1 to 5 P.M. Sunday.*

Newest of East Bay art developments is the University of California's Art Museum in Berkeley, scheduled for completion in time for the University's centennial year in 1968. ("Westward the course of empire takes its way," wrote Bishop Berkeley of Cloyne in the 18th century, never dreaming that it would go that far west and boast a university town named in his honor.) A total of 366 architects submitted designs for the museum to an award jury headed by Lawrence B. Anderson, chairman of the department of architecture at Massachusetts Institute of Technology. Winning architect was Mario Ciampi, well known in his native San Francisco for his Corpus Christi Church, Daly City Community Center, and the master plan for downtown renewal.

The prize-winning Art Museum, which was hailed by the jury as one of the outstanding contributions to museum design in our time, will provide the University and the community with 90,000 square feet of space for the University's permanent art collection and changing exhibitions. Galleries, studios, conference rooms radiate from a central axis like the pleats of two open fans.

The new museum, which will replace the University Art Gallery, built in 1905 as a steam heating plant, had its genesis in a gift of 45 paintings from the celebrated abstract expressionist painter, Hans Hofmann. Hofmann was invited from Munich to teach at the Berkeley summer sessions of 1930 and 1931, and was fortunately spared the holocaust that was about to engulf his native land. Hofmann opened his own school in New York and became a most powerful influence in the emergence of that modern American abstract painting that was to establish New York as a new capital of the art world. Fame and fortune came to Hofmann, but he never forgot Berkeley. The University of California had rescued him from the Nazi catastrophe. Thirty-four years later he expressed his gratitude in a monumental way, not only with the gift of 45 major paintings but with $250,000 from the sale of other pictures to provide a gallery in which to house them.

One of the seven galleries in the new $4,000,000 art museum will be the Hans and Maria Hofmann memorial. Here on permanent display will be a unique ensemble of some of the most important pictures of our time—bold, brilliant, sometimes baffling canvases which challenged the visual concepts of traditional painting and imposed a new way of looking at art.

KEEPING UP WITH ART IN THE BAY AREA

In addition to San Francisco's three major art museums there are some 50 galleries in the city which change exhibits every month. Each Sunday the *San Francisco Examiner and Chronicle* lists museums and galleries alphabetically and indicates all the group and one-man exhibitions of the week. The daily *San Francisco Chronicle* also runs a selective list of outstanding art exhibitions every Thursday.

Art critic of the *Chronicle* is Alfred Frankenstein. His reviews and his articles in art magazines have earned him an international reputation in the field. Knowledgeable and outspoken Alexander Fried has long been covering the cultural waterfront as art and music critic of the *San Francisco Examiner*. Another Bay Area art critic, widely respected for her insight and her stimulating reviews, is Miriam Dungan Cross of the *Oakland Tribune*.

Artforum Magazine covers exhibitions in San Francisco and the Bay Area in its usual lively and literate style. The local pundits are Palmer D. French, James Monte, Elizabeth M. Polley, and Knute Stiles. They all have the indispensable tools of their trade: a wide frame of reference, strong legs, keen eyes, and sharp pens.

RUGGED AND SOLID AS THE MESAS, Maynard Dixon's Earth Knower *symbolizes the American Indian's oneness with the earth. Fresno-born Dixon worked as an illustrator, graduated to painting, found inspiration in landscapes of the Southwest. (Oakland Art Museum.)*

"Art must not imitate physical life," said Hofmann, who died at the age of 85 in February, 1966, before ground was broken for the museum. "Art must have a life of its own, a spiritual life."

You will see the record of his own spiritual life on the walls of the museum he helped to found. The thick impasto and joyous colors vibrate with the same impulsive energy and human warmth that characterized their creator, a beloved teacher who will continue to teach here at his American alma mater.

Aside from the Hofmanns, Berkeley has an excellent painting by Mark Rothko, and a number of treasures which have been accumulating during the first century of the University's existence. Among them are 1,600 Japanese wood block prints, a dynamic sculpture of chromium plated steel by Jason Seley, a rare painting, *Daphnis and Chloe*, by Puvis de Chavannes, an important Italian Renaissance painting by Giovanni Savoldo, and a Baroque sculpture by Diego Carlone. The last two are recent acquisitions.

In various tunnels and basements of the University new discoveries are being made daily. One of the latest, uncovered as recently as 1964, is Emanuel Leutze's *Washington Rallying the Troops at Monmouth*, a huge historical tableau painted in 1854.

COMPLETING THE EAST BAY COLLEGIATE CIRCUIT

MILLS COLLEGE ART GALLERY. *Mills College, Oakland, California. Hours 1 to 4 P.M. Sunday, Wednesday, Friday. Graphic arts collection, German Expressionists.*

CALIFORNIA COLLEGE OF ARTS AND CRAFTS. *Broadway at College Avenue, Oakland, California. Call ahead for operating hours. Changing exhibitions of contemporary painting, sculpture, ceramics, and graphic art.*

ROBERT H. LOWIE MUSEUM OF ANTHROPOLOGY. *Kroeber Hall, University of California, Berkeley. Hours 1 to 5 P.M. daily except Monday.*

Several schools in the San Francisco Bay Area have made national contributions to the artistic life of America. Mills College in Oakland has long been known for its creative arts program. One of its most beloved art professors, Dr. Alfred Neumeyer, directed this program for many years. Under his egis, the college rescued Lyonel Feininger from Nazi Germany in 1936 and brought this fine artist to the United States to the great enrichment of American cultural life. The

*WROUGHT IRON GATES swing open, welcoming
visitors to a ceramics exhibition at Oakland's
Mills College Art Gallery, organized by outstanding
East Bay ceramist, Anthony Prieto. Mills, noted
for its creative arts program and internationally famous
artists in residence, is one of a dozen Bay Area schools
providing the community with frequent art exhibits.*

GALLERIES AWAY FROM THE BAY

Wherever you drive from San Francisco: over the Golden Gate Bridge into beautiful Marin County, over the Bay Bridge to the bustling East Bay cities, down to the wooded suburbs of the Peninsula, you'll find attractive art galleries displaying paintings, sculpture, ceramics, jewelry.

North

SAUSALITO	*Horizons*, 759 Bridgeway
CORTE MADERA	*Anderson Gallery*, 5615 Paradise Drive
FAIRFAX	*Buffs*, 28 Bolinas Road
NOVATO	*Smalle Gallery*, 828 Grant Avenue
SAN ANSELMO	*San Francisco Theological Seminary Gallery*, Alexander Hall
SAN RAFAEL	*Musée d'Art International*, 507 Francisco Boulevard
SAINT HELENA	*Hatchery*, 1345 Railroad Avenue

East

BERKELEY	*Arts and Crafts Cooperative* *Nicole*, 2400 Telegraph Avenue
EL CERRITO	*Arts and Crafts Cooperative*, 1751 Eastshore Boulevard
OAKLAND	*Harbor Gallery*, 567 Fifth Street
WALNUT CREEK	*Arts and Crafts Cooperative*, 1510 Geary Road and 1295 South Main Street

South

BURLINGAME	*Garden Cafe*, 1447 Burlingame Avenue
SAN MATEO	*Artell's*, 20 West 41st Avenue *Sherman Clay*, 250 Hillsdale Mall
MENLO PARK	*Gallery House*, 280 Ladera Shopper, Alpine Road.
PALO ALTO	*Circle*, 616 Cowper Street. *El Palo Alto*, 555 Ramona Street
LOS ALTOS	*Mark Gallery*, 111 Main Street
SARATOGA	*Villa Montalvo*, off Saratoga-Los Gatos Road. *Paint Brush*, 14583 Big Basin Way
LOS GATOS	*El Gatito*, 3 Montebello Way
SAN JOSE	*San Jose Art Center*, 482 South Second Street *Art*, 1114 Brace Avenue *Cameo*, 393 West San Carlos Street

college has an attractive art gallery with important collections of graphic arts, textiles, and ceramics, and an active exhibitions program which attracts some 5,000 visitors a year to the campus.

Oakland's California College of Arts and Crafts also has a distinguished history. Its teachers have included Richard Diebenkorn, Sabro Hasegawa, and Leon Goldin, and its alumni such well-known artists as Nathan Oliveira, Paul Wonner, Alexander Nepote, and Peter Voulkos. The school has frequent shows at its exhibition center in Treadwell Hall, 5212 Broadway, Oakland.

There are new shows every month at the lively Richmond Art Center (Civic Center at Barrett, Richmond), and frequent exhibits at Saint Mary's College in Moraga (east of Oakland), renowned for its permanent collection of paintings by William Keith.

The Robert H. Lowie Museum of Anthropology, on the Berkeley campus of the University of California, has some 400,000 items in its ethnographic and archeological collections. But quite apart from its value as a research center for anthropology, the museum has numerous works of art whose appeal is not restricted to the specialist.

There are some wonderful examples of Peruvian art here, especially the ceramic sculpture portraits of the Early Chimu pottery. There are examples of Eskimo sculpture and dance masks that will make you look upon our northern neighbors with deep respect. And there are some very fine Etruscan bronzes collected at the turn of the century by Dr. Alfred Emerson for Mrs. Phoebe A. Hearst.

Mrs. Hearst also sponsored the University's 1905 archeological expedition to Egypt under the direction of Dr. George A. Reisner. Among the 17,000 entries in the Reisner Collection is the great slab-stela of Prince Wepemnofret. Contemporaneous with the famous pyramid of Cheops, 2700 B.C., this funerary slab of one of Cheops' relatives was sealed up so securely in its tomb that its colors never faded. The stela shows us a royal personage, the owner of the tomb, seated at his funerary meal. The hieroglyphics are fascinating. Note the rich brown loaves of bread, the stylishly drawn goat and steer heads, the subtle brush strokes suggesting the texture of the owl's wing, the mottled skin of the frog, and the rich orange and yellow tones of the baby quail. Forty-five hundred years old, this bas-relief, with its fresh, clear colors, makes life and death in ancient Egypt as real and vivid as events in the morning paper. The hieroglyphic inscriptions on the stela are instructive.

TIEPOLO'S MASTERY *of light and color is evident in drama-filled 18th-century sketch of* The Crucifixion. *The airy grace of his pen stroke does not diminish the heaviness of Christ's hanging body or the sombre tragedy of the event, glimpsed in a lightning flash of high Baroque illusionism. (Achenbach Foundation for Graphic Arts.)*

EMOTION BEGINS ITS CONQUEST *of Byzantine style in Luca di Tommè's* Crucifixion *of 1366, a Sienese painting. Note the fainting Madonna robed in black. (Kress Collection: De Young Museum.)*

THREE CENTURIES *of the crucifixion*

EVERY LINE of Rembrandt's drypoint, The Three Crosses, *leads the eye to the figure of suffering Christ. The artist's astonishing range of tonality from white to velvet black creates a veil of mystery through which the dramatic climax of the passion is perceived. (Achenbach Foundation for Graphic Arts.)*

A STERN SITTER and childhood charm

THE VANITY OF POSING *seems to have been condemned by Joshua Henshaw, a man of forceful character, decided opinions, and severe expression. The Boston patriot's portrait is now in the California Palace of the Legion of Honor, and is one of the rare paintings by John Singleton Copley on the West Coast.*

CHARM OF CHILDHOOD *is captured in the endearing portrait of* Lord Seaham as a Boy, *by Sir Thomas Lawrence, who succeeded Reynolds as English court painter in 1792. Better known as* The Red Boy, *the picture is one of best loved in the California Palace of the Legion of Honor.*

METAMORPHOSIS *of the female form*

STRIVING TO FREE HIMSELF from the powerful influence of Picasso, Arshile Gorky abstracted female forms in Enigmatic Combat. *(San Francisco Museum of Art.)*

LEGER REMAINED *attached to reality of the feminine figure, delineated pen and ink drawing of* Two Nudes *in 1941. (Mills College Art Gallery.)*

ALWAYS A CHAMELEON, Picasso *varied form within a single picture as in* Women of Algiers, *a bravura performance in the collection of San Francisco Museum of Art.*

HIGH JINKS in the
low countries

PIETER BREUGHEL the Younger painted frolicking
Flemish peasants with brutal realism, giving
detailed attention to physical types and 17th-century
costumes. He often copied the work of his more
famous father, Pieter Breughel I, the greatest landscape
painter of the 16th century. The lively Peasants
Dancing is in the collection of the Crocker Gallery.

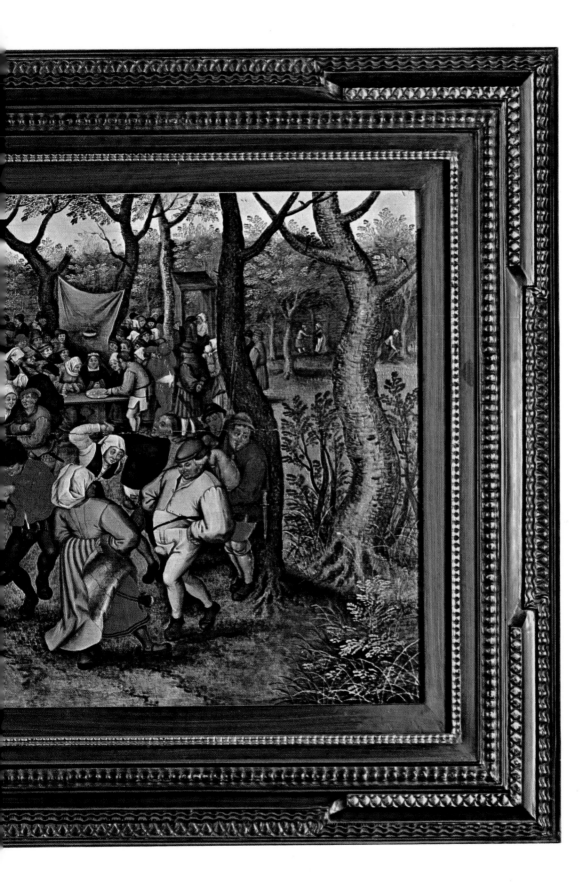

ALESSANDRO MAGNASCO created a melodramatic setting for Soldiers Feasting, *giving it an almost cinematic sense of light and movement, typical of 18th-century mannerism. (De Young Museum.)*

REVELRY *and ribaldry in dark and light*

PAUL CADMUS, an American, was not concerned with light, shows his sailors enjoying themselves outdoors in his high-spirited Shore Leave, *a 1936 etching from the Achenbach Foundation for Graphic Arts. (Legion of Honor.)*

VIEW OF ROME, by Corot, was painted during the artist's first trip to Italy in 1825.
The limpid scene reflects Corot's philosophy that beauty in art is truth bathed in an impression
received from nature. (Legion of Honor.)

RIVER SCENE, by Charles François Daubigny, shows the influence of the Barbizon painters,
whose aim was to provide exact rendering of scenery painted outdoors on the spot. Note the play of
light and reflections in the water. (Legion of Honor.)

MOODS *of nature on canvas*

YOU CAN FEEL the moisture-laden air of Holland in Jan van Goyen's evocative painting,
The Thunderstorm. *The low horizon and architectural details are typical of this 17th-century*
landscape painter, whose sensitively brushed pictures, washed with silver light, present a realistic
view of the Netherlands, on constant guard against the menace of the sea. (De Young Museum.)

West of the Sierra

Once a congeries of goldrush settlements with names like Grub Gulch and Cassady's Bar, Fresno (the name is Spanish for white ash) emerged as a town on the Central Pacific Railroad in 1872 and became a city as recently as 1900. It is now the thriving market center of the San Joaquin Valley and the home of a great winery and a large raisin packing plant. Tourists know Fresno as the gateway to three national parks (Yosemite, Sequoia, and General Grant) and for the famous Fresno Underground Gardens seven miles north of the city. This maze of grottoes and flowering subterranean rooms (there are 65 of them) were created by a single man, Baldasare Forestiere.

The art-mindedness of the San Joaquin Valley may be measured by the growth of the Fresno Arts Center, a nonprofit organization incorporated in 1949. A decade later it had raised a building fund which, matched by the city, has produced the modern home you see today in Radio Park. The interest and the growth continue. The Center has actually outgrown its quarters and has now extended its gallery space to include the city hall, the county courthouse, and the Fresno air terminal!

Exhibitions (sometimes as many as four at a time), lectures, art classes for children and adults, art rental, gallery tours—all are in the day's work at this busy place, not to mention such fun and fund-raising events as the annual Beaux Arts Ball. If your visit to the city doesn't coincide with the Arts Center's visiting hours, you can arrange to see the galleries by appointment.

After a visit to the Arts Center don't fail to take a stroll along the Fresno Mall. The very model of a civic esplanade, it is embellished by more than a dozen examples of modern sculpture, displayed out of doors and in the round as sculpture should be. Most of the pieces are gifts of anonymous art-minded and public-spirited citizens. One of the favorites is James Lee Hansen's cast bronze sculpture, *Talos*. This sturdy tripodal structure may remind you of those three-footed Chinese Shang dynasty wine beakers. *Talos* also suggests the forms of Indian totem poles. These resemblances are not accidental. Having grown up in Portland, Oregon, near the art museum, the sculptor was familiar with both.

TWO MONUMENTAL WOMEN GOSSIP all day long on Fresno's Civic Mall, embellished since 1964 by work commissioned by local businessmen. The women are by sculptor Clement Renzi; other contributing artists are Bruno Groth, James Lee Hansen, Peter Voulkos, François Stahley. There are also fountains by George Tsutakawa and Stan Bitters.

STARTING YOUNG in Stockton, a visitor teethes on velvet rope while admiring a Bierstadt view of the High Sierras in the Haggin Galleries. The museum recently launched a class for three-year-olds, teaches them art and French.

A MARRIAGE OF ART AND HISTORY

PIONEER MUSEUM AND HAGGIN GALLERIES. *Victory Park, Stockton. Hours 1:30 to 5 P.M. every day but Monday. Sunday afternoon films and concerts.*

One hundred and twenty-four miles north of Fresno is Stockton. An inland port connected by an 88-mile channel to San Francisco, it was chartered as a city in 1850.

Established in 1931, Stockton's San Joaquin Pioneer Museum and Haggin Art Galleries are a happy marriage of art and history. They have two objectives: first, perpetuating the cultural heritage of the pioneers who settled in the San Joaquin Valley; second, keeping the community informed on current trends in the field of fine art.

The Pioneer Museum does the former with its fascinating relics and authentic reconstructed rooms of the last century. And the Haggin Art Galleries does its job from the cradle up. Its trustees recently authorized funds for a brand-new prekindergarten art school, a project that will expose toddlers not only to art but to the elegant cadences of the French language. This *"Ecole du Musée,"* a pet project of the Haggin's young director Stephan Gyermek, is one of the most advanced things of its kind in the West. The pioneer spirit of Stockton is far from dead.

The museum's exhibitions schedule features frequent shows of contemporary artists in painting, sculpture, prints, drawings, and photography. These are supplemented by regular lectures on art and art history. Check with the museum for schedules.

The permanent collection of the Haggin Art Galleries is of more than passing interest. It includes numerous examples of painting long despised for its photographic realism—a realism that is making a comeback: works by J. L. Gérôme, Vibert, and Bouguereau. And don't overlook the huge collection of Leyendecker's original *Saturday Evening Post* covers.

The Haggin's American collection, strong on 19th century landscapes, includes 14 paintings by Albert Bierstadt. An unusual picture is William F. Cogswell's *Portrait of Lincoln*, painted from photographs and memory in 1866, one year after the President's assassination. Another version of this portrait hangs in the White House.

Don't leave this interesting museum without looking at the graphic arts collection on the second floor. It includes six drawings by Delacroix, etchings by Whistler, Childe Hassam, and Anders Zorn, and 47 works by another of our grandparents' favorites: the redoubtable Maxfield Parrish.

ART IN CALIFORNIA'S CAPITAL

Some 37 miles north of Stockton and 75 miles northeast of San Francisco is the state capital of California, Sacramento. The first U.S. settlement in California, Sacramento was founded in 1839 by Captain John A. Sutter on a land grant from the Mexican Government.

At Sutter's Fort, western terminal of the pioneer wagon trains, you'll see the stage coaches and prairie schooners that transported the first gold from the Mother Lode. Discovery of the precious metal at Sutter's Mill in 1848 made Sacramento rich as the center of mining activities. Fifteen years later the first transcontinental railroad was begun here, financed and promoted by the citizens of Sacramento. In the main reading room of the State Library you will see these and other events of California's colorful history depicted in a mural by Maynard Dixon.

DELICATE STRENGTH and nostalgia of Pont San Irmita are caught in the etching by Joseph Pennell, an American. Note how reflections are shown by a few simple lines. (Crocker Gallery.)

HUGE PICTURE *depicting the driving of the last spike measures 8 by 11 feet, is best known work of Thomas Hill, who once decorated coaches. Picture is in Capitol building, Sacramento.*

Adjoining the library is the State Capitol, a domed building of classic style with a gleaming white portico, the form of whose Corinthian columns is accentuated by the magnificent Indian cedar trees in the surrounding park. You may be tempted to linger in this park, listening to the music piped through amplifiers high in the trees and watching the antics of bluejays and squirrels, irresistible scolds and beggars of the animal kingdom. But pictures of great historic interest await you inside the capitol.

Perhaps the grandest is *The Driving of the Last Spike* by Thomas Hill. An outstanding California artist, Hill was commissioned to paint this huge canvas in 1875 to immortalize that moment on May 10, 1869, when the mythical Strait of Anian was finally realized in steel. Leland Stanford is shown as he drives the golden spike that linked the Central and Union Pacific Railroads at Promontory Point, Utah. It is one of the most populous pictures ever painted. There are some 400 figures depicted, ranging from the Big Four who conceived the railroad to the Chinese coolies who worked on it for fifty cents a

HEAD OF BEARDED MAN, by Peter Paul Rubens, was one of hundreds of old master drawings acquired by Sacramento collector Edwin Bryant Crocker on grand tours of Europe in the 19th century. Not highly regarded at the time, the drawings and prints now have enormous value. Judge Crocker's acquisitions of drawings by Rembrandt, Van Dyck, Carracci, and others made the Crocker Art Gallery's collection one of the finest in the nation.

day and rice. Seventy-one of the figures in this canvas are actual portraits; you can identify them by means of a diagram.

In the rotunda under the capitol's soaring dome (237 feet above street level) you will see twelve panels by Arthur F. Mathews illustrating other great moments in the history of the West. Painted on canvas in 1913, these murals celebrate the spacious landscapes and luminous cloud-swept skies of California with all the charm of a children's story book.

The spacious corridors of the ground floor form a portrait gallery of California personalities beginning with Sutter and continuing through such latter day figures as Hiram Johnson and Earl Warren. Don't miss W. S. Jewett's portrait of Captain Sutter. Turned out in full military rig with gold epaulets and gilded feathers in his cap, he looks like the reigning prince of New Helvetia.

NO PAINTINGS...NO DRAWINGS

E. B. CROCKER ART GALLERY. *216 O Street, Sacramento. Hours 10 A.M. to 5 P.M.; closed Monday. Drawings, prints, oils, and a 19th century ballroom.*

A more recent reigning prince of Sacramento was Edwin Bryant Crocker, elder brother of San Francisco's Charles Crocker. Born in New York in 1818, E. B. Crocker became a lawyer in Indiana, noted for his abolitionist activities and his defense of fugitive slaves. In 1852, at the age of 34, Crocker arrived in Sacramento, opened a law firm, and was eventually appointed to the State Supreme Court by Governor Stanford. Prospering as chief counsel, general agent, and a director of the Central Pacific Railway, Judge Crocker wanted to build up a fine collection of art and leave it to his adopted city. Traveling in Germany he bought art in wholesale lots, some of it from barons who were being ruined by Bismarck's heavy taxes to finance the German Empire.

Returning to Sacramento with 700 paintings and 1,200 drawings which dealers insisted he buy ("No drawings, no paintings," said they), he built an art gallery to house his treasures which he hoped would compare favorably with any private collection in the world. The gallery was a complement to the Crocker home which the judge had purchased in 1868, and whose scale may be deduced from the fact that its basement was large enough to encompass a billiard room, a bowling alley, and a skating rink.

The museum, which will fortunately be left intact when new galleries are added, is a historic monument that would warrant a visit even if it were empty. Black walnut, Honduras mahogany, and rare Oregon myrtle are some of the woods used in the interior, a model of exquisite Victorian cabinet work. The ballroom, with its gilded Corinthian columns and pilasters and its glistening parquetry floor of polished fir and cedar, has been lovingly preserved. It was the scene of lavish parties given by the Crockers' daughter, Amy Isabella, whose name was Gallicised to Aimée when she became the Princess Galitzine. These parties were the talk of the nation, let alone the town, and it is easy to imagine this ballroom in its glittering heyday with Victorian belles and their beaux whirling around the floor by gaslight to the strains of the Blue Danube Waltz.

By one of the ironies of changing taste, the drawings and prints which Judge Crocker was obliged to buy to secure his paintings are now the chief glory of the Crocker Art Gallery. Drawings were considered inconsequential in those days; few museums showed them and few collectors sought them. So the drawings and prints that were forced on Judge Crocker were stored away in drawers and remained there for nearly 60 years. When they came to light in the 1930's the director called in Dr. Alfred Neumeyer and other experts who gasped at the sight of Rembrandts, Dürers, Rubenses, and Van Dycks. The two Dürers, a voluptuous drawing, *Nude with Herald's Wand*, and a virile etching, *Saint George and the Dragon*, are works which many a larger museum would envy. And well they might. If you want to find old master drawings as distinguished as these you will have to go to New York.

FESTIVAL AND FANDANGO

If Judge Crocker was less lucky in his purchase of paintings, his gallery has a number of treasures all the same, and they are increasing, thanks to the activity of the Crocker Art Gallery Association which in 1964 bought the brilliant Tamayo painting, *Laughing Woman*. Judge Crocker's taste leaned toward genre painting, and

DRAWING FROM THE NUDE was frowned on in Europe in 1498, when Dürer did this pen and ink, titled Nude Woman with Harold's Wand. *The drawing is part of the Crocker Gallery collection.*

you will enjoy some of the Dutch and Flemish pictures of popular life. Outstanding is the colorful country festival, *Feasting and Dancing in the Low Countries*, attributed to Pieter Breughel the Younger. This picture makes an interesting comparison with another country fiesta, *Fandango*, by Charles Nahl. Although Nahl's frolicking Californians are more elegant than the Flemish peasants of Breughel, the same spirit of fun permeates both paintings. And, though more than two centuries and the widest cultural differences separate these two works, their affinities are greater than their dissimilarities. The composition and the handling of figures in an outdoor setting are almost identical, to such an extent that one wonders if Nahl had at one time seen and admired this particular Breughel picture in Judge Crocker's collection.

Speaking of Nahl, don't miss his picture *Sunday Morning in the Mines*, an animated genre painting that depicts a score of miners in every mood from reverent to ribald, and re-creates, as only art can, the crude and lusty life of an important moment in California history. For a more poetic view, turn to Thomas Hill's radiant *Great Canyon of the Sierras*, in which the tiny figures of campers, dwarfed by the pines, serve to punctuate the grand mountain solitude that makes up much of beautiful California.

HAND RAISED in peaceful benediction, this Siamese walking Buddha undergoes a bath of sodium sesqui-carbonate. Old bronze pieces become "diseased" from moisture attacking the copper salts; soaking helps to counteract the oxidation process.

REALISTIC RHINOCEROS, dating from late 11th century B.C. is one of oldest Chinese bronzes in collection. It has no known counterpart.

ORIENTAL wonders in Golden Gate Park

The Avery Brundage Collection of Oriental Art became a permanent part of the San Francisco cultural scene in 1966, when its 6,000 pieces, spanning 4,500 years of Oriental history, were installed in a specially designed new wing at the M. H. De Young Memorial Museum. Indian, Tibetan, Cambodian, Nepalese, and Japanese art are included in the collection, but its most important section is Chinese, typical treasures of which are shown here. About a third of the collection is on display at any one time. The best way to visit the collection is by guided tour conducted by docents Monday through Friday at 11 A.M., 12 noon, 2 and 3 P.M.

LO-HAN, Buddhist ascetic (above) is 11-inch carved jade from Ch'ing Dynasty (1644–1911). The rare T'ang (618–906) horse is glazed ceramic.

225

THE WOMAN *who has never been seen*

THE FAVORITE MODEL of the Middle Ages and Renaissance was a woman no one had even seen—the Mother of God. The Madonna, symbol of maternal tenderness and merciful intercessor between humanity and God, was the object of millions of prayers, subject of thousands of pictures and statues. She is portrayed in many guises, many settings, but always with appropriate reverence. As the Christian world moved from the pious Middle Ages into the more worldly atmosphere of the Renaissance, it became the fashion to paint her not in the simple surroundings of a stable but in the sumptuous setting of a palace.

COLD LIMESTONE is imbued with a warm sense of life and wonder by an anonymous 14th-century French sculptor of Madonna and Child, symbol of radiant Gothic faith. (De Young Museum.)

CESARE DA SESTO, early 16th-century Milanese painter, seats his Madonna on a throne of classical ruins, flanks her with John the Baptist in Biblical attire, St. George in armor. Renaissance painting is from the Kress Collection of the De Young Museum.

THE ADORATION OF THE SHEPHERDS
SCHOOL OF PROVENCE
END OF 15th CENTURY
KRESS COLLECTION

PROVENCAL VILLAGERS of 1500 would have recognized their neighbors in this unadorned
and touching Nativity. Only the halo distinguishes the Madonna from an ordinary peasant woman;
the men are as any of the local folk. (Kress Collection: De Young Museum.)

EXOTIC EYES *in timeless portraits*

NEARLY NINETEEN HUNDRED years separate the women of Fayoum, Egypt, from the models of Henri Matisse, but the old in this case is just as modern in feeling as the new. The resemblance is especially striking in the vigorous but simple delineation of features, the almond eyes, the clear definition of sensuous lips, the strongly marked brows. The tragic, masklike face of Sarah Stein suggests a simplification of the Fayoum mummy mask. Both portraits—as well as the etching—are redolent of the dark and mystic exoticism of the Near East.

EXOTIC INFLUENCE of Orient persists in Matisse's Seated Figure, a 1929 etching in the Crocker Art Gallery. "It is through the human figure," said the artist, "that I best succeed in expressing the nearly religious feeling I have towards life."

BOLDLY PAINTED portrait of Sarah Stein reflects Matisse's affection for a sensitive San Francisco collector who befriended him, promoted his work. (San Francisco Museum of Art.)

PORTRAIT OF A WOMAN from Fayoum, Egypt was painted from life in 2nd century A.D. The portrait, painted in encaustic on wood, was placed over the face before the body was mummified. (Stanford Museum.)

NORTHERN CALIFORNIA   **229**

BENNY *is San Francisco's pride and joy*

FIVE FEET TALL and with the air of a mischievous monk, Beniamino Bufano is San Francisco's own special sculptor. His guiding light is the patron saint of the city; he has always wanted San Francisco "to come to terms with the spirituality mandated by her saintly name." He himself has done his best to beautify the city with a statue of St. Francis near Fisherman's Wharf, another of Sun Yat Sen in Portsmouth Square, a peace statue at the International Airport, a mosaic mural in Moar's Cafeteria.

SMOOTH PLANES of semi-abstract Bear and Cubs arrest attention of mother and child on San Mateo's Hillsdale Mall.

GIRL MEETS MOUSE, fascination seems mutual. Bufano did this Hillsdale piece in 1956, infused it with so much spirit it looks ready to jump.

SIMPLICITY IS ART; BEYOND LIES ONLY PRIDE. This is the philosophy of Benny Bufano, who has been called a great artist of great talent. Born in San Fele, Italy, in 1903, Bufano came to San Francisco in 1924 at the age of 21, has spent almost half a century working in his adopted city. A man of peace and loving kindness, he can sometimes deliver a sharp riposte, if the mood so strikes him.

A STUDY in human emotions by Rubens

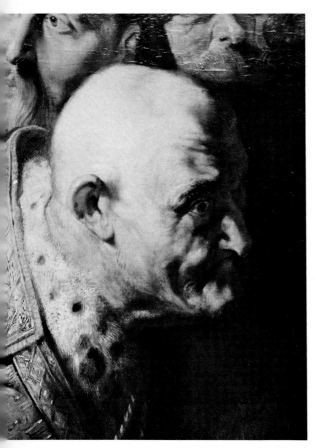

GREATEST FLEMISH artist of the 17th century, Peter Paul Rubens used the familiar Bible story of the tribute money to paint a masterpiece of human emotions revealed in a moment of drama. The priestly sect of the Sadducees tried to trap Christ into disobeying Roman law by asking if it was right to pay tribute money. Jesus replied by ordering them to bring him a penny. Having examined the coin with its graven image of the Roman emperor, He returned it, saying, "Render unto Caesar the things that are Caesar's and unto God the things that are God's." It is this moment, with the varying reactions of the Sadducees, that Rubens has recorded in paint.

CLOSEUP OF FACE of Sadducee reveals consternation and frustration of man who is confounded by the wisdom of Christ.

THREE HANDS, with the coin being returned, are a composition in themselves, show Rubens' superb drawing in microcosm.

FROM THE VERY BEGINNING Rubens designed
The Tribute Money *in terms of color and light,*
floodlighting the faces of the Sadducees with a golden
beam worthy of Caravaggio, illuminating Christ's face
with a mystic nimbus. The picture, a brilliant example
of the high Baroque, was painted in Antwerp in 1612,
now hangs in the De Young Museum.

"NO TEMPLE MADE WITH HANDS can compare with Yosemite," said naturalist John Muir. The point is underlined by Thomas Hill's Yosemite Valley. (Gift of Mrs. Ira Coe.)

234   NORTHERN CALIFORNIA

CALIFORNIA'S *romantic history and scenery*

THROUGHOUT THE LATTER HALF of the 19th century, the opening of the American West made newspaper headlines from the Mississippi to the Volga. The romantic history and scenery of California were especially attractive to people in such established capitals as New York, Paris, and Rome, and art exhibitions featuring landscapes of the vanishing Western frontier were eagerly attended. California's beauty was recorded in thousands of paintings like these three in the Oakland Art Museum, which is fast becoming an archive of California art.

DISCOVERY of San Francisco Bay was painted in 1896 by Arthur F. Mathews. (Lent by San Francisco Art Institute.)

PLEASURES OF LIFE in California were recorded by William Hahn. Return from the Bear Hunt, which he painted in 1882 helped win him national acclaim. (The Kahn Collection.)

Pacific
Northwest

ORGANIC VITALITY IN THE LAND AND ART

The primordial forms of the rugged Pacific Northwest are and have always been an inspiration to artists. Everything about the region is sculptural, says sculptor Mark Sponenburgh—the peaks of the Cascades, the slopes bearded with trees, and the ever-changing coastal wall. Another sculptor, Czech-born Jan Zach, speaks of the immense organic vitality of his adopted land, its endless variety of shapes

Native-Born Kenneth Callahan, who spent two years working as a forest ranger in the wilderness not far from his native Spokane, was fascinated by the interrelation of man, rock, and elements in the landscapes. Ladislos Kardos left his native Hungary at the age of 47 and moved to Vancouver under a compulsion to live and paint in the light of the Pacific Northwest. Softened by veils of mist, that light is similar to the luminous shawl that wraps the ancient cloud-hung capitals of Japan—Kyoto and Nara—whose marine climate is so similiar to that of this region.

Oregon painter Carl Morris has noted this correspondence and has suggested further affinities:

"In the Northwest the similarity in landscape and atmosphere brings to us the same sources in nature that nourished traditional Oriental art. The powerful urge to look inward, so great among Oriental artists, also exists in us.

AN EVER-LIVING BREATH OF VITALITY.
Merchant Holding a Wine Skin Vessel *owes its realism to a T'ang Dynasty (619-906 A.D.) Chinese sculptor. Models of people and objects were fashioned in ceramics and buried in tombs to serve the dead. (Seattle Art Museum.)*

237

Oregon Abloom with Art

Five years ago Oregon was generally regarded, even by Oregonians, as the no man's land of the art world, a kind of vacuum between the booming markets of Seattle and California. Today the Portland newspapers list as many as forty exhibitions a month. Art galleries have sprouted at Ashland, Bend, Eugene, Corvallis, Klamath Falls, Medford, and Salem, and the state, to quote one of its collectors, Mrs. William A. Haseltine, is abloom with art interest.

YOU CAN SEE HIS MISSING HORSE

UNIVERSITY OF OREGON MUSEUM OF ART. *Eugene, Oregon. Hours 1 to 5 P.M. daily. Murray Warner Collection of Oriental Art, Haseltine Collection of Pacific Northwest Art. Paintings by Morris Graves, Paul Horiuchi.*

Few states in the Union are more conscious of their regional qualities than Oregon, and few are more actively aware of the rich heritage and limitless potential of Pacific Northwest Art than the University of Oregon Museum of Art in Eugene. Its director, Wallace S. Baldinger, has traveled and studied much in Japan, and his lively interest in Oriental and contemporary art is reflected in the museum's lively and interesting exhibitions.

Built in 1933 to house the Murray Warner Collection of Oriental Art, the museum was designed as the heart of the university's famed School of Architecture and Allied Arts.

The museum's Oriental treasures range from a beautiful little Wei Dynasty tomb statuette, *The Turkish Groom*, to the fantastic Chinese *Imperial Jade Pagoda*, which stands nine feet tall. The *Groom*, though barely 14 inches high, is a masterpiece of ceramic sculpture, an individualized portrait with his right hand raised in a gesture so articulate that you can almost see his missing horse.

Outstanding in the sculpture department is Tom Hardy's *Flying Horse*, an arresting composition in welded steel that recalls the dynamics of futurism, the spirit of Han Dynasty horses, and the essential beauty of vertebrate structure.

Among the paintings at the University of Oregon Museum of Art are Morris Graves' mystic *Effort to Bloom*, Carl Morris' *Land, Sea, and Sky* (a shining abstract synthesis of the vast elemental spaces of the Northwest), and Paul Horiuchi's *Autumn in Kyoto* and *Summer Breeze*. Outstanding is *Figures and Boats* by Clayton S. Price. He was a prophetic painter; you can sense his influence on Carl Morris and Richard Diebenkorn. Though Price died in poverty in 1950 at the age of 76, his genius is now recognized. You'll probably find yourself lingering long before the grave and somber *Figures and Boats*. It has the eternal solidity of the coastal rocks of Oregon, touched here with the tragic apprehension of the human spirit.

FUNDS, $1,000—WORKS OF ART, NONE

PORTLAND ART MUSEUM. *Southwest Park at Madison Street, Portland, Oregon. Hours noon to 5 P.M. daily; closed Monday. Rasmussen Collection of Northwest Indian Art, Kress Collection of Renaissance Art, Ladd Collection of Japanese Prints, paintings and sculpture by Northwest artists, Chinese sculpture, bronzes, ceramics.*

In December 1892 seven citizens of Portland met to found the Portland Art Association. Their resources were: funds, $1,000; works of art, none. They wanted to make a collection of works of art, erect and maintain a suitable building to house them, and develop and encourage the study of art. They would be pleased to see their handsome museum and its flourishing art school today.

The Portland Art Museum has a fine collection of sculpture, ranging over a broad field from pre-Columbian figures and Palmyra funerary portraits to Brancusi and Mario Marini. Among the carefully chosen Chinese pieces are two horses that New York's Metropolitan might envy—a glazed one from the T'ang Dynasty, and a wooden one of the Han Dynasty, both noble works of exceptional quality. In European sculpture, a rare and beautiful *Standing Woman* by Lehmbruck is outstanding. Modern Northwest sculptors James Lee Hansen, Manuel Izquierdo, Lee Kelly, and Fred Littman are also represented, along with painters Carl Morris (don't miss his striking oil *Expanding Elements*), Mark Tobey, Louis Bunce, Morris Graves, and Darrel Austin. The modern collection is constantly augmented, for the Portland Art Museum is the scene each April of the well-attended Artists of Oregon Annual.

The Portland Art Museum is most famous for its Rasmussen Collection of Native Arts of the Pacific Northwest. Its 5,000 pieces were collected over a quarter century by Axel Rasmussen, Superintendent of Schools at Skagway, Alaska, from 1937 to 1945. Portland raised the money to buy the collection by public subscription in 1948.

In this collection are painted Tsimshian and Kwakiutl wooden masks that rival the African Negro sculpture which had so powerful an effect on Picasso. The vitality of the Pacific Northwest informs every stroke of adz and brush. The masks are painted with pigments of blue copper oxide, black charcoal mixed with mud, and vivid red and yellow ochres of the northern earth. What did the artists use for oil? The red caviar of Chinook salmon. Art has seldom been so ingenious, never bolder than as represented by this collection.

SHOWS AND EXHIBITS AROUND OREGON

At Klamath Falls the Klamath Art Association sponsors frequent shows in all media. So does the Rogue Gallery at Medford. At Eugene you'll find exhibits at the Student Union Gallery, at the 12th Avenue Gallery, and at the Maude I. Kerns Art Center. While in this attractive university town take a look at Tom Hardy's welded bronze fountains in the court of the Erb Memorial Union on the campus and in front of Eugene's prize-winning city hall.

You'll see more of Hardy's work back in Portland: *Flocks of Birds* at the Lloyd Center, and *Oregon Country*, a series of huge welded bronze panels at Portland State College. Another prolific Northwest sculptor, Fred Littman, is well represented in Portland with a wood carving in the First Unitarian Church, grilled bronze doors for the Ark of the Covenant at Temple Beth Israel, a *Madonna and Child* at the University of Portland.

The Portland Museum Art School and Reed College exhibit works of art in the Civic Theater, Adele's Restaurant, in banks, high schools, and just about every place that has walls for painting and a spare inch for sculpture. The public libraries of Beaverton and Lake Oswego feature monthly shows. So do Portland's Jewish Community Center, Masonic Temple, Image Gallery, and Fountain Gallery of Art. Take the small fry to the Junior Museum to see the work of their contemporaries (you'll enjoy it too), and be sure to see the first-rate pots and sculpture at Portland's justly famed Oregon Ceramics Studio.

See the murals in the State Capitol at Salem, and the art exhibit in historic Bush House. And don't miss the WPA murals by Clayton S. Price in Timberline Lodge at Mount Hood.

*FIVE BEAUTIES, by Hokusai,
illustrate feminine virtues of
education, entertainment, domesticity,
art, and writing. The early
19th-century painting on silk is in
the Seattle Museum.*

*JAPANESE SAMURAI dressed up in
Western ruff, carries a crucifix and
musket brought to Japan by
"barbarians" from Europe. The gold
leaf and color screen panel is typical
of the Momoyama Period—1573-1615.
(Seattle Art Museum.)*

OREGON 241

Washington's Children

The Oriental influence, so marked in the painting and sculpture of Oregon, is even more apparent in the work of such Washington artists as Mark Tobey, Morris Graves, James Lee Hansen, George Tsutakawa, and Paul Horiuchi. In the Seattle Art Museum, Graves and Hansen found the Chinese Shang bronzes that would inspire them, and Tobey got his first taste of Japanese calligraphy.

Tobey and Graves went subsequently to the Orient in search of themselves. The instinctive mysticism of Graves was given definition by Zen Buddhism. He was also inspired by the sea-laced atmosphere of the Washington coast, so similar in character to that of Japan. Tobey studied Chinese calligraphy in Shanghai, *sumi* and brushwork

BEAUTIFUL GIRL, BIBULOUS OLDSTER are typical of the realism of Greek Tanagra figurines given by the Queen of Greece to the Maryhill Museum.

FOUNTAIN OF NORTHWEST splashes in courtyard of Seattle Center Playhouse. Sculpted by James Fitzgerald in 1962, the 23-foot, 3-ton bronze structure recalls forms of Washington's Cascade Mountains.

at a Zen monastery in Japan, and then returned to America in 1934 to begin the "white writing" that made him world famous. In Seattle at this time he met the Japanese-born painter Paul Horiuchi, an artist whose remarkable plastic development owes much to Tobey's influence. Tobey was 44, Horiuchi 28 when they met.

"I was introduced to the enlightenment of Oriental philosophy by an Occidental, Mark Tobey," Horiuchi recalls.

SAM HILL'S CASTLE

MARYHILL MUSEUM OF FINE ARTS. *Maryhill, Washington. Open March 15 to November 15. Hours 9 A.M. to 5:30 P.M. daily, including Sundays and holidays.*

A hundred miles east of Portland, up on the northern rim of the Columbia Gorge, stands the Maryhill Museum of Fine Arts. The place was founded by Samuel Hill, a friend of Queen Marie of Rumania, who dedicated the museum November 3, 1926.

"I am a dreamer," said the queen, "and there is a dream built into this place." You will read the rest of her speech on a bronze plaque located within the museum.

To make Sam's own dream come true, Queen Marie made gifts to

POPULAR FEATURE of Seattle Center, Paul Horiuchi's
free-standing glass mosaic mural looks like a
launching pad for the Space Needle in background.
The painter's abstract collage sketch, using scraps of
Japanese paper and 16 colors, was re-created on a
parabolic wall of 54 concrete slabs. Note the interesting
color correlations between the mural and the
flowers, as well as the sky.

the museum: her coronation robes, signed photographs, the throne of gilded wood from her summer palace outside Bucharest. These and other personal souvenirs were the nucleus of one of the most heterogeneous museum collections in the world.

You will find something for every taste at Maryhill. Outstanding among the authentic art treasures is a group of 18 Tanagra figurines, which the Queen of Greece chose for Sam Hill from the National Museum in Athens. There are also 22 original Rodin drawings, selected by the sculptor's friend Loie Fuller for Alma de Bretteville Spreckels, who donated these and other "leftovers" from the California Palace of the Legion of Honor in San Francisco. What leftovers! One of them is the original plaster cast of one of Rodin's greatest statues to be found in the United States, *Eve*.

A large collection of chessmen, the largest in America outside the Philadelphia Museum of Art, is a popular feature of the museum. Indian artifacts, French high fashion dolls, glass, ceramics, and hundreds of photographically realistic paintings make up the rest of the exhibits. In spite of the restless, brooding presence of Rodin, Maryhill is a stronghold of academic art. Star of the show is R. H. Ives Gammell, whose classical and biblical tableux have the fascination of stills from the silent movies.

"The function of Maryhill," says its hospitable director Clifford R. Dolph, "is to preserve the beauty of traditional painting while abstract fashions come and go."

SEATTLE—A CULTURAL CAPITAL

The 1962 World's Fair in Seattle left that city with one of the most beautiful civic centers in the nation: the Seattle Center. Take time to stroll along its tree-lined walks, to admire the leaping fountains, to contemplate Paul Horiuchi's free-standing glass mosaic mural. Walk under the airy arches of Minoru Yamasaki's Pacific Science Center, a space age adaptation of Gothic architecture that has been called the most beautiful public building to be constructed in America since World War II. Visit the handsome modern opera house, embellished by paintings by Mark Tobey, Morris Graves, Guy Anderson, and other Northwest artists.

Focal point of art activity in the Seattle Center is the Seattle Art

Museum Pavilion, which began life in 1962 as the British Pavilion of the fair and has now been remodeled for the permanent display of art. An adjunct to Seattle's famed Museum of Art, the pavilion is open daily from noon to 9 P.M. Visit it in October to see the Northwest Annual, now in its fifty-first year. Artists from Washington, Oregon, British Columbia, Alaska, Montana show their best work.

WINDOW ON THE ORIENT

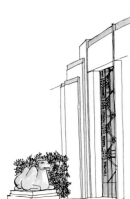

SEATTLE ART MUSEUM. *Volunteer Park, Seattle. Hours 10 A.M. to 5 P.M. Tuesday-Saturday; noon to 5 P.M. Sunday; closed Monday. Internationally famous jade and Oriental art collections, European art, 600 works of Pacific Northwest artists.*

The Seattle Art Museum stands at the top of one of the city's seven hills with a magnificent view over Puget Sound. If that inland sea, warmed by the Japanese current, is the Northwest gateway to the Orient, the museum is a window opening onto Oriental culture. Few institutions have had more influence in shaping the taste and art of an entire region.

As a plaque in the foyer will inform you, the museum was donated to the city of Seattle in 1933 by director Richard E. Fuller and his mother "for the recreation, education, and inspiration of its citizens."

The city of Seattle maintains the building; the art treasures are mostly gifts, beginning with the Chinese and Japanese works which the Fullers had the foresight to collect on trips to the Orient as early as 1919. The Oriental treasures range over the whole history of Asiatic Art from Shang Dynasty bronzes 4,000 years old to 20th-century Japanese landscapes of the late Edo period, whose influence on expressionist painting is marked. In between are the plastic wonders of the Chinese Han and T'ang dynasties, splendid 6th-century A.D. Haniwa figures from Japanese burial mounds, rare paintings by such great Japanese masters as Sesshu, majestic mountain landscapes of the Ming Dynasty, great Japanese scrolls and screens, vibrating with birds and blossoms on gold and silver backgrounds. How the brushes of these painters tingled with life! No wonder they tempted Tobey and Graves to try their hand at calligraphy.

The creative genius of many other lands and periods is illuminated by carefully chosen art treasures from Sumerian sculpture, 3,000 B.C.,

EAGLES PERCH on a snowy branch in the six-panel screen, The Five Eagles, *in Seattle Art Museum. Gold leaf, color, and ink were used with gorgeous decorative effect.*

DEER PRANCE WITH ABANDON in this portion of a 17th-century Japanese scroll by Nonomura Sotatsu and Honnami Koetsu. The ink, gold, and silver piece is in the Seattle Art Museum.

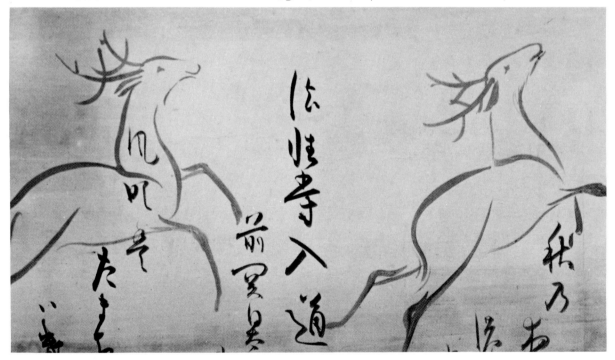

WATER LILIES were a favorite subject of Claude Monet. Painting them many times over, he influenced abstract art with his shimmering pools of light and color. (Portland Art Museum.)

to the works of a hundred living Northwest artists. You'll find good examples of Egyptian, Indian, Greek, and Roman art, some excellent primitive sculpture, and the Kress Collection of Renaissance and Baroque painting. This includes Rubens' sketch for *The Last Supper* (the finished painting was destroyed by a fire in the Antwerp Cathedral) and a Tiepolo ceiling, installed here just as it once was in the Palazzo Porta in Vicenza.

WESTERN SUCCESS STORY

CHARLES AND EMMA FRYE ART MUSEUM. *Terry at Cherry, Seattle. Open every day of the year but Christmas. Hours 10 A.M. to 5 P.M. weekdays; noon to 6 P.M. Sundays and holidays.*

The small and attractive Charles and Emma Frye Art Museum symbolizes a western success story that began with Charles Frye's birth in Iowa in 1858 and reached its climax in 1952 with the opening of the free public art museum which he and his wife endowed for the people of Seattle. With little formal education, Charles Frye became the best corn husker in Iowa, the proprietor of a small butcher shop in Butte, Montana, and in 1891 co-owner of a small meat packing plant in Seattle that became a multi-million dollar business. As Charles Frye and his art-minded wife Emma prospered they began to travel to their ancestral Germany and soon accumulated the paintings you will see in the museum. Their taste, as the 230 ultra realistic pictures in the museum show, was remarkably consistent.

The Frye Museum, entirely supported by funds from the Frye Foundation, is a haven and refuge for all those who have never been able or willing to accept abstract art. Typical of the collection is *Susanna and the Elders*, a painting by Francis Xavier Winterhalter. Though he is forgotten today, he was once the rage of Europe, a hundred years ago, greatly admired by Queen Victoria, and court painter of Napoleon III and the Empress Eugénie. He often painted the latter and her ladies in waiting. The latter detested the Impressionists. She used to slap their pictures with her fan. She would have loved the paintings in the Frye Museum as do 50,000 annual visitors.

Among the handsomely displayed pictures are works by the leading academic painter of the late 19th century, William Adolphe

Bouguereau. Another nearly forgotten French master represented here in Adolphe Joseph Thomas Monticelli, a neglected painter whose orchestration of color was highly admired by Van Gogh. There is a delightful landscape by Manet, another by the American impressionist Childe Hassam, and there are three pictures by the precursor of impressionism, Eugene Boudin, whom Corot called "the King of Skies."

ON THE CAMPUS AND AROUND SEATTLE

HENRY GALLERY. 15th Avenue N.E. and N.E. Campus Parkway, Seattle. Hours 10 A.M. to 5 P.M. Monday–Saturday; 1 to 5 P.M. Sunday.

Up on the University of Washington campus you'll find the Henry Gallery, a modern brick structure with Gothic trim, built in 1926. Though the names of Rembrandt, Holbein, and other old masters appear in Old English lettering on the facade, the gallery is devoted to works of the late 19th and early 20th centuries, the collection of the gallery's donor, Horace C. Henry of Seattle. There is a good small group of works by Northwest artists, including Tobey, Graves, and Callahan. Outstanding are Callahan's poetic *Mountain Landscape* and Spencer Moseley's *Red Rondo Tondo*, a circular picture that anticipates hard-edge and op.

The Henry Gallery has a fine modern print collection and features stimulating shows of contemporary art, with such frequency that the permanent collection is seldom on view. Among the annual exhibits well worth attending are Artists of Washington, Northwest Craftsmen, and Northwest Printmakers.

In downtown Seattle see James Fitzgerald's fountain in the plaza of Yamasaki's IBM Building at 5th Avenue and University and the work of several artists in the new Seattle Public Library, 4th Avenue at Madison Street. On the third floor terrace is Ray Jensen's *Pursuit of Knowledge*, an imaginative and spirited sculpture in which the pursuers are a trio of high hurdlers. George Tsutakawa's bronze fountain in the library garden creates a pleasing balance of abstract forms and space, evoking once more those subtle correspondences between the sculptor's Northwest home and the Orient of his ancestors. Unveiled in 1960, it led to a veritable fountain explosion in the Pacific Northwest.

British Columbia

Impressive examples of the Indian culture of the Pacific Northwest await you everywhere in this beautiful Canadian province. You will find them in the Vancouver City Museum at 401 Main Street and in the thousand cedar-scented, water-girdled acres of Vancouver's famous Stanley Park. Near Brockton Point you'll come to a clearing in the forest where heraldic totem poles, carved with grotesquely stylized effigies of killer whale and salmon, raven, wolf, and grizzly bear, stand out in color against the green of the encircling cedars.

More of these polychrome columns stand in Totem Park on the 1200-acre campus of the University of British Columbia at Grey Point. Here in the Museum of Anthropology you will find a collection of more than 8,000 Northwest Indian artifacts. Many of the pieces, notably the painted ceremonial masks of the Kwakiutl, Tlingit, Haida, and Bella Bella people, transcend all limits of regional folklore and emerge as stunning works of art, invested with the indwelling universal spirit of creative genius. Across the hall from the Anthropology Museum, the University's Fine Arts Gallery has no permanent collection but features exhibitions that range from the work of young Vancouver artists to traveling shows reflecting the latest trends in international painting and sculpture. Hours of gallery are 10:30 A.M. to 5 P.M. Tuesday through Saturday.

VANCOUVER AND THE REGIONAL ARTISTS

VANCOUVER ART GALLERY. *1145 West Georgia Street, Vancouver, B.C. Hours 10 A.M. to 5 P.M. Tuesday–Saturday; 2 to 5 P.M. Sunday; open from 7 to 10 P.M. Friday evenings; closed Monday.*

The scenic grandeur and Indian lore of British Columbia have tempted many artists, none more than that local pioneer of painting, Emily Carr (1871-1945), who literally paddled her own canoe and took the whole of British Columbia as her subject matter. Her art is a perceptive esthetic record of the villages, totems, and customs of the coastal Indians whose culture she observed at first hand during arduous trips into remote regions. The Vancouver Art Gallery has

*VIOLENT AS WAR ITSELF are two etchings by Georges Rouault from a series titled Miserere.
On the left*, This Will be the Last Time, Father; *on the right*, Onward, Dead Men! *(Henry Gallery.)*

nearly 200 of her oils, watercolors, and sketches in its permanent collection along with works of other Canadian artists, De Tonnancour, Shadbolt, Roberts, Borduas, Lemieux, and Binning, to name a few. There is a small but select collection of outstanding British moderns (among them Wyndham Lewis, Graham Sutherland, Ben Nicholson, W. R. Sickert, and John Bratby) and a fine international print collection worth a visit in itself.

The Vancouver Art Gallery assumes the role of discovering and bringing British Columbia painters to the attention of the art world in annual jury shows and such major invitationals as New Talent B.C., widely circulated in 1964-65.

Across the Strait of Georgia from Vancouver, the North American culture boom continues with the construction of Victoria's

British Columbia Archives and Provincial Museum, both of which are scheduled for completion in 1968.

From the dock on Vancouver Island the bus will take you past rolling English farms and country gardens to Thunderbird Park, named for that horned and fabled eagle who perches like a family crest atop the totem poles. There are a score of these primitive yet highly sophisticated columns here, where you can also visit an authentic painted Kwakiutl Indian house. Combined with smaller exhibits in the Provincial Museum in the east wing of the nearby Parliament Building, they form one of the most important Northwest Indian collections in existence. At the present writing the Provincial Museum is open only on Saturdays and school holidays from 9:30 A.M. to 5 P.M. and on Sundays from 1 to 5 P.M.

PEACEFULLY pastoral, and in contrast with Rouault's maledictions against war, facing page, is the Goatsherd, by Claude Lorraine. (Art Gallery of Greater Victoria.)

FRUITFUL AND PROMISING EFFORTS

ART GALLERY OF GREATER VICTORIA. *1040 Moss Street, Victoria, B.C. Hours 11 A.M. to 5 P.M. Tuesday–Saturday; 2 to 5 P.M. Sunday; 7:30 to 9:30 P.M. Thursday; closed Monday. Afternoon tea served from 3 to 4:30.*

Victoria's isolation from the world's major art centers, says Art Gallery Director Colin Graham, requires the most strenuous efforts to offset this drawback by building up a rich local collection. The efforts are fruitful and promising.

The Art Gallery is a pleasant place to refresh yourself with art discoveries and good English tea. Among the paintings inspired by the local environment is Brian Travers-Smith's *Tidal Patterns*, a spacious delta scene reveling in the play of light over vast expanses of water, sand, and sky. Another is Jack Shadbolt's *New Snow From My Studio Window*, in which the firs and hemlocks of Vancouver's Burnaby Mountain are limned in ink with a calligraphic line.

RAPT ATTENTION is evident in the faces of a group of sixth-grade students on a tour of the Vancouver Art Gallery. The exhibition was titled Yugoslav Frescoes.

IN PITY AND TERROR, an encaustic by Mitchell Jamieson, has the stunning aspect of the accident it depicts, plus symbolic overtones. (Henry Gallery.)

BRITISH COLUMBIA   255

A *SYMBOL of power and menace*

MEN OF MANY CIVILIZATIONS have been fascinated by the symbolic image of the bull. It first appears on the walls of prehistoric caves in France and Spain, painted there some 25,000 years ago. It haunts Greek legend in the form of the dreaded Minotaur. It remains a vital force in the art of contemporary Spain and Mexico. Even when yoked, as in Albert Bierstadt's painting on page 194, the bull remains a symbol of latent power and menace. The four bulls shown on these two pages are all from the collection of the Seattle Art Museum.

TERROR OF BULL dominates Francis Picabia's Barcelone. *Painted in 1924, it achieves pictorial dynamism through simultaneous contrasts.*

BLACK BULL from a Japanese scroll titled The Ten Fast Bulls. *The scroll, painted about 1280, records great power and volume with only ink on paper.*

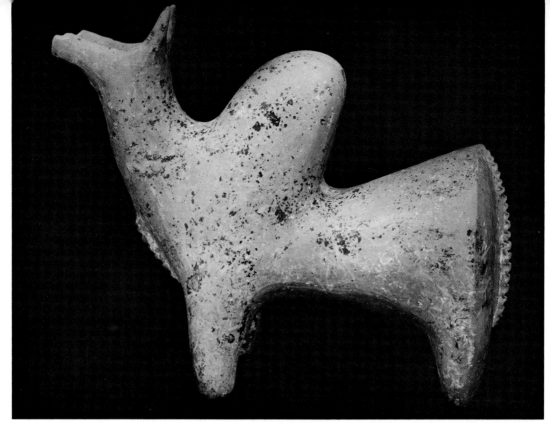

ABSTRACT VERSION of high-humped bull from ancient Persia (7th century B.C.) was found at Amlash in Iran. This earthenware figure was used as a vessel.

ROMAN BULL dates from 1st century B.C. The sturdy, realistic bronze is like the symbol of a young republic already in the process of conquering the world.

FIGURES AND BOATS, a moody and haunting work by C. S. Price, is as solid in construction and form as rocks on the Oregon coast. (University of Oregon Museum of Art.)

WASHINGTON Cascades grandeur is recorded in Mountain Landscape, by Kenneth Callahan, which reflects the artist's experience as a forest-fire lookout in the wilderness near Seattle. (Henry Gallery.)

NORTHWEST *forms and figures*

PAINTERS AND SCULPTORS of the Pacific Northwest speak of the organic vitality of their land, its primordial forms, its cloud-filtered light. These are palpable things which often appear in the art of one of the most individual regional schools in America. So strong is the mutual impact of nature and art that one cannot see the work of Northwest artists without gaining a keener, a deeper perception, without sensing the influence of the earth.

FORMS FOLLOW MAN was painted in 1941 by Washington's famed Mark Tobey. The sharp, angular shapes keep the eye darting from one form to another. (Seattle Art Museum.)

INFLUENCE of the Orient in the Pacific Northwest

ORIENTAL ART, brought to the Pacific Northwest by collectors and installed in the Seattle and Portland Art Museums and the University of Oregon Museum at Eugene, has exerted a powerful influence on the artists of the region, many of whom had their first contacts with art in these very galleries. Of all the objects imported from China, few are more impressive than the bronze ritual vessels of the Shang Dynasty (1523 to 1028 B.C.), whose tombs have disclosed fine Bronze Age works.

FERTILE IMAGINATION of Morris Graves took flight in 1947 watercolor, Ceremonial Bronze Taking the Form of a Bird. *(Seattle Art Museum.)*

JAMES L. HANSEN of Vancouver was influenced by Shang bronzes, used their forms in his own bronze sculpture. This example, in the Seattle Art Museum, is called The Neo Shang. A similar Shang-inspired sculpture, Tales, adorns the civic mall in Fresno, California.

MODEL FOR ARTISTS was the early Shang Dynasty chueh, or ritual tripod-shaped wine goblet, used in religious ceremonies. This one in the Seattle Art Museum, dating from the 15th century B.C., was excavated from a tomb in China's Honan Province.

Inter-Mountain States

RICH IN ART AND NATURAL WONDERS

Daniel Webster, who had a certain reputation for far-sighted states-manship, once dismissed the region between the Rockies and the High Sierra as a barren waste of prairie dogs, cactus, and shifting sands, incapable of producing anything, and therefore not worth retaining. He died in 1852, seven years before Nevada's Comstock Lode began to yield the billion-dollar bonanza that did more to save the Union than all the oratory of Webster's silver tongue. Sheep and cattle now graze contentedly on the barren wastes of Arizona. Citrus groves bear golden fruit among the shifting sands. The prairie dogs have long since given way to bipeds in search of sunshine and a salubrious climate, and a new industrial bonanza is in full swing.

If riches come can art be far behind? In what used to be regarded as a cultural dustbowl art now blooms like the flowering saguaro cactus. Annual art festivals flourish in Boise, Idaho. Iranian art is shown in Reno, and an airlift delivers oil paintings to the farthest corners of Utah. In these inland states there are contemporary Mexican paintings and Chinese ceramics; there are works by Americans ranging from Copley to Wyeth; there is sculpture by Calder, pottery by the Hopis, sand paintings by the Navajos.

GORGEOUS BYZANTINE TRADITION.
Its essence is perpetuated by 14th-century Sienese
artist Taddeo di Bartolo in his Coronation of the
Virgin, with its appealing cherubs and warm expression
of Christ and Virgin. The work is from the Kress
Collection at the University of Arizona.

263

Arizona

Arizona, the Grand Canyon State, is almost as rich in art, architecture, and artifacts as it is in natural wonders. Three hundred years before Columbus discovered America, Arizona's Indians had the modern idea of set-back apartment houses, as you will see when you visit the Hopi pueblos, notably Oraibi, which, dating from A.D. 1200, is the oldest continuously-inhabited community in the United States. The vigor of native Indian art continues in Navajo weaving and silverwork, in Hopi, Yuma, and Mohave pottery. You'll see fine examples at the Museum of Northern Arizona in Flagstaff. Here you will also find the first oil landscapes of Arizona, painted by intrepid artists like Frederic Dellenbaugh and Elbert Burr who strapped their easels to the backs of mules and explored the trails of the Grand Canyon back in the 1870's, painting as they went.

A LONG WAY FROM MOOSEJAW

PHOENIX ART MUSEUM. *1625 North Central Avenue, Phoenix, Arizona. Hours 10 A.M. to 5 P.M. Tuesday–Saturday; 1 to 5 P.M. Sunday; closed Monday and entire month of August. French and American art, Luce Collection of Chinese art.*

Back in 1957 the Phoenix Art Museum was a gleam in the eye of certain civic leaders who felt it was time that Phoenix became a city in fact as well as name. The land for a civic center had been donated by Mrs. Dwight Heard, and the trustees of the Fine Arts Association were looking for a founding director of a museum that did not exist. Their choice fell upon Dr. Forest Melick Hinkhouse, director of the art history department at the University of Buffalo's Albright Art School. At a fund raising dinner for the still non-existent museum, actor-connoisseur Vincent Price said, "To be a major city you've got to have a major art museum. If a Phoenician wants to see a real museum he has to go as far west as Los Angeles, as far east as Denver, as far south as Mexico City, as far north as Moosejaw, Saskatchewan!" The point was a good one.

This caught the city fathers at the point of their maximum sensibilities. The 400 persons attending that dinner pledged $400,000 on the spot. The rest is civic history of which Phoenix can be proud; a $500,000 bond issue, voted by the citizens and matched again by private contributions. Gifts poured in from generous collectors: French impressionists from the Donald Harringtons, Han and T'ang art from the Henry Luces, Renaissance art from the Lewis Ruskins, Sung and Ming porcelains from the Matthew Wongs. The museum had hardly opened its doors in 1959 before it became apparent that its 25,000 square feet of floor space would have to be tripled to accommodate the collections. This has now been accomplished with the addition of the new wing, opened in 1966. When you visit it you'll know you're a long way from Moosejaw.

A magnet for excellence, a watering hole for art: this is the down-to-earth way in which the Phoenix Museum has been described. It would be hard to imagine a more attractive watering hole than this clean-cut, functional but warmly human art center.

ART IN AND AROUND PHOENIX

There's so much art activity everywhere in and around Phoenix that it's hard to tell at times whether you're in a bank, an automobile salesroom, or an art gallery. Three Phoenix banks, Valley National, Southwest Savings, and the Guaranty Bank actually have art galleries on the premises with one-man and group shows changing with your monthly statement. Collector Read Mullan has a handsome Gallery of Western Art above his Ford Agency at 1550 Camelback Road. Here you can browse happily among Indian and Western paintings, beautiful Navajo rugs, and Indian jewelry. The Heard Museum at 22 East Monte Vista Road has prehistoric relics, wonderful examples of Indian weaving, and changing exhibits of Indian painting in a charming Spanish Colonial house, open daily except Monday from 10 A.M. to 4 P.M.

There are more than two dozen commercial galleries in Phoenix and in neighboring Scottsdale, Tempe, and Goodyear. They are listed with their hours and the exhibitions of the week every Sunday in the art pages of *The Arizona Republic.*

Taliesin West, the famous school established and designed by Frank Lloyd Wright, is another must for visitors to Phoenix. Just off Shea Boulevard, this remarkable example of desert architecture is open daily, June through October; thrice weekly (Wednesdays, Saturdays, Sundays), November through May. Hours 10 A.M. to 4 P.M. Guided tours: $1.

ANDREW WYETH aimed to submerge his craft, make it a handmaiden of beauty and emotional content. How well he succeeded is evident in The Tolling Bell, *a haunting watercolor at Arizona State University.*

Among the French works on view you'll see a masterly seascape by Courbet, *The Wave*, a vibrant realistic painting imbued with the rhythm and menace of the sea, the incipient violence of a livid sky. Derain, Renoir, Millet, David, Odilon Redon, and the Douanier Rousseau are a few of the other stars of the French galaxy.

The Phoenix Art Museum's American collection spans a century and a half from Copley's *Portrait of John Graham* (1795) through Charles Wimar's naturalist Western study, *Buffalo Drinking* (1861), to Andrew Wyeth's sensitive watercolor, *Dune Landscape*.

Of historic as well as esthetic interest is Stuart Davis' very early *Cornfield*. Painted in 1919 when the artist was 23, it is a strongly brushed figurative landscape in which you can already see the elements of that abstract vocabulary that was to dominate his own and American painting two decades later.

For an artist who remained faithful to a more realistic idiom turn to another Davis, Lew, a native son of Arizona. His picture, *Little Boy Lives in a Copper Camp*, is a poignant human and economic commentary, tinged with social protest. Compare it with Richard Diebenkorn's *Woman by a Window*, a work of similar subject matter and composition in which the painter has been more exclusively concerned with plastic or "painterly" problems.

PAINTERS OF THE WESTERN SCENE

ARIZONA STATE UNIVERSITY ART COLLECTIONS. *Arizona State University, Tempe, Arizona. Hours 8 A.M. to 10 P.M. Sunday–Friday; 8 A.M. to 5 P.M. Saturday. Important collection of American paintings and prints; Kress Collection of Renaissance painting. Works are displayed in lobby, lounge, and gallery of the Matthews Library.*

On the south bank of the Salt River ten miles east of Phoenix is Tempe, so named by an English traveler because of its resemblance to the beautiful Vale of Tempe in Greece. Here amidst the cottonwoods and tamarisks you'll find the 40-acre campus of Arizona State University. In its administration building a fresco by Jean Charlot depicts man's wisdom in subduing the aggressive forces of nature. An Indian medicine man and modern techniques of extracting rattlesnake venom figure in this allegory.

The University art collections have recently expanded into what used to be a library. Here there is a remarkable collection of American art. One of the early paintings is Gilbert Stuart's portrait of Mrs. Stephen Peabody who recorded how disagreeable it was "to sit down to be looked at and to look up into a stranger's face."

You'll find the painters of the Western scene here: Frederic Remington, Frank Tenney Johnson, and that master of the bucking bronco, Charles M. Russell. They all provide vivid reminders of the vanishing frontier. So does that great birdwatcher John James Audubon. His frontier is the Northwest, his subjects an osprey and an otter about to stage a battle royal over a large Chinook salmon. Among the romantic landscapes on hand are two by Albert Pinkham Ryder, *The Canal* and *White Horizon*, haunting night scenes of infinite space and eerie luminosity. The Ash Can School is represented by Robert Henri, George Luks, John Sloan. Georgia O'Keeffe's *Horse's Skull on Blue* is bleached with the dazzling light of the desert, and Charles Sheeler's *Barn Variations*, a marvel of precise form, is as clean and exhilarating as the Arizona air outside.

MODERN ART IN OLD TUCSON

UNIVERSITY OF ARIZONA GALLERY. *Tucson, Arizona. Hours 10 A.M. to 5 P.M. Monday–Saturday; Sundays 2 to 5 P.M. Gallego's Altar Piece from the Cathedral of Ciudad Rodrigo, Gallagher Collection of Modern Art.*

One of the oldest Spanish towns in the United States, Tucson was described in the 19th century as a resort for horse thieves, murderers, vagrant politicians, and a place where men who were no longer permitted to live in California went for their health.

The Old Pueblo, as the town is still affectionately called, is still a health resort. It is also a cultural center. In 1954 the local art colony buzzed with excitement as the University of Arizona received the first of some 150 paintings and sculpture presented by Baltimore businessman and collector Edward Joseph Gallagher, Jr., in memory of his son. It was a fine nucleus of modern art.

The collection covers most of the major trends in modern art from the soft, introspective color harmonies of Mark Rothko to the slam-bang fireworks of Georges Mathieu. It includes an inspired example of abstract action painting by Jackson Pollock and an equally powerful figurative action painting by Willem de Kooning. There's a great Matisse ink drawing, *Girl with a Gold Necklace;* there are three Légers, a handful of vibrant canvases by Irene Rice Pereira, and a memorable watercolor, *Along the Ramapo River,* by John Marin.

The Kress Collection, given to the Gallery in 1951, includes two extraordinary Tiepolos; Tintoretto's luminous and sensuous *Venus Lamenting the Death of Adonis;* a great Hispano-Flemish masterpiece: Fernando Gallego's *Altar Piece from the Cathedral of Ciudad Rodrigo;* and a rare example of the 14th-century Sienese School, *The Coronation of the Virgin* by Taddeo di Bartolo.

A magnet for local painters and sculptors is the Tucson Art Center at 325 West Franklin Street. Founded in 1925, the center offers a varied program of art exhibitions, lectures, courses, concerts, and films, all designed to unlock the treasures of abundant living. In addition to exhibitions of international art, the center stages two important local shows each year: The Arizona Craft Annual, and the Annual Tucson Festival Art Show. The Tucson Art Center is open to the public from 10 A.M. to 5 P.M. Monday through Saturday; Sunday afternoons from 2 to 5 P.M.

AUDIENCE PARTICIPATION *is order of the day at the Phoenix Art Museum as mother and child mirror posture of Anthony Van Dyck's* Holy Family *and young art lovers admire Labille-Guiard's portrait of* Adelaide de France.

IDEAS, NOT THINGS, AT FLAGSTAFF

MUSEUM OF NORTHERN ARIZONA. *Flagstaff, Arizona. Fort Valley Road. Open March 1 to December 24. Hours 9 A.M. to 12 noon and from 1 to 5 P.M. weekdays; 1:30 to 5 P.M. Sunday. During June, July, August weekday hours are 9 A.M. to 5 P.M. without interruption. Indian art and Southwest American paintings.*

Three miles north of Flagstaff, in the shadow of the San Francisco Mountains, the Museum of Northern Arizona is primarily a scientific research center for local archeology, ethnology, and geology. It also has a collection of Western Art of the Colorado Plateau. Among the artists represented are Frank Swinnerton, Gunnar Widfores, Karl Oscar Borg, John Frost, Edgar Payne, Jay Bartlett, and E. A. Burbank. There are also fine examples of Indian art and artifacts in this fascinating museum, which displays "ideas, not things."

Utah

As early as 1855 Brigham Young was urging his missionaries to convert artists to Mormonism so that they could embellish the temples of Deseret. His Salt Lake Theater was a godsend for painters like George Ottinger, Daniel Weggeland, and John Tullidge, brought from New England, Norway, and England respectively and employed as scene painters. When they weren't painting scenery they bartered their landscapes for onions, potatoes, and home-knit sox. In 1863 these three men founded the Deseret Academy of Fine Arts, first thing of its kind in the West. It soon closed, but the spark had been struck. In our times it has been revived by the Springville Art Association, the Utah State Institute of Fine Arts, and three universities: University of Utah in Salt Lake City, Utah State University at Logan, Brigham Young University at Provo.

KEEPER OF THE FLAME

SALT LAKE ART CENTER. *54 Finch Lane, Salt Lake City, Utah. Hours 1 to 5* P.M. *Tuesday–Saturday; 2 to 6* P.M. *Sunday; guided tours at 8:30 Tuesday nights.*

Perhaps the staunchest keeper of the flame is the Salt Lake Art Center, the only gallery in the nation that uses an airplane to take art to the people. Every three months Junior Leaguer Mrs. Richard K. Reuling hops into *Nancy*, a Cessna 182 specially equipped to transport oil paintings, and takes off for outlying communities. Her usual load is 25, selected from some 200 works by 60 artists in the Center's rental gallery. This service has proved so popular that a Cessna 206 was added to the airlift in 1966 for transporting larger works. It's a good example of bringing art to the people.

The Art Center's ground activities include organizing the Utah Biennial of Painting and Sculpture and, in odd-numbered years, the Intermountain Biennial, which presents a broad view of current production by the artists of Utah, Idaho, Nevada, Colorado, Montana, and Wyoming.

The center's program includes films, art classes, traveling exhibitions, and an occasional survey of local collectors' taste.

A LUXURY APARTMENT

UTAH MUSEUM OF FINE ARTS. *Fourth Floor, Park Building, University of Utah, Salt Lake City. Hours 8:45 A.M. to 4:45 P.M. Tuesday–Friday; 2 to 5 P.M. Sunday, 12:30 to 4:45 P.M. Monday.*

Just a pleasant stroll up the hill from the Salt Lake Art Center is the Utah Museum of Fine Arts. Founded in 1951, the museum has the charm of a luxury apartment furnished in many styles. Nucleus of the collection is Mrs. Richard A. Hudnut's ensemble of French, Spanish, and English furniture and decorative art, to which has been added the Egyptian things of her daughter, Natasha Rambova. Among the art treasures are an Egyptian funerary barge (1500 B.C.), a painting by Turner, *Men in Boats*, and, looking very wild in this polite setting, a spirited cast of Frederic Remington's *Bronco Buster*. Another surprise: a whole series of Utah-born John Held Junior's flapper girls who used to cavort on *New Yorker* covers back in the roaring twenties. There is a large modern gallery for the University's changing exhibitions and another one, brand new in 1966, over in the Union building. Don't miss the Sunday music recitals.

IF THE PEOPLE can't come to the art, then take the art to the people. James Haseltine, Salt Lake City Art Center, helps pilot unload paintings after a flight to bring a cargo of rental works to Ephraim.

UTAH   271

Idaho

Watershed of the Continental Divide, Idaho has gorges deeper than the Grand Canyon, cascades higher than Niagara, caves whose ice has never melted, boiling springs whose steam heats the houses of Boise. It has, as well, some important centers of art.

In the State Capitol at Boise you will see pioneer Charles Ostner's statue of George Washington, along with murals that have tried to capture the evergreen forests, topless mountains, and eternal sunsets of the state. Outside on the lawn you'll see Gilbert Riswald's cast bronze memorial to Governor Frank Steunenberg, who was killed by a bomb in 1905 at the height of bitter labor strife between employers and unions of Idaho's rich lead and silver mines.

EXCITING EXHIBITIONS IN AND NEAR BOISE

BOISE GALLERY OF ART. *Julia Davis Park, Boise, Idaho. Hours 12 noon to 5* P.M. *Tuesday-Sunday. Collection of Japanese netsuke.*

Ten blocks south of the Capitol building in Boise you'll come to lovely Julia Davis Park, setting for Idaho's Historical Museum and the Boise Gallery of Art. The latter is headquarters for the Boise Art Association, which has been sponsoring the Annual Exhibition for Artists of Idaho since 1935. The exhibition presents a graphic survey of Idaho art production in all media and encourages artists with a series of cash prizes and subsequent circulation of the best work. Thirteen loan exhibitions a year keep Idaho abreast of current art trends.

Another event staged by the Boise Art Association is the annual Art Festival. A two-day outdoor-indoor gala, it attracts thousands each September to see—and buy—the work of Idaho's artists.

At nearby Caldwell, west of Boise, The College of Idaho's art department features many traveling exhibitions from the museums of New York, California, and Europe. Its interests range from Primitive African Sculpture to the latest cross-currents of American and European art, and it is building up an impressive print collection.

Nevada

The oldest visible signs of art in the Silver State are in the Valley of Fire in Clark County near the California and Arizona borders. Here you can visit caves whose walls are etched with remarkably preserved petroglyphs. The prehistoric Indians, as you will see, did "white writing" long before Washington's Mark Tobey.

The Nevada State Museum in Carson City is a storehouse of historic and artistic mementos. The building used to be the Mint; it turned out millions of silver dollars from 1866 to 1893.

To keep up with more current developments on the local and international art fronts, go north a few miles to Reno. At 643 Ralston Street the Nevada Art Gallery exhibits work by members of such groups as the Nevada Artists Association, who also have a big spring art festival each May. The Gallery shows range from pre-Columbian sculpture to contemporary Iranian painting, from New York oils to the annual exhibit of the California Watercolor Society. The Nevada Art Gallery is open daily except Friday from 1 to 4 P.M. There are frequent art lectures, craft demonstrations, recitals on Sunday afternoons at 2 P.M. Between this gallery and the excellent traveling exhibits and student shows at the nearby University of Nevada, the citizens of Reno and their guests lack not for art.

NETSUKE *were carved from wood or ivory by the Japanese, were used as purse or medicine-bottle fobs. Many are less than an inch high. (Boise Art Association.)*

HUMAN FACES *and the classic mode*

ALTHOUGH ABSTRACT expressionism almost removed the human face and figure from contemporary art, certain artists continued to paint it in the great traditions of Greece and Rome, reaffirmed by the classical French revival under Jacques-Louis David (1450–1523). Even the fiery Mexican, Orozco, despite the expressionist violence of his social protest, clung to a classic principle. "We have to fall in line and learn our lesson from the Master," he said. "If there is another way it has not been discovered yet. The line of Culture is continuous."

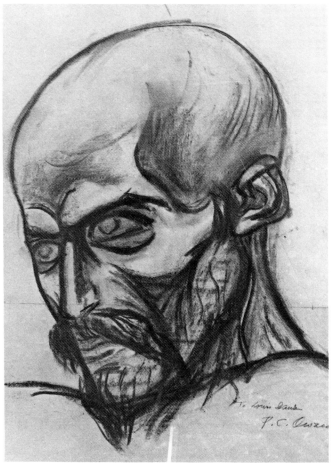

SURREALIST DALI, EXPRESSIONIST OROZCO, remained faithful to classic ideal. Dali's Gala Placida (above), for which his wife was model, is in Gallagher Collection at University of Arizona Art Gallery. Orozco's Head of a Man (Phoenix Art Museum) is a sketch for the central figure in a Guadalajara orphanage fresco.

HAUNTING STUDY of a man's head, by Jacques-Louis David, who set neo-classical style in post-Revolutionary France. Sketch was made in 1806 in preparation for official picture commissioned by Napoleon: The Emperor Distributing the Eagles on the Field of Mars. *David supported overthrow of monarchy. (Phoenix Art Museum.)*

FIGURATIVE art in the Southwest

ALTHOUGH PROPAGANDIST tendencies of some modern Mexican art have caused it to be bypassed by historians whose chief concern is stylistic evolution, there is much good Mexican painting which avoids the tinted photograph look that so often afflicts social realism. In remaining figurative, many Mexican and Southwestern American painters seem to be following Diego Rivera's quest for "an art extremely pure, precise, profoundly human, and clarified as to its purpose . . . It is necessary that the worker find aesthetic satisfaction and the highest pleasure appareled in the essential interest of his life."

ELOQUENT PROTEST against economic conditions of the thirties, Arizona-born Lew Davis' lonely Little Boy in a Copper Camp combines stark realism with pathos, bony torso with skeletal landscape. (Phoenix Art Museum.)

PRE-COLUMBIAN INDIAN influence marks Ricardo Martinez' luminous Mother and Child. The self-taught Mexican artist gave the mother the stylized face of an early Indian sculpture. (Phoenix Art Museum.)

VOLUMINOUS FORMS of Two Women, by Francisco Zuniga, are typical of Costa Rican artist who became major Mexican sculptor after an apprenticeship with his father as a stone carver. The chalk sketch for a sculpture is in the Phoenix Art Museum.

A RARE PAINTING by David Alfaro Siqueiros, a political activist who spent more time agitating than painting. The Sleep, done in 1939, recalls the rounded forms, flesh, and hair of many of the earlier Baroque masters. (Arizona State University.)

Hawaii

A FINE BLENDING OF EAST AND WEST

The fiftieth state, as millions of tourists can attest, is more than a tropical paradise; it is a brilliant mosaic of races, each of which has brought its germinal contribution to a still-evolving culture. With traditional Hawaiian *aloha* as a catalyst, East became West, West East in these beautiful islands.

The fusion took several generations—the icebergs of prejudice melt slowly even under the genial sun of Hawaii—but the state motto, "Above All Nations Is Humanity," now seems to be a working philosophy in a community that has become America's showplace of race relations. As a trustee said to Rush Kress when he came to present Italian Renaissance paintings to the local art museum, "A little isle shall lead them."

That museum has been a leader in bringing the best of Asian as well as Occidental art to this once remote island community, whose desire has grown to supplement the collections of Polynesian artifacts with other great works of art from over the world.

The Honolulu Academy of Arts building itself is a delightful amalgam of Polynesian, Western, and Oriental architectural forms. It speaks for the fine admixture so characteristic of Hawaii. With a Chinese court reminiscent of a Peking garden, a Spanish patio that recalls the fountain-cooled charms of the Alhambra, it is a tranquil oasis in downtown Honolulu, almost as popular with tourists as the Kodak hula show at Waikiki.

TWO NUDES ON A TAHITIAN BEACH.
A powerful early statement (1890) by French artist
Paul Gauguin, who revolted against conventional
restraints, found inspiration in the primitive atmosphere
of the South Seas. He influenced modern art by
freeing it from copying. (Honolulu Academy of Arts.)

279

NEW CULTURE, OLD STRAIN

HONOLULU ACADEMY OF ARTS. *900 South Beretania Street, Honolulu. Hours 10* A.M. *to 4:30* P.M. *Tuesday–Saturday; 3 to 6* P.M. *Sunday. Oriental Collection of Korean ceramics, Japanese screens, Chinese scrolls.*

Founded by Mrs. Charles Montague Cooke and her family, descendents of missionary teachers, the Academy was dedicated to "our children of many nationalities and races, Hawaiians, Americans, Chinese, Japanese, Koreans, Filipinos, North and South Europeans . . . so that, contacting through the channel of art those deep intuitions common to all, they may perceive a foundation on which a new culture, enriched by all the old strains, may be built in these Islands."

The physical embodiment of this ideal, designed by Bertram Goodhue, was opened to the public in 1927. Its airy galleries are filled with the art treasures of Occident and Orient. The collecting Cookes had taste as well as high ideals, and in the museum's latter days they were aided by the generosity of another great and discerning collector, the late Robert Allerton of Chicago and Kauai. In building up a splendid collection of Oriental art, the museum also had the services of such discriminating directors as Robert P. Griffing, Jr. and Edgar C. Schenck.

The Academy's Oriental Collection is one of extraordinary quality. The museum has what may well be the most important collection of Korean ceramics between Boston and Seoul, the finest range of Japanese screens west of the Mississippi, and, thanks to the generosity of author James A. Michener, one of the best collections of Japanese prints in the Western World.

European sinologists come 6,000 miles to see the Chinese treasures. Most extraordinary of all is the famous *Hundred Geese Scroll* by the 12th-century master Ma Fen. A masterpiece of descriptive brushwork, it lifts the spirit with each vibration of the whirring wings. A similar effect is produced by *The Seven Thuja Trees*, a handscroll dated 1532 in which the artist Wen Cheng-ming has delineated every curve and contortion of these gnarled junipers with a brush bursting with vitality. Compare this expressionistic brushwork with that of Van Gogh's *Wheat Fields* elsewhere in the Academy, and you will sense a plastic kinship between the 16th-century Chinese and the modern Dutch master. Another outstanding Chinese treasure is the long, hanging scroll, *Coming of Autumn* by Hung

Jen. A 17th-century work which is a serene distillation of nature, it has been called the greatest Ch'ing painting outside China.

In the Japanese department you'll find several galleries aglow with those folding screens that were the glory of the castles of the Momoyama lords of the 17th century. On these lavish screens traditional Chinese brushwork combines with the Japanese love of brilliant but discreetly handled color to achieve one of the high moments in the history of decorative art.

Of equal importance is the Academy's superb collection of Asian sculpture. It ranges from a unique marble mask of the Shang Dynasty through a comprehensive collection of 5th century B.C. Hui Hsien tomb sculptures of dancing figures to a great 12th-century polychrome wood statue of Kwan Yin, Chinese goddess of mercy.

NEW STAB AT OLD TECHNIQUE of woodblock carving is made by a junior citizen of the 50th state in a children's class at Honolulu Academy of Arts.

COURT OF ASIAN ART WING at Honolulu Academy of Arts was inspired by Peking garden, frames 10th-century granite statue, Dvarapala, from South India.

HONOLULU'S HISTORY OF WESTERN ART

The history of Western Art is traced at the Academy from notable examples of antique sculpture and mosaic to such modern masters as Gauguin, Van Gogh, Braque, Picasso, and Matisse.

The Kress Collection of Italian Renaissance painting is one of the most important bequests of the Kress Foundation. It is in recognition of the receipts at the local Kress store in Honolulu; they are the highest in the nation. Here the greatest picture is the smallest: Veronese's *Descent from the Cross*, a profoundly moving composition, so strongly designed that local artists have been known to spend hours copying it.

Local artists love the Academy; many of them have had their first contacts with art here in children's classes, and some are alumni of the Academy's Art School. The museum has been encouraging Hawaii's painters and sculptors for nearly four decades, and stages an annual Artists of Hawaii Exhibition in which you can see the best work currently being produced in the Islands.

Among Island painters who have gained national and international attention are the late Isami Doi, Kauai-born, Paris-trained artist whose work combines Oriental mysticism with a poetic cosmic piety; Tseng Yu-ho, Peking-trained mistress of Chinese brush drawing who has revived the ancient Oriental art of collage with subtle effect and employed it in modern composition; John Young, Hawaii-born Chinese artist of dazzling virtuosity; Tadashi Sato, who cultivates a serene and personal Zen-inspired art in the tranquillity of his native Maui; Willson Y. Stamper, whose paintings of local girls recall the sensuous charm of Proust's *Within a Budding Grove*; the University of Hawaii's Ben Norris, whose new paintings and collages reflect experiment with traditional Japanese and European techniques; Edward Stasack, an outstanding abstract painter who teaches at the University; J. Halley Cox, Hawaii's leading watercolor painter, and Jean Charlot, an original member of the Mexican Renaissance who has been in the Islands since 1949.

You can see Charlot's frescoes in the University of Hawaii's administration building, where he has depicted Hawaiians in all stages of development and costume from loincloth to cap and gown. In the Waikiki branch of the First National Bank of Hawaii you will find an original collage mural by Ben Norris.

Restaurants, hotels, and shopping centers have employed Hawaii's artists with happy results, as you will see if you visit the Ala Moana Center at Ala Moana and Atkinson Drive. This may be the handsomest shopping center in the nation. Helping it to be so are Bumpei Akaji's *Fountain of the Gods*, Claude Horan's *Bamboo* and *Children's Fountains*, and the *Petroglyph Fountain* by Edward Brownlee, who also sculpted the huge Tiki figures outside the McInerney Store.

THE ETERNAL HAWAIIANS

THE TENNENT ART FOUNDATION. *201-203 Prospect Street, Honolulu. Hours 3 to 5 P.M. Sunday; 10 A.M. to noon Tuesday; 7 to 9 P.M. Thursday; also by appointment.*

Madge Tennent's voluminous portraits of Hawaiians are displayed in a handsome modern gallery designed by award-winning architect Vladimir N. Ossipoff. Paris-trained as a child prodigy, Madge came to the Islands early in the century and very soon found her subject matter in the Hawaiian race, whose dignity and nobility she has recorded in the sure line and thick glowing impasto of a highly personal art. One critic has said that if the Hawaiians were to vanish as a race they would still live forever in her paintings. Inevitably, Mrs. Tennent, painting in this tropical paradise for nearly half a century, has been called the Hawaiian Gauguin, not because of any resemblance of style but because she did for Hawaiians what Gauguin did for the Tahitians. The Polynesian race emerges from the Giotto-blue walls of this most impressive gallery robed once again in the ancient glory of a long-vanished kingdom.

IF YOU WANT TO SEE the artifacts of the Hawaiians you should hie yourself to the Bishop Museum at 1355 Kalihi Street. Here you will find the fabulous feather cloaks and helmets worn by Hawaiian chiefs, idols carved from wood and stone, temple drums, and the outrigger canoes in which the dauntless Polynesians traveled the high roads of the sea. The museum is open Monday through Friday from 9 A.M. to 4:30 P.M., Saturday from 10 A.M. to 1 P.M., Sunday afternoon from 2 to 5 P.M. Special express buses of the Honolulu Rapid Transit will take you there from your Waikiki hotel on weekday mornings at 9:30 for a guided tour.

*AN OUTSTANDING EXAMPLE of cubism, George
Braque's still life,* La Pomme (The Apple), *shows modern
master's desire to create a new unity, a "lyricism
which grows completely from pictorial means."
(Honolulu Academy of Arts.)*

ORIENTAL TREASURES *near the Orient*

HUNDRED GEESE HANDSCROLL *is a pilgrimage picture in that it attracts visitors from the world over to admire the delicate brushwork of 12th-century Chinese artist, Ma Fen. (Detail: Honolulu Academy of Arts.)*

FIREFLY CATCHING is the subject of this exquisite 18th-century Japanese color woodblock print by Eishosai Choki, one of a comprehensive collection given to the Honolulu Academy of Arts by the author James Michener.

COMIC STRIP technique was utilized by the Japanese in the Kamakura Period (1185-1392) with e-makimono or handscrolls illustrating popular stories. The fragment from Life of Konin Shonin is from the Honolulu Academy of Arts.

HAWAII   287

CHINA...and the
South Seas

EARLY T'ANG sculptor infused
limestone with the sap of life
in a 7th-century statue of
Sakyamuni, the historic Buddha. The
Chinese masterpiece is in the
Honolulu Academy of Arts.

HAWAIIAN GIRL has the
monumental quality of sculpture in a
wash and sepia drawing by
Madge Tennent, one in a series of
her striking South Sea Scrolls.
(Tennent Art Foundation.)

Special Supplement

A compilation of useful information prepared by the Editors

GUIDE to WESTERN MUSEUMS

GLOSSARY of ART TERMS

CAPSULE ART HISTORY

BIOGRAPHIES of the ARTISTS

SELECTED READINGS

GUIDE to WORKS ILLUSTRATED

SUBJECT INDEX

WESTERN GALLERY GUIDE

MUSEUM	HOURS	COLLECTIONS	REGULAR SHOWS
SOUTHERN CALIFORNIA			
The Fine Arts Gallery of San Diego (27) Plaza de Panama, Balboa Park, San Diego, Calif.	10 A.M. to 5 P.M. Tues–Sat; 12:30 to 5 P.M. Sun; closed Mon	Works by Velasquez, Rembrandt. Spanish, Italian old masters. Goya's *Marques de Sofraga*	Two open shows a year: Spring, local all California artists; Fall: all country artists
Timken Gallery (31) Plaza de Panama, Balboa Park, San Diego, Calif.	10 A.M. to 4:30 P.M. Tues–Sat; 1:30 to 4:30 P.M. Sun; closed Mon	Superlative collection of old masters	None at present
La Jolla Museum of Art (33) 700 Prospect St., La Jolla, Calif.	12:30 to 4:30 P.M. Tues–Sun; 7 to 10 P.M. Wed; closed Mon	Contemporary American art. Primitive African and pre-Columbian art objects	Works of selected local artists in one-man shows throughout year
Long Beach Museum of Art (36) 2300 East Ocean Blvd., Long Beach, Calif.	10 A.M. to 5 P.M. Tues–Fri; 1 to 5 P.M. Sat–Sun; closed Mon	Contemporary art of the American West. African sculpture	Annual Southern California show
J. Paul Getty Museum (39) 17985 Pacific Coast Highway, Malibu, Calif.	2 to 4 P.M. Wed and Sat by appointment	Works by Tintoretto, Veronese, Rubens, Titian. Classical sculpture. French art, furniture	None at present
Los Angeles County Museum of Art (52) 5905 Wilshire Blvd., Los Angeles, Calif.	10 A.M. to 5 P.M. Tues–Sun; closed Mon	Egyptian, classical, Oriental, modern art. Renaissance and baroque paintings. Decorative arts. Textiles and costumes	Check in *Los Angeles Times* or with museum
University of California at Los Angeles Art Galleries (62) 405 Hilgard Ave., Los Angeles, Calif.	12:30 to 5 P.M. Mon–Fri; 1 to 5 P.M. Sun	Lehmbruck, Picasso, Kirchner. 19th, 20th-century prints. Lipchitz' *The Song of Vowels.* Matisse's *La Gerbe*	Annual student show. Occasional shows featuring local artists
University of Southern California Fisher Gallery (62) University Park, Los Angeles, Calif.	12 to 5 P.M. Mon–Fri	American landscape paintings. Flemish and Dutch portraits, *genre* paintings	None at present
Southwest Museum (69) 234 Museum Drive, Highland Park, Los Angeles, Calif.	1 to 5 P.M. Tues–Sun; closed Mon	Indian handicrafts, artifacts. Pueblo pottery, woven baskets	Periodically features Indian handicrafts, pictures about American Indians
Pasadena Art Museum (70) 46 North Robles Ave., Pasadena, Calif.	10 A.M. to 5 P.M. Wed–Sat; 2 to 5 P.M. Sun; 10 A.M. to 9 P.M. Tues; closed Mon	Works by Blue Four. German expressionist painting. 20th-century painting and sculpture. Contemporary American art	None at present
Henry E. Huntington Art Gallery (76) 1151 Oxford Road, San Marino, Calif.	1 to 4:30 P.M. Tues–Sun; closed Mon. Closed month of Oct and certain holidays	British paintings of Georgian period. 18th-century French decorative art, sculpture. Renaissance bronzes	None at present
Rand-Lang Galleries (85) Scripps College, Claremont, Calif.	1:30 to 5 P.M. daily	Works by Scripps art faculty, art graduates, recipients of MFA degree from Claremont graduate school. American paintings	Annual local show Claremont Artists Invitational
Pomona College Gallery (85) Montgomery Art Center, Pomona College, Claremont, Calif.	1 to 5 P.M. daily. Closed during college vacations	Renaissance and baroque paintings. Matisse's *Jetty at Collioure.* Chirico's *Furniture in a Landscape*	None at present

...*The Museums and Their Activities*

ACTIVITIES	MEMBERSHIP	RENTALS	REMARKS
Adult art and art appreciation classes. Children's and young adults' classes and lectures. Library, 5,500 vols	Annual dues: $10 individual; $15 family	Approx 45 paintings, sculptures. Monthly rent: $5 minimum to 10% of purchase price	In center of one of the West's largest and most handsome parks, near zoo
None at present	None at present	None at present	Same area as Fine Arts Gallery. Houses Putnam Foundation's old masters
Periodic lectures. Occasional art auctions. Music, theater programs, Christmas open-house for children. Library, approx 3,000 vols	Annual dues: $10 individual; $15 family. Previews, discounts	Approx 300 paintings, drawings, sculpture; $5 to $27/ two months; option to purchase	Housed in former private home, with a commanding view of the Pacific Ocean
Children's classes (ages 6–15). Museum receptions (opening–Sun of exhibition), film series (2 to 4 P.M.), concerts, lecture series. Art auction	Annual dues: $10 individual; $25 family. Educational and social programs	Paintings; fee (per three months) dependent upon value of work	Monthly exhibitions; originate arts of Southern California Survey which tours Western Association of Art Museums
Evening lectures by visiting scholars. Library, approx 3,000 vols	None at present	None at present	A stroll through courtyard reveals well-kept gardens, marble statues, sights of Pacific Ocean
Junior Art Workshop (ages 4–17), membership only. Lectures, musical, dance concerts. Film festival, series. Library, (non-circulating) approx 32,000 vols. Book shop	Annual dues: $18 active; $30 participating. Exhibition previews, receptions, art calendar, discounts, members' room	Approx 100 paintings, sculpture; $4 to $22 per two months	A fine example of pavilioned, modern architecture. Be sure to spend some time on the sculpture court and various terraces
Annual Art Council lecture series. Library, approx 50,000 vols	None at present. Annual Art Council and Dept of Art dues: $5 individual; $8.50 couple. Preview openings, discounts	None at present	Don't miss Picasso's *Head of Woman*, Henri's *Whistling Boy*
None at present	None at present	None at present	Visit the Rodia towers in the Watts district, not far from the campus
Las Posadas (Christmas folk festival). Gift shop	Annual dues: $10 minimum. Discounts, preview invitations	None at present	Casa de Adobe, at foot of museum hill, is authentic replica of Spanish colonial *hacienda*
Art lectures. Periodic art auctions. Concerts, recitals, film programs. Junior and adult art workshop	Annual dues: $15 general; $25 family. Discounts, museum calendar, previews, travel programs	None at present	One of the West's liveliest museums, both in its temporary exhibitions and activities
Guided tours for school children, by appointment. Periodic lectures, recitals (membership only)	By invitation. Annual dues: $15 minimum. Discounts, invitations to lectures, special occasions	None at present	Huntington library, adjacent to art museum, houses Gutenberg Bible, original Shakespeare quartos, manuscripts
Art programs in connection with Scripps College. Some adult art classes. Art lectures	Annual dues: $10	Approx 150 paintings, other works of art; $10 to $30 per month	Don't miss the fine Martinez fresco in Margaret Fowler Memorial Garden
None at present	None at present	None at present	Before leaving campus, stop by Frary Hall to see Rico Lebrun's mural *Genesis* and Orozco's fresco *Prometheus*

WESTERN GALLERY GUIDE

MUSEUM	HOURS	COLLECTIONS	REGULAR SHOWS
Santa Barbara Museum of Art (113) 1130 State St., Santa Barbara, Calif.	11 A.M. to 5 P.M. Tues–Sat; 12 to 5 P.M. Sun; closed Mon	Classical sculpture, American painting, old masters, modern drawings. Collection of antique musical instruments, dolls	None at present
University of California at Santa Barbara Gallery (116) Goleta, Calif.	10 A.M. to 4 P.M. Mon–Sat; 1 to 5 P.M. Sun	Renaissance medals and plaquettes. Renaissance and baroque paintings	Annual faculty exhibition; annual student exhibition

NORTHERN CALIFORNIA

MUSEUM	HOURS	COLLECTIONS	REGULAR SHOWS
M. H. De Young Memorial Museum (147) Golden Gate Park, San Francisco, Calif.	10 A.M. to 5 P.M. daily	Encyclopedic collections of Western art. Brundage Collection of Asian Art. Rubens' *Tribute Money*. El Greco's *Saint John the Baptist*	None at present
California Palace of the Legion of Honor (153) Lincoln Park, San Francisco, Calif.	10 A.M. to 5 P.M. daily	French art and furniture. Achenbach Foundation for Graphic Arts (West's largest print collection). Sculpture by Rodin	Midwinter Invitational Exhibition of Bay Area artists
San Francisco Museum of Art (161) Civic Center, McAllister Street at Van Ness Ave.	10 A.M. to 10 P.M. Tues–Fri; 10 A.M. to 5 P.M. Sat; 1 to 5 P.M. Sun; closed Mon	Modern European and American art. Matisse's *Girl with the Green Eyes*	Host Annual Exhibitions of San Francisco Art Institute. San Francisco Women Artists
San Francisco Art Institute (163) 800 Chestnut St., San Francisco, Calif.	10 A.M. to 4 P.M. daily; closed Sun	Diego Rivera mural	Annual juried art show open to local artists and those throughout the country
Leland Stanford Junior Museum (169) Stanford University, Palo Alto, Calif.	10 A.M. to 5 P.M. daily	Classical antiquities. Leventritt Collection of Asian art	None at present
Oakland Art Museum (192) Tenth and Fallon Streets, Oakland, Calif.	10 A.M. to 5 P.M. daily	Archives of California art. 19th and 20th-century California painters	None at present
University of California Art Museum (195) University of California, Berkeley, Calif.	12 to 6 P.M. daily	Paintings by Hofmann, Rothko; sculpture by Jason Seley	Annual UC Arts Festival (Special student exhibition)
Mills College Gallery (198) Mills College, Oakland, Calif.	1 to 4 P.M. Sun, Wed, Fri	Graphic arts collection. German expressionist drawings	Annual student art show

...The Museums and Their Activities

ACTIVITIES	MEMBERSHIP	RENTALS	REMARKS
Children's art program. Art lectures, film programs. Periodic concerts. Annual Treasure Sale, Bal au Musée	Annual dues: $10 individual; $15 family. Invitations to opening exhibitions, monthly calendar, lecture-luncheon series, discounts	None at present	An abandoned post office transformed into a Mediterranean structure houses art treasures
None at present	None at present	None at present	Visit Mission Santa Barbara—the "Queen of Missions"—an interesting blend of Roman and mission architecture
Art classes for children. Lectures. Library, approx 14,000 vols. Guided tours by appointment. Book shop	Annual dues: $12.50 regular; $25 contributing	None at present	Next to art museum is Japanese tea gardens where you can sip tea and munch fortune cookies. Close by are natural history museum, aquarium
Art lectures, guided tours. Weekend organ concerts; frequent recitals. Library, approx 3,500 vols (use on premises only). Book shop	Annual dues: Patrons of Art and Music, $12.50 minimum. Tickets to musical events in little theater, previews of loan exhibitions	None at present	From entrance way is spectacular view of Golden Gate Bridge, Pacific Ocean
Children's art, dance classes. Occasional lectures, concerts, film programs. Reference library, approx 3,300 items. Book shop	Annual dues: $15 (minimum). Preview major exhibitions, members' room.	Members only. Approx 650 items; $7.50 to $33.50 per three months	More than 200,000 visitors in 1965
Art classes for high-school students, adults. Lectures, films, concerts, panel discussions (members only). Occasional art auctions, art and architectural house tours, artists' studio tours, art symposiums	Annual dues: $15. Special previews, receptions, tuition discount on certain college classes, use of library and art store	None at present	Rent exhibitions of contemporary California art to museums, galleries, and qualified institutions
Art auction (preview to members)	Annual dues: $10; $25 associate	None at present	A work of art in itself is awe-inspiring Stanford Memorial Church where Byzantine style mosaics decorate interior walls, apse, facade
Art lectures. Annual craft sale. Concour D'Antiques. Library, approx 8,000 vols; largest collection of California art reference material. Book shop (contemporary pottery, jewelry, sculpture, prints by local artists)	Annual dues: $12 per couple, Oakland Museum Association. $10 Art Guild. Invitations, discounts	Available to residents of Bay Area. 500 paintings; $6 to $25 per three months	*New* three-tiered complex to house Oakland art, history, and natural science museums scheduled for spring, 1968, opening
Art lectures, concerts, dance, music recitals, film programs. Museum tours. Library (extensive collection of art books)	None at present	None at present	*New* University Art Museum scheduled to open 1968. Currently, temporary art exhibitions also held at: Student Union Lobby, 8 A.M. to midnight, Mon–Sat; 12 P.M. to 12 A.M. Sun; Worth Ryder Hall, 12:30 P.M. to 4 P.M. Tues–Sat; 1 to 5 P.M. Sun
None at present	None at present	None at present	A few steps away from gallery along eucalyptus-lined path is the tea shop where student works are frequently exhibited

WESTERN GALLERY GUIDE

MUSEUM	HOURS	COLLECTIONS	REGULAR SHOWS
Fresno Art Center (215) 3033 E. Yale Ave., Fresno, Calif.	12 to 4 P.M. Tues–Sun; 7:30 to 9:30 P.M. Wed	Good permanent collection—chiefly American painters	San Joaquin Valley Art Annual, open to artists from Stockton to Bakersfield
Pioneer Museum and Haggin Galleries (217) Victory Park, Stockton, Calif.	1:30 to 5 P.M. Tues–Sun; closed Mon	Works by Renoir, Gauguin. 19th-century French and American schools. Graphic arts. Marie Laurencin's *Les Deguises*	Stockton Art League Annual Spring Exhibition
E. B. Crocker Gallery (221) 216 O Street, Sacramento, Calif.	10 A.M. to 5 P.M. Tues–Sun; closed Mon	Works by Tamayo, Breughel the Younger. Prints, drawings, oils	Two annual exhibitions, competitive shows. Open to artists of specified perimeter of Sacramento. Biennial All California Crafts exhibition

PACIFIC NORTHWEST

MUSEUM	HOURS	COLLECTIONS	REGULAR SHOWS
University of Oregon Museum of Art (238) Eugene, Oregon	11 A.M. to 5 P.M. Tues, Thurs; 1 to 5 P.M. Wed, Fri, Sat	Paintings by Morris Graves, Paul Horiuchi. Oriental art. Art of Pacific Northwest	Annual show devoted to some aspect of Pacific Northwest arts and crafts
Portland Art Museum (239) Southwest Park at Madison St., Portland, Oregon	12 to 5 P.M. daily; closed Mon	Painting and sculpture by Northwest artists. Northwest Indian art. Kress Collection of Renaissance Art. Japanese prints	Annual show of Oregon artists
Maryhill Museum of Fine Arts (243) Maryhill, Wash.	9 A.M. to 5:30 P.M. daily. Open March 15 to November 15	Rodin sculpture. Tanagra figurines. Personal souvenirs of Queen Marie of Rumania	None at present
Seattle Art Museum (246) Volunteer Park, Seattle, Wash.	10 A.M. to 5 P.M. Tues–Sat; 12 to 5 P.M. Sun, Holidays; 7 to 10 P.M. Thurs	Internationally famous jade, Oriental art collections. European art. 600 works of Pacific Northwest artists	Annual exhibition of residential architecture. Northwest Painting Annual
Charles and Emma Frye Art Museum (249) Terry at Cherry, Seattle, Wash.	10 A.M. to 5 P.M. Mon–Sat; 12 to 6 P.M. Sun–Holidays	19th, 20th-century European, American paintings	Puget Sound Area Exhibition. Competitive exhibitions of contemporary West Coast art (juried, prizes.) Annual American Watercolor Society Traveling Exhibition
Henry Gallery (250) 15th Ave., N.E. and N.E. Campus Parkway, Seattle, Wash.	10 A.M. to 5 P.M. Mon–Sat; 1 to 5 P.M. Sun	19th, 20th-century European and American paintings. Northwest artists. American, Japanese 20th-century ceramics	Annual Art Faculty Exhibition. Annual Northwest Printmakers' Regional Exhibition. Biennial Northwest Craftsmen
University of British Columbia (251) Vancouver, B.C.	1 to 5 P.M. Mon, Wed–Fri	Northwest Indian artifacts. Masks of the Kwakiutl, Tlingit, Haida, Bella Bella	None at present
Vancouver Art Gallery (251) 1145 West Georgia St., Vancouver, B.C.	10 A.M. to 5 P.M. Tues–Sat; 2 to 5 P.M. Sun; 7 to 10 P.M. Fri evenings; closed Mon	Contemporary Canadian paintings	British Columbia Annual Exhibition

...The Museums and Their Activities

ACTIVITIES	MEMBERSHIP	RENTALS	REMARKS
Children's, adults' art classes. Children's dance classes. Workshops with painters, sculptors throughout year. Lecture series. Tours. Beaux Arts Ball	Annual dues: $10; $25 business. Previews, discounts. Can display own works at Art Center	Approx 300 paintings; rent per three months dependent on value of painting	Lively monthly exhibitions in all media and from many sources
Children's art classes. Art auctions every two years. Film program Sunday afternoon. Periodic concerts, recitals. Library, approx 5,000 vols (California history)	Annual dues: $12 contributing membership; $25 sustaining membership. Free art classes for children, special previews, social activities, announcements	None at present	Huge collection of Leyendecker's original *Saturday Evening Post* covers
Lectures, tours for children, adults. Sunday concerts. Reference, research, general arts library, approx 400 vols	Annual dues: $10 individual; $12.50 family. Exhibitions, previews, receptions, special music programs. Bulletins, discounts	Works by California artists; rent 1% of value	At State Capitol Building, see the collection of Western historical paintings
Library lecture series, gallery tours, art-in-the-schools program. Mother-daughter tea, family day at museum. Flea Mart	Annual dues: $10 regular; $25 sustaining. Preview-receptions, special events, discounts	Members only. Approx 300 paintings; $3 flat rate plus $4 to $7 per three months	Located in the Willamette Valley, Eugene is state's leading lumbering, logging city
Art classes for students, children, adults. Art lectures, films. Library, approx 3,500 vols	Annual dues: $10 individual; $25 family. Previews, monthly calendar, annual meeting	Members only. $15 to $30 per month	It's worth a special visit to 100-acre Washington Park, where International Rose Test Gardens are located
None at present	None at present	None at present	Pleasant scenic drive from Seattle along Columbia River; museum sits on top of 900-foot bluff overlooking river
Chamber music concert series, Sun. Seattle Art Museum Guild Lectures; P.T.A. Day; Senior Day. Library, approx 7,000 vols	Annual dues: active member $15. In conjunction with Seattle Art Museum Pavilion	None at present	Situated on top of one of Seattle's seven hills, museum overlooks Puget Sound
Guided tours. Friday at the Frye	None at present	None at present	Be sure to take one of the ferry trips on Washington's Puget Sound. Trips range from 7 minutes up to 4 hours
Film series, art auction	None at present	None at present	Art gallery is part of University of Washington, oldest state university on Pacific coast
None at present	None at present	None at present	Fine Arts Gallery, across hall from Museum of Anthropology, features traveling shows
Adult art classes. Children's gallery, painting classes, print library, class tours. Art reference library, gallery shop	Annual dues: $10 individual: $15 family. Library privileges, painting classes for adults, members' children; preview invitations and discounts	Members only. Approx 150 works; rental 1% of purchase price. Fifty works in businessmen's rental gallery	Sponsors gallery clinic where curatorial staff will comment on attribution and artistic merit, but not on monetary value of attic masterpieces, heirlooms

WESTERN GALLERY GUIDE

MUSEUM	HOURS	COLLECTIONS	REGULAR SHOWS
Art Gallery of Greater Victoria (254) 1040 Moss St., Victoria, British Columbia	11 A.M. to 5 P.M. Tues–Sat; 7:30 to 9:30 P.M. Thurs; closed Mon	Contemporary Canadian paintings. Chinese art	Annual Vancouver Island Jury Exhibition

INTER-MOUNTAIN STATES

Phoenix Art Museum (264) 1625 North Central Ave., Phoenix, Ariz.	10 A.M. to 5 P.M. Tues–Sat; 1 to 5 P.M. Sun	Oriental, American, Mexican art. 18th, 19th-century French paintings, drawings, sculpture	Arizona Annual
Arizona State University Art Collections (267) Tempe, Ariz.	9 A.M. to 5 P.M. Mon–Sat; 1 to 5 P.M. Sun	American art (paintings, graphics, sculpture); Kress Collection of Renaissance paintings	None at present
University of Arizona Gallery (268) Tucson, Ariz.	10 A.M. to 5 P.M. Mon–Sat; 2 to 5 P.M. Sun	Works by Pollock, Rothko. Modern art. Altar piece from Cathedral of Cuidad Rodrigo	None at present
Museum of Northern Arizona (269) Fort Valley Road, Flagstaff, Ariz.	9 A.M. to 12 NOON, 1 to 5 P.M daily; 1:30 to 5 P.M. Sun; open March to Dec 24	Southwest American, Indian art	Annual Hopi, Navajo arts and crafts exhibition
Salt Lake Art Center (270) 54 Finch Lane, Salt Lake City, Utah	1 to 5 P.M. Sat; 2 to 6 P.M. Sun; closed Mon and approx June 15 to Sept 15	Contemporary American, European paintings. Works of local artists	Utah Biennial of Painting and Sculpture. Intermountain Biennial of Painting and Sculpture. Annual Utah Craft Show. One-man, group invitational exhibitions, featuring local regional artists
Utah Museum of Fine Arts (271) Park Bldg., University of Utah, Salt Lake City, Utah	8:45 to 4:45 P.M. Tues–Fri; 2 to 5 P.M. Sun; 12:30 to 4:45 P.M. Mon	19th-century French, American paintings. 19th-century Japanese woodcut prints. French, Spanish, English furniture, decorative arts	None at present
Boise Gallery of Art (272) Julia Davis Park, Boise, Idaho	12 to 5 P.M. Tues–Sun	Oriental art. Contemporary American, Idaho art. Japanese netsuki	Annual Exhibition for Artists of Idaho
Nevada Art Gallery (273) 643 Ralston St., Reno, Nevada	1 to 4 P.M. daily except Friday	American paintings, French vases	Spring art festival

HAWAII

Honolulu Academy of Arts (280) 900 South Beretania St., Honolulu, Hawaii	10 to 4:30 P.M. Tues–Sat; 3 to 6 P.M. Sun; closed Mon	Korean ceramics. Japanese screens; Chinese scrolls	Artists of Hawaii

...The Museums and Their Activities

ACTIVITIES	MEMBERSHIP	RENTALS	REMARKS
Art classes for children, adults. Periodic lectures, art films, recitals. Library, approx 800 vols	Annual dues: $7.50 individual; $10 family. Free admission to gallery, discounts, museum bulletin	Members only. 190 paintings; $1 to $2.50 per month	Don't miss Thunderbird Park, its totem poles, authentic Kwakiutl Indian house
Art classes for children, adults. Lectures, monthly concerts. Library, approx 2,500 vols	Annual dues: $10 associate; $15 family. Discounts at book shop, on art classes, use of members' lounge. Free authentication or examination of works of art. Preview invitations, museum bulletin	None at present	Visit Heard Museum's American Indian weaving and painting exhibits; also see Taliesin West, Frank Lloyd Wright's school
Panels, lectures, guided tours on request. Color-slide rental program—various art works	None at present	None at present	University's exhibitions are housed in three locations on campus: gallery, Memorial Union, Gammage Auditorium
Lectures, guided tours	None at present	None at present	Tucson Art Center, 325 West Franklin St., offers art exhibitions, lectures, courses, concerts, films, two local shows a year
Library, approx 10,000 vols. Gift shop (Indian arts and crafts)	Annual dues: $5 individual; $10 family	None at present	Scouting surrounding area, you'll find Indian pueblos, one of which dates back to 1200 A.D.
Children's, teenage, adult art classes year-round. Art lectures, art appreciation series. Monthly television program. Periodic concerts. Guided tours Tues evening	Annual dues $10 regular; $25 family (minimum). Invitational previews, bulletin, discounts	Available to members only. Approx 150 paintings, sculpture by Utah artists; $2.75 to $6.50 per month. Option to purchase	On Capitol hill you'll see murals, statuary, paintings in marble rotunda of Capitol building; also on exhibit are pioneer costumes
Periodic lectures. Art library, approx 17,000 vols, maintained by College of Fine Arts at University	None at present	None at present	A pleasant stroll down the campus takes you to the Salt Lake Art Center
Children's, adults' art classes. Lectures. Association membership contest. "Art-for-Christmas" sale	Annual dues: $5 individual; $10 family. Bulletin, annual report, discounts, preview invitations. Association functions. Slide lending library	Check with museum for details	Several blocks north of Julia Davis Park you'll see State Capitol and Osiner's statue of George Washington, murals depicting Idaho's landscapes
Art lectures. Sunday afternoon recitals. Craft demonstrations	Annual dues: $2 minimum	None at present	In Carson City area, a pleasant stop is the state museum where former Mint houses historic, artistic mementos
Children's, adults' art classes. Library, approx 17,000 vols	Annual dues: $10 individual; $15 family. Discounts, use of members' Lanai in Kinau Court, preview invitations, special lectures, recitals	None at present	In Honolulu, don't miss the Tennant Art Foundation or the Bishop Museum

GLOSSARY OF ART TERMS

Abstract Expressionism. The dominant school of American painting in the forties and fifties, it is a kind of abstract art which expresses the subjective or interior life of the artist. See *Expressionism.*

Academic. A term, usually opprobrious, used by critics and artists to express contempt for the rigid formal rules of any established tradition of art. Those in revolt against academicism often become as rigid as the academicists.

Action Painting. An athletic branch of abstract expressionism in which the artist's physical engagement in the act of painting is emphasized. Flinging the paint at the canvas, dripping it on, spattering, and trampling the picture underfoot are some of the techniques that have been used. Despite its circus aspects, action painting in the hands of certain modern masters, such as Jackson Pollock and Willem de Kooning, has greatly enriched the technical means at the disposal of the contemporary painter.

ORNATE HERALDIC ANIMALS prance, writhe, dangle in woodcut masterpiece by Albrecht Dürer (note initials at lower right), Emperor Maximilian I, *from Portland Art Museum.*

Avant Garde. This French term, which sounds artier than its English equivalent, vanguard, refers to the latest experimental fads in modern art. Synonyms: hip, far out, way out, in, with it, ahead of it. Antonyms: old-fashioned, out of date, not of our times, square.

Barbizon School. A group of 19th-century French painters inspired by the rustic scenes around the village of Barbizon in the Forest of Fontainebleau. Their fondness for outdoor painting of the actualities of nature made them precursors of impressionism. Theodore Rousseau, Daubigny, and Millet were three of the Barbizon painters. Their forerunner, sometimes considered a member of the school, was Corot (1796-1875). (See their work at the California Palace of the Legion of Honor.)

Baroque. Derived from the Portuguese word *barrocco* (an irregularly shaped pearl), this term denotes that dramatic, exuberant, and highly decorative post-Renaissance style of the 17th and 18th centuries which reached America in the gilded Spanish altarpieces of the California Missions. You'll find other facets of the baroque style in Rembrandt and in Rubens' paintings (*The Nativity* in the Fisher Gallery at USC; *The Tribute Money* at San Francisco's De Young Museum), in the mystic ecstasies of El Greco (Fine Arts Gallery of San Diego), and in the pompous portrait of Louis XIV by Rigaud (Getty Museum).

Bauhaus. A school of design founded by Walter Gropius in Weimar, Germany, in 1919. Its educational philosophy sought an ideal synthesis of all the plastic arts to create the building of the future that would combine painting and sculpture with architecture. It believed in manual as well as intellectual training and wanted to create a guild without distinction between craftsman and artist. Among the many artists and teachers associated with the Bauhaus were Kandinsky, Paul Klee, Lyonel Feininger, Mies van der Rohe, Josef Albers, Marcel Breuer, Laszlo Moholy-Nagy. When the Nazis closed the Bauhaus in 1932 most of these men came to the United States where they were able to continue their work to the great and lasting enrichment of all American art and architecture.

Blue Four. This name was adopted in 1924 by four painters, Kandinsky, Klee, Feininger, and Jawlensky, friends who exhibited together in Germany. Their American agent, Madame Galka Scheyer, advanced the cause of German expressionism in the United States and left a large collection of the Blue Four's paintings to the Pasadena Art Museum.

Classicism. A term primarily indicating the principles of ancient Greek and Roman art. By extension it denotes the objectivity, formality, elegance, harmony, symmetry, restraint, lucidity, and order of such art as opposed to the unbridled subjectivity and the strong and violent emotion of romanticism and expressionism.

Collage. Literally a pasting, this term is applied to pictures made up wholly or in part of objects, usually flat ones, pasted to a canvas. Picasso and Braque started collage in 1913 as an experiment with texture in building up

...*Language of the Art World*

synthetic cubist pictures. The surrealists soon latched onto collage, since it gave them a chance to juxtapose previously unrelated images in a bizarre and incongruous manner. More recently collage has been used by certain artists to create lyrical abstract compositions through the superimposition of rice paper (Paul Horiuchi in Seattle, Tseng Yu-ho in Hawaii), colored foil, and the like.

Construction.   A term applied in modern art to abstract compositions of metal, wire, glass, and other materials; it is an outgrowth of collage, closely linked with assemblage. (See Schwitters' *Construction for Noble Ladies,* Los Angeles County Museum of Art.)

Contemporary.   Another term for 20th-century art. It had its basis in the end of the 19th century with Cézanne and his solid analysis of form. Artists such as Dali, Tamayo, Park, Picasso, Moore, Calder, Matisse, in trying to build new vocabularies of form, produced fauvism, cubism, futurism, surrealism, and abstract expressionism.

Cool Art.   First employed in the mid-sixties by critic Irving Sandler, this term is applied to that impersonal, emotionless painting at the opposite end of the spectrum from expressionism. Art ought to be depersonalized, say the cool artists, and should not represent anything but itself.

Cubism.   This movement, one of the most important in modern art, had its origins in France in 1907 when Cézanne wrote, "You must see in nature the cylinder, the sphere, and the cone." Under this influence and the inspiration of African Negro sculpture, two giants of modern art, Braque and Picasso, began reducing the forms of nature to basic geometric shapes. "Little cubes," said one critic, and the name has stuck ever since.

Dadaism.   Begun in Zurich in 1916 by the Rumanian poet Tristan Tzara and others, this movement, whose name derives from the French word for hobby horse or simply from a baby's babbling, was dreamed up by artists and writers in protest against the civilization that they blamed for the carnage of the first World War. Wishing to kick over the traces of such a civilization, the Dadaists struck at its cultural values, its conventions, and its inhibitions with nihilistic force. At once cynical and romantic, the Dadaists glorified the irrational, the amoral, the art of the unconscious. Their manifestoes denounced such qualities as taste and harmony and glorified the antiesthetic. Dada's hostility to naturalism, combined with its rejection of polite inhibitions, paved the way for two diametrically opposed developments: abstract art and surrealism. The latter was a direct consequence of Dada.

Docent.   From Latin *docere,* to teach—a combination guide and lecturer in a museum. Most art museums have docents on their staffs.

Expressionism.   The theory and practice of freely expressing one's emotions and sensations. Expressionist painting, whether figurative or abstract, asserts the artist's feelings

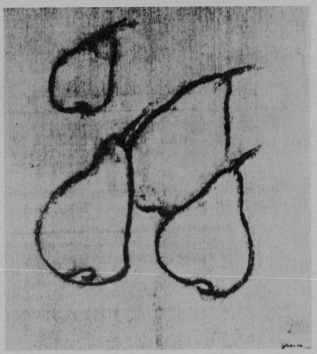

AUTUMN PEARS, by Morris Graves—an oil painting on 300-year old, gold woven Chinese fabric—is from Gallagher Collection of University of Arizona.

and moods above all else. On a more objective level the artist portrays what he conceives to be the expressive qualities of the object he is painting: the violence of the sea or the convulsive nature of the sky, as in the paintings of Van Gogh. (One of the best places to see expressionist paintings in the West is the Pasadena Art Museum.)

Fauves.   French for wild beasts, this term was applied by art critic Louis Vauxcelles to Matisse, Derain, Vlaminck, and other expressionist painters who exhibited in the famous Autumn Salon in Paris in 1905. Their brilliant, violent, and arbitrary colors (Matisse wanted colors to match his sensations, and often painted blue nudes) were a revolt against the hazy effects of impressionism and the deliberate scientific methodism of neo-impressionists such as Seurat and Signac. (See Matisse's *Jetty at Collioure* at the Pomona College Art Gallery. The biggest collection of fauve painting in the West is at the San Francisco Museum of Art.)

Figurative Painting.   As the term implies, this is representational painting with more or less specific references to figures and objects in nature. In the avalanche of abstract expressionism the figure almost disappeared from modern American painting. It was restored, and with great authority, in the 1950's by California artists David Park, Richard Diebenkorn, and Elmer Bischoff. (You can see good modern figurative painting at the Oakland Art Museum.)

GLOSSARY OF ART TERMS

SOFT PASTEL renders a delicate, rhythmic feeling in Edgar Degas' Dancer Adjusting Her Dress, captures delicate and fleeting moment of repose. (Portland Art Museum.)

Futurism. An Italian idea, rife about 1911, whose aim in painting and sculpture was to portray the dynamics of movement. Galloping horses and cars zipping along at unheard-of speeds up to fifty miles an hour were among their favorite subjects. Though the movies soon made futurism a thing of the past, its contribution to modern art was great. Two famous futurist pictures were produced in 1912: Giacomo Balla's *Dog on a Leash* (it had as many legs as a centipede) and Duchamp's *Nude Descending the Stairs*, which the artist explained as "an organization of kinetic elements, an expression of time and space through the abstract presentation of motion."

Genre Painting. Painting that depicts homey scenes from everyday life.

Hard-Edge Painting. This term applies to painting, usually abstract, whose forms are sharply defined by a clean, hard line. Ellsworth Kelly is a well known American hard-edge painter. Gene Davis is known for painting colored vertical stripes, one inch wide. Lorser Feitelson is a West Coast pioneer of the hard-edge school.

Impasto. The thick application of pigment to a canvas.

Impressionism. A way of painting which had its recognizable beginnings about 1865, impressionism was concerned with the study of light and its effects in visual communication. The impressionists preferred to paint nature outdoors in all its shifting light, and they expressed this luminosity by a series of scintillating spots or points of pure color. Monet was the great technician of the movement; Pissarro was its high priest; Renoir was one of its foremost exponents.

Kinetic Sculpture. Mobile or moving sculpture, activated by wind, water, or mechanical impulse. It's as old as the Greeks, having begun with their water clocks, and it was popular in the Middle Ages, as the still-operating figures on medieval belfries attest. Children's wind-up and electrical toys are a form of kinetic sculpture. Alexander Calder's mobiles are outstanding examples in contemporary art. (See his watermobile at the Los Angeles County Museum of Art.) Far-out kinetic sculpture reaches its paroxysm in motor-driven machines.

Middle Ages. A term used by Renaissance Italians to denote the thousand-year interim between the fall of Rome in A.D. 476 and the rebirth of humanism. The term is still used to designate roughly the period from the 5th to the 15th century.

Neo-Impressionism. A style founded by Seurat in the 1880's involving the methodical use of the pointillist technique (the application of tiny points of color) to achieve the brilliance of impressionist light. Though Seurat emphasized design and personal emotion in his great pictures, the scientific method soon became academic in the hands of lesser artists and it helped to a great extent to bring on the revolt of the fauves.

Non-Objective Painting. Purely abstract painting which attempts to create a plastic reality of its own on its own terms without reference or intellectual association with any other material reality. The non-objective painter is not interested in portraying people, events, still life, or anything but the forms and designs proceeding from his own creative imagination. Kandinsky (whose work you can study in the Pasadena Art Museum and Los Angeles County Museum of Art), is the best example of a non-objective painter in Western collections. In spite of its negative name, the non-objective movement has been a positive force in the emancipation of painting from literary, historical, and other extraneous considerations.

Op Art. Art which is closely related to the science of optics. The op artists are interested in testing the retinal possibilities of certain experimental patterns of color and line. Their researches have been especially valuable in revealing the vibrations of color. Josef Albers, with his structural constellations and his geometric series called *Homage to the Square,* is one of the early masters of this rather mechanistic movement. Vasarely in France and Larry Poons in America are two of the most brilliant of the op artists working today.

...Language of the Art World

Plastic. From Greek *plastikos*, capable of being molded, this adjective originally applied to the modeling of sculpture. Now in a wider sense it refers to those qualities of art that derive from the means of expression at the artist's disposal and the way in which he exploits these means for his own creative ends. In a painting like Van Gogh's *Starry Night*, the artist achieves a dazzling nocturnal atmosphere and an effect of loneliness; these are expressionistic values, extraneous to the plastic values. The bold brush strokes, thick impasto, vigorously defined forms, and vibrant colors are the plastic elements of the picture.

Pop Art. A reaction against abstract expressionism, this is an impassive, mechanistic, representational art, using images from comic strips, soap boxes, soup cans, and other phenomena of our culture to satirize or glorify that culture.

Provenance (also Provenience). A fancy way of saying where something came from. Applied to art, it means a full documentation of the source and history of a picture or object: who made it, when, where, and what collections it has belonged to.

Renaissance. This term, referring to a period roughly from 1300 to 1600, was a conscious effort to revive classical learning and art. It began when the Italian poet Petrarch proclaimed that the medieval age of faith was a dark age by comparison with which classical antiquity was a golden age of enlightenment. New freedom of thought led to artistic experiment, development of perspective, scientific research, invention (printing press), exploration, religious reform, and the increase of humane (secular) studies over religious scholasticism.

Rococo. An elaboration and refinement of Baroque, this 18th-century style was characterized by shell ornament, curved shapes, ornate and intricate design. Artists such as Fragonard, Watteau, Boucher used fantasy and much frivolity to create an intimate, sensual feeling.

Surrealism. Literally super-reality, this literary and artistic movement began in France in 1924 with a manifesto published by André Breton. In art, surrealism is the pictorial equivalent of Freudian psychology. The dream world and the subconscious mind are the sources of its inspiration. Opposed to naturalism and abstract art, surrealism grew out of Dadaism. Its greatest exponent, Max Ernst, was one of the pioneers of the Dada movement. Uninhibited expression of the subconscious is a supreme virtue, a tenet that links surrealism with expressionism. Going farther back in history, surrealism has obvious affinities with the fantastic paintings of Hieronymous Bosch and William Blake. The chief objection to surrealism as art is that its values are apt to be more literary and psychological than plastic. The most famous of surrealist artists in America is Salvador Dali.

Synchromism. A doctrine promulgated and practiced from 1913 by Stanton Macdonald-Wright (most of whose long career has been spent in Southern California) to the effect that the proper aim of painting is the juxtaposition of pure colors in an abstract design. Asserting that color automatically extends itself into an emotional third dimension, Macdonald-Wright claimed that the impressionists had failed to exploit all the intermediate tones between their extremes of yellow and violet.

Zen. A sect of Buddhism which disregards the canonical books and insists that truth and self-knowledge can be attained only through introspective meditation. At a certain point in the Zen discipline, the contemplator can expect a sudden intuitive revelation of the principle underlying the universe. The Zen sect became powerful in Japan in the 15th century. Many of the Zen priests were also painters. Under the influence of Zen, and inspired by Chinese Sung dynasty paintings, these Japanese artists made swift ink sketches of nature: a single spray of plum blossom, a bird on a snowy branch, the fleeting glimpse of a mountain through the mist. The theme was not so important as what it evoked in the spectator's mind.

FINE, DETAILED LINES emphasize facial features and hair of Bibi Lalouette, an 1859 etching by James McNeill Whistler (1834–1903). (Fine Arts Gallery of San Diego.)

CAPSULE ART HISTORY

PERIOD/SCHOOL	DATES	CULTURAL/POLITICAL CHANGES
ANCIENT		
Egyptian (Old Kingdom)	4500 to 2500 B.C.	Egyptian pyramid building. Neolithic culture spreads in western Europe and Nile Valley. Bronze Age
Egyptian (Middle and New Kingdoms)	2160 to 1090 B.C.	War against Hyksos, followed by period of prosperity, cultural refinement. End of Hittite Kingdom
Sumerian and Persian	4000 to 331 B.C.	Persians occupy Babylon (539 B.C.). Darius builds Persepolis (c. 500 B.C.)
Aegean	3000 to 1100 B.C.	Minoan civilization in Crete. Potters strengthen fragile vessels with painted designs. Frescoes and statues honor the mother goddess
Archaic Greek	1100 to 480 B.C.	The Homeric Age. City-states of Sparta, Athens
Classic Greek	480 to 404 B.C.	Golden Age of Athens. Building of Parthenon. Peloponnesian War
Hellenistic	404 to 1st century B.C.	Decline of Greece, rise of Macedonian society. Death of Alexander
Etruscan and Roman	1000 B.C. to A.D. 500	Etruscans expelled from Rome. Ascendancy of Julius Caesar. Fall of Roman Empire
MEDIEVAL		
Byzantine	A.D. 323 to 1453	Founding of Constantinople. Establishment of Holy Roman Empire. Ottoman Turks capture Byzantium. Greek scholars, artists seek refuge in Italy
Romanesque	500 to 1150	Destruction of Gallo-Roman civilization. Romanesque style develops chiefly in France
Gothic	1150 to 1453	Age of the Crusades. Hundred Years War. Joan of Arc at Orleans. Magna Carta accepted
Gothic	13th century	Byzantium sacked. Latin Empire established in the East. Gothic architecture reaches its peak
Gothic	15th century	Rise of Medici family in Florence. End of War of Roses. Emergence of Renaissance. Invention of printing. Discovery of the New World
RENAISSANCE		
Florentine	15th century	Controlled by Medici, Florence becomes center for art, architecture, literature
Florentine	Late 15th, early 16th century	Machiavelli and *The Prince*
Venetian	Late 15th, early 16th century	Rise of Venetian economic power and its attendant effect on patronage of the fine arts
Flemish	16th century	Religious wars split Protestant Holland and Catholic Belgium. Rise of burgher society in Flanders and Holland, resulting in a wealthy art patronage
German	Late 15th, early 16th century	Protestant Reformation. Voyages of exploration by Columbus, Vespucci, Magellan
Mannerism	Late 16th century	Italian states come under Spanish influence. Italy loses her cultural primacy

ART & ARTISTS	EXAMPLES IN THE WEST
Pyramids and royal tombs. Carved and painted bas-reliefs with scenes from daily life. Sculpture in the round	Funeral stela of Prince Wepemonfret, and Egyptian collection: Lowie Museum. Limestone relief, *Bulls and Figures:* Seattle Art Museum
Carving of human and animal forms in obsidian. Brightly painted, low reliefs. Gigantic temples, colossal statues	Reliefs and sculpture: Stanford Art Museum; Seattle Art Museum; Lowie Museum; L.A. County Museum of Art
Assyrian and Babylon art in Tigris-Euphrates Valley. Immense bas-reliefs: bulls, winged lions. Copper reliefs, gold ornaments and jewelry	Assyrian bas-reliefs: Honolulu Academy of Arts; L.A. County Museum of Art. Luristan and Amlash pottery bronzes: Seattle Art Museum. Fragment of Persepolis bas-relief: Seattle Art Museum
Naturalistic frescoes at Knossos. Golden masks from Mycenaean royal tombs. First known figures of female nude produced by sculptors of Greek Cycladic islands	See typical works in Seattle Art Museum; Honolulu Academy of Arts. Cypriot sculpture: Stanford Museum
Geometric designs on vases. Earliest free-standing stone statues of human figure	Phoenician statuettes: Seattle Art Museum
Phidias, Polyclitus set ideal proportions for glorified human figure, establish classical esthetic standard for 2,000 years	Various works in Honolulu Academy of Arts; Stanford Museum; L.A. County Museum of Art; Getty Museum; De Young Museum
Lysippos, court sculptor to Alexander the Great, puts personal charm into sculpture. Statues become more slender, graceful	Tanagra Figurines: Maryhill Museum. Various works in Santa Barbara Museum of Art; Getty Museum; L.A. County Museum of Art; Honolulu Academy of Arts
Etruscan clay, bronze sculpture shows archaic Greek flavor. Rome assimilates Etrurian, Greek art. Portrait sculpture, decorative mosaics, wall paintings	Mosaic fragments, bronze and marble statues: Seattle Art Museum; Honolulu Academy of Arts. Biographical sarcophagus: L.A. County Museum of Art. Palmyra tomb sculpture: Portland Art Museum
Construction of Santa Sofia (532–537). Rich Byzantine mosaics enlighten mysteries of Christian faith	See various reproductions of mosaics and marble figuring in museum bookshops
Culture kept alive by Church. Revival of stone sculpture. Hand-lettered and illuminated manuscripts.	See reproductions in museum bookshops. Works in Huntington Museum
Soaring cathedrals with stained glass windows—France. Religious sculpture. Roman-type basilicas with frescoes–Italy	See works in De Young Museum; L.A. County Museum of Art; Honolulu Academy of Arts
Giotto, in Florence and Padua, frees painting from Byzantine style, strives for natural form, human drama. Sienese painters add human feeling to richness of Byzantine formula	Examples in Fine Arts Gallery of San Diego. See also the Kress Collections of Italian Renaissance paintings in various museums
Van Eyck brothers record light, air of Low Countries. Van der Weyden explores human emotion in religious art. Bosch's pessimistic painting foreshadows 20th-century expressionism and surrealism	See various *Madonna* paintings: L.A. County Museum of Art; Huntington Gallery. *Christ Taken Captive:* Fine Arts Gallery of San Diego
Massaccio paints realistically with three-dimensional effects. Piero della Francesca, Botticelli, Ghirlandai, Lorenzo di Credi	See various works in L.A. County Museum of Art; Getty Museum. See also various Kress Collections
Leonardo, Michelangelo, Raphael make Italy fountainhead of European art	See Kress Collections in various museums
Color, rich textures, gorgeous pageantry are exploited. Giovanni and Gentile Bellini, Carpaccio, Giorgione, Titian, Tintoretto, Veronese	Representative works in Fine Arts Gallery of San Diego; Fisher Gallery; Getty Museum; Kress Collections
Demand for religious pictures declines in Protestant north. Pieter Breughel, followed by son Pieter Breughel the Younger, develops landscape, genre painting	See works in Timken Gallery; Crocker Art Gallery
Cranach, Grunewald, Dürer, though Italian influenced, retain own strong style. Holbein the Younger gains reputation in England as portrait painter at court of Henry VIII	Legion of Honor; De Young Museum; Achenbach Foundation for Graphic Arts
Pontormo, Parmigianino, Bronzino rebel against slavish imitations of nature, employ heightened esthetic effects, exaggerated forms, clever lighting. Tintoretto, El Greco convey religious ecstasy through paintings	See works in Portland Art Museum; Fine Arts Gallery of San Diego; De Young Museum. See sculpture of Giovanni da Bologna: Huntington Gallery. *Il Rosso Fiorentino:* L.A. County Museum of Art

CAPSULE ART HISTORY

PERIOD/SCHOOL	DATES	CULTURAL/POLITICAL CHANGES
BAROQUE		
Italian	1600 to 1750	Rome capital of Catholicism. City-states disunited politically; advanced culturally and intellectually
Flemish	*1600 to 1750*	Flanders, Spanish territory. Revocation of the Edict of Nantes
Dutch	*1600 to 1750*	William of Orange curtails French advances into Holland. Peace of Westphalia. Netherlands independent of Spain
Spanish	*1600 to 1750*	Peace of Pyrenees. War of Spanish Succession. Peace of Utrecht-Rastadt
French	*1600 to 1750*	Age of Cardinal Richelieu, Louis XIV
MODERN		
Neoclassicism	19th century	Napoleon, Emperor of France. French invasion of Russia. Battle of Waterloo, end of Napoleonic Empire
Independents	*19th century*	Louis Napoleon creates second French Empire
Romanticism	*19th century*	English, American Industrial Revolution. Crimean War. British Antarctic exploration. End of the Tory regime in England
Genre	*19th century*	Monroe Doctrine. Missouri Compromise. American Civil War. American painters travel to West
Realism	*19th century*	French July Monarchy overthrown. Barricade fighting in streets of Paris
Realism	*19th century*	Spanish Peninsular War, civil strife. Rule of Spanish Bourbon family
Impressionism	*19th century*	Franco-German War. Third French Republic. Unification of Germany and Italy
Neo-Impressionism	c. 1886	Revival of the labor movement in France. Scandal of the Dreyfus affair.
Post-Impressionism	19th century	French alliance negotiations with Austria, Italy. Commercial expansion in Holland
CONTEMPORARY		
Fauvism	Early 20th century	Separation of Church and State in France. Cultural repercussions evidenced in the arts
German Expressionism	*Early 20th century*	Socialism spreads widely in Germany, has both positive and negative influence on artists
Blue Rider Group	1910	Potsdam agreement between Russia and Germany. Artists become allied in their work
Cubism	1908 to 1915	Second Moroccan Crisis causes crisis in French-German relations
Neo-Plasticism	1912	Liberals in power in Holland, but are ineffectual
Fantasy	Early 1900's	World War I causes many painters to protest its horrors in their work

...*European and American*

ART & ARTISTS	EXAMPLES IN THE WEST
Caravaggio is great influence on painters of France, Spain, Netherlands. Bernini, Borromini hi (leading sculptor-architects) decorate Roman churches, palaces	See various reproductions of paintings, sculpture, architecture in museum bookshops
Rubens creates forms alive with swirling movement, dramatic tension. His pupil, Van Dyck, makes reputation in England as portrait painter	*Tribute Money:* De Young Museum. *Sketch for Last Supper:* Seattle Art Museum. *Susanna and the Elders:* Fisher Gallery
Rembrandt reveals through flashes of light depths of human character	See works in Timken Gallery; Fine Arts Gallery of San Diego; De Young Museum; Legion of Honor. See also etchings in Achenbach Foundation for Graphic Arts
Velasquez, influenced by Caravaggio and Rubens, masters light and shadow. Sculpture is highly ornamental, glorifies religion of Counter-Reformation. Style reaches New World where it is further enriched by Indians	See works of Cotan and Zurbaran: Santa Barbara Museum of Art; Fine Arts Gallery of San Diego. See gilded altarpieces in California and Arizona mission churches
Baroque reaches culmination at Court of Louis XIV	*Sun King:* Getty Museum. See French 17th-century paintings at Legion of Honor
French Revolution sweeps decorative frivolity of Boucher out of fashion; painters try to recapture classic feeling of ancient Rome. David depicts Napoleon as Roman Emperor. Other artists of the times: Gros, Ingres, Houdon	See works of Gros at L.A. County Museum of Art; Ingres at Legion of Honor. See Roman-style portrait busts at Huntington Gallery
Daumier, Corot, Millet remain free of neoclassical formula, create satirical prints, pictures of rural life	Works at Legion of Honor; also in Achenbach Foundation
Back-to-nature reaction against baroque and neoclassical "artificiality" Mystical, visionary, personal paintings by Blake, landscapes by Constable, Turner	See various and representative works at Huntington Gallery
American painters: Homer, Hill, Bierstadt, Keith, Nahl	See works in Oakland Art Museum. See also *Sunday Morning in the Mines:* Crocker Art Gallery; *Rape of the Sabines:* De Young Museum
Courbet, objective as a camera, tries technical experiments devoid of sentimentality, morality	*The Wave:* Phoenix Art Museum
Goya, Spanish genius of the century, creates penetrating portraits, realistic engravings, aquatints	See representative works in Fine Arts Gallery of San Diego. *The Disasters of War:* Achenbach Foundation
Extension of realism. Leading impressionists: Monet, Renoir, Pissarro, Morisot, Cassatt. Degas, considered an impressionist, refuses to paint outdoors	See *Waterlilies:* Portland Art Museum and Honolulu Academy of Arts. Other works in Legion of Honor; Phoenix Art Museum; La Jolla Art Museum; L.A. County Museum of Art; Santa Barbara Museum of Art
Seurat and Signac turn intuitive impressionism into a science, develop *pointillism*, creating pictures from tiny dots of color	See representative works in L.A. County Museum of Art
Cézanne reacts against ephemeral surface quality of impressionism. Van Gogh paints agitated landscapes, introspective portraits; Gauguin evolves flat, decorative style with brilliant color	See works in L.A. County Museum of Art; Honolulu Academy of Arts
Matisse, strongly influenced by Gauguin, uses violent color, bold distortion. Rouault expresses rage and compassion, religious fervor and social criticism	Works in San Francisco Museum of Art; Pomona College Gallery; UCLA Art Galleries; Honolulu Academy of Arts; Henry Art Gallery
Kirchner, Kokoschka, Beckmann are influenced by pioneer Norwegian artist Edvard Munch	Works in L.A. County Museum of Art
Kandinsky, Klee, Marc, and others stage avant garde exhibitions in Germany	Representative works in Pasadena Art Museum; L.A. County Museum of Art
Picasso and Braque experiment with Cézanne's solid analysis of form. Armory Show in New York, 1913, introduces avant-garde art to the United States	San Francisco Museum of Art; Honolulu Academy of Arts; Seattle Art Museum
Piet Mondrian develops nonrepresentational geometric style	See representative works in L.A. County Museum of Art
Chirico, Marc Chagall, Paul Klee	San Francisco Museum of Art; Santa Barbara Museum of Art; Achenbach Foundation; Pasadena Art Museum

CAPSULE ART HISTORY

PERIOD/SCHOOL	DATES	CULTURAL/POLITICAL CHANGES
Dadaism	1916 to 1922	War runs its course. Formation of the League of Nations. European aftermath of the conflict
Surrealism	1924 (founded)	Dawes Plan. Death of Lenin. World Depression. Nazi dictatorship of Germany. Spanish Civil War
Mexican	First half of 20th century	Mexican Revolution
Abstract Expressionism	1940's and 1950's	World War II and its after-effects are felt by all nations. Start of Cold War
Abstract Expressionism	1949 to 1957	Korean War. Suez Crisis
Figurative	1957	Initiation of American, Russian space race
Current Trends	1966	Great advances in scientific space exploration. Acceleration of Vietnamese War
CHINESE ART Shang Dynasty	1766 to 1122 B.C.	Feudal rule. Warfare with neighboring states. Cities surrounded by walls of pounded earth
Chou Dynasty	1122 to 255 B.C.	Chous overthrow Shangs. Ascendancy of Confucius, Lao-tzu
Han Dynasty	206 B.C. to A.D. 221	Powerful centralized government. Indirect trade with Rome
Wei and Six Dynasties	216 to 618	Buddhism takes hold in China
T'ang Dynasty	618 to 906	Age of Humanism, scholar statesmen. Empress Wu
Sung Dynasty	960 to 1280	Sungs unite China after Civil Wars. Zen Buddhism gains importance
Ming Dynasty	1368 to 1644	Mongol overlords overthrown by Hung-Wu. Relations established between China and Malay states
Ch'ing Dynasty	1644 to 1911	Manchus invade China, remain in control until 20th century
JAPANESE ART Tumulus or Tomb Period	1st to 6th century A.D.	Buddhism established in Japan
Nara	8th century	Chinese-Japanese relations deteriorate
Heian or Fujiwara	10th–12th centuries	Civil wars throughout country
Kamakura	1185 to 1390	Great advances in painting and sculpture
Muromachi	15th century	Continuous civil wars
Momoyama	1573 to 1615	Peace comes to Japan
Tokugawa	1600 to 1868	Edo (today's Tokyo) becomes economic, political, cultural capital of Japan
Contemporary	20th century	Russo-Japanese War. Japanese suffer first atomic bomb attack

...Chinese and Japanese

ART & ARTISTS	EXAMPLES IN THE WEST
Non-sense and anti-art protest against war, traditional art, and other phenomena by Dada Group	Representative works in L.A. County Museum of Art
Outgrowth of Dadaism. Psychic automatism free from reason or any esthetic or moral purpose. Ernst, Miro, Dali, Tanguy	Santa Barbara Museum of Art; Honolulu Academy of Arts; Achenbach Foundation
Realism and social protest expressed by Rivera, Orozco	Phoenix Art Museum; University of Arizona; San Francisco Art Institute
Action painting in New York: Pollock, de Kooning	Works in San Francisco Museum of Art; University of Arizona
Sculpture: Moore, Calder, Kricke	See works in L.A. County Museum of Art, also Arizona State University
California Bay Area Figurative Show at Oakland Art Museum	Oakland Art Museum
Pop art, op art, top art, cybernetic sculpture	See latest trends in galleries on La Cienega Blvd., Los Angeles. Also see works in L.A. County Museum of Art
Ceremonial bronze vessels, made by piece molds. Decoration zoomorphic, spirals symbolizing nature over animals	Sculpture, vessels: Seattle Art Museum. Marble demon mask: Honolulu Academy of Arts
Work in bronze, jade: Motifs become dynamic, explosive, settle down into playful rhythms. Subject matter changes to hunting scenes, religious rites, magic practices	*Dancing Girl:* Seattle Art Museum. *Standing Figure of Woman:* Honolulu Academy of Arts. Wood, ceramics: Portland Art Museum
Paintings, stone reliefs, pottery tiles, concerned with daily life. Art shows linear rhythm, dimension, background	See Brundage Collection of Asian Art: De Young Museum. Also see works in Portland Art Museum
Sculpture of Buddha surrounded by paintings depicts lives of Buddha. Wall paintings show depth and reality	Guardian figures from Buddhist caves of Lung Men: Honolulu Academy of Arts
Golden age of Chinese sculpture. Wares covered with colorful lead glazes; shapes clearly articulated	*Polo Player:* University of Oregon Art Museum. Glazed *Bactrian Camel:* Art Gallery of Greater Victoria. *Merchant with Wine Skin Vessel:* Seattle Art Museum. Stone life-size Buddha: Honolulu Academy of Arts. Glazed horses: Brundage Collection (De Young Museum)
Development of handscroll; landscapes with peaks and clouds. Ceramics with monochrome glazes, more polished than T'ang	See *Figure of Priest, Hundred Geese Scroll:* Honolulu Academy of Arts
Sumi and watercolor landscape by Shen Chou; many styles, moods. Fan paintings. Long horizontal scrolls of changing landscapes. Porcelains with three-color enamels	*Shen Chou:* University of Oregon Art Museum. Fan painting (only one on North American continent): Art Gallery of Greater Victoria. Works at Seattle Art Museum; Honolulu Academy of Arts
Jade, ivory carvings	See Brundage Collection (De Young Museum). *Imperial Jade Pagoda:* University of Oregon Art Museum. *Coming of Autumn:* Honolulu Academy of Arts
Haniwa, sculptured pottery, placed around burial mounds	*Helmeted Haniwa Warrior:* Seattle Art Museum. Works in L.A. Museum of Art; Brundage Collection (De Young Museum)
Chinese T'ang style dominates arts. Esoteric Buddhism leads to heavier images with multiple arms, heads	*Standing bronze Kwannon:* Honolulu Academy of Arts
Fan paintings reflect court life	Cypress wood sculpture: Seattle Art Museum; University of Oregon Art Museum; Honolulu Academy of Arts
Adopted strength, realism in art. Sculptures; handscrolls	Seattle Art Museum; Honolulu Academy of Arts; Brundage Collection (De Young)
Sculpture lessens in importance. Painting is influenced by Sung, Ming masters	Seattle Art Museum; Art Gallery of Greater Victoria
Emphasis on two-dimensional design, three-color patterns	Seattle Art Museum; Honolulu Academy of Arts
Decorative screens, paintings, Japanese wood blocks	Representative works in Portland Art Museum; Honolulu Academy of Arts; University of Oregon Museum of Art; L.A. County Museum of Art
Japanese calligraphy, paintings, prints. New departures in modern abstract paintings	See works in University of Oregon Museum of Art; Achenbach Foundation

BIOGRAPHICAL NOTES

The following biographical notes are a brief review of the life, times, and accomplishments of the principal artists whose works are illustrated in this book. The page numbers immediately following an artist's name refer to pages on which his work is shown. At the end of entries are listed his chief works in the West and some of the places—museums and public locations—where they may be seen.

Audubon, John James. p. 138. American. 1785–1851. Ornithologist, artist, keen observer of nature, he did 435 hand-colored folio plates for his monumental *Birds of America.* Several prints in Achenbach Foundation for Graphic Arts. Painting in Arizona State University Art Gallery.

Bellini, Giovanni. p. 96. Italian. *c.* 1429–1516. One of the best and most influential of Venetian painters, he taught Giorgione and Titian, painted devotional pictures of Madonnas and saints, striking portraits of his contemporaries. Work in Fine Arts Gallery of San Diego.

Bellows, George. p. 127. American. 1882–1925. An outstanding high-school athlete, Bellows became a leading painter of realistic sports scenes, found his subject matter in the boxing ring and slums. Work in Los Angeles County Museum of Art.

Bierstadt, Albert. pp. 123, 143, 194. American. 1830–1902. German-born, Dusseldorf-trained landscape painter who specialized in mountain scenery. Accompanied General Lander's expedition across Rockies to Pacific Coast in 1857. Had studio in San Francisco in 1872-73, made Yosemite sketches for subsequent paintings exhibited in Paris, London, Moscow, Vienna, Berlin. See works in Oakland Art Museum.

Bischoff, Elmer. p. 181. American. 1916–. Berkeley-born artist has been called "lyricist of the Bay Area realists," teaches at San Francisco Art Institute, has exhibited at California Palace of the Legion of Honor, M.H. De Young Memorial Museum, Richmond Art Center. Works in the Oakland Art Museum.

Bologna, Giovanni da. p. 83. Italian. 1529–1608. Sculptor whose work can be seen in Huntington Art Gallery.

Bosch, Hieronymus. p. 26. Flemish. 1450–1516. Obsessed by late Gothic visions of original sin, this artist expressed the crimes and punishments of mankind with nightmarish fantasies which probe the subconscious to such an extent that modern surrealists claim him as a spiritual ancestor. Fine Arts Gallery of San Diego.

Botticelli, Sandro. p. 32. Italian. *c.* 1445–1510. Leading painter of early Renaissance in Florence, brought exquisite, decorative line to delineation of human emotion in mythical and religious scenes. You can see his work in the Los Angeles County Museum of Art.

Braque, Georges. p. 285. French. 1882–1963. Co-founder, with Picasso, of cubism, he became a specialist in vibrant, harmonious still life, believed that nobility grows out of contained emotion, is considered one of the greatest masters of modern French art. Excellent examples of his painting are in the San Francisco Museum of Art and Honolulu Academy of Arts.

Breughel, Pieter. p. 122. Flemish. *c.* 1525–1569. Known as "Peasant Breughel," because of his love of rustic scenes, he was the greatest landscape painter of his age, and founder of a dynasty of artists which included sons Pieter II or Pieter Breughel the Younger, Jan Breughel, and grandson Jan Breughel II. Work in Crocker Art Gallery.

Breughel, Pieter, the Younger. p. 209. Flemish. 1564–1638. Was also known as "Hell Breughel" because of his affection for nightmare scenes. He often copied his father's works; the Crocker Gallery's *Feasting and Dancing in the Low Countries* is a case in point.

Brookes, Samuel Marsden. p. 89. American. 1816–1892. Born in England, he came to America in 1833, settled in San Francisco in 1862, specialized in still life, genre, and portrait painting, became a master in all three. Works in Oakland Art Museum.

Bufano, Beniamino. p. 230. American. 1903–. Italian-born (San Fele), Benny—as he is familiarly known around San Francisco—came to the Bay Area when he was 21. See his captivating sculptured animals at Hillsdale Mall, San Mateo; his mosaic mural at Moras Cafeteria on Powell Street, San Francisco; his *St. Francis,* near Fisherman's Wharf, San Francisco.

Burchfield, Charles. p. 95. American. 1893–. Began as a romantic nature painter, turned to realism, eventually combined both tendencies in the "expression of a completely personal mood," his chief aim in art. *Rainy Night* in Fine Arts Gallery of San Diego is typical of his moody evocation of atmosphere.

Cadmus, Paul. p. 211. American. 1904–. In the realist tradition of the Ash Can School, he found preferred subject matter among the common people, was especially fond of drawing crowds at beach, sailors with their girls, as in *Shore Leave* in the Achenbach Foundation Collection.

Callahan, Kenneth. p. 258. American. 1906–. Spokane-born painter is one of foremost Pacific Northwest regional artists. You will find his strong cosmic landscapes in the University of Washington's Henry Gallery, Seattle Art Museum (where he spent 15 years as a curator), Portland Art Museum, San Francisco Museum of Art, Santa Barbara Museum of Art.

Cassatt, Mary. p. 117. American. 1845–1926. The talent of this Pittsburgh-born artist was so great that confirmed misogynist Edgar Degas stopped hating women long enough to persuade her to exhibit with the impressionists. See her *Maternity* in the Los Angeles County Museum of Art.

Cézanne, Paul. p. 120. French. 1839–1906. Born in Aix-en-Provence, Cézanne was the son of a rich provincial banker who took a dim view of painting as a career for his offspring. This strange son, who once shocked his family with a dinner table prayer to the Virgin "to keep your eye on me because I am surrounded by idiots," joined the impressionists in Paris, but abandoned them in 1879 in search of a deeper reality beneath the dazzling surface. See work in Los Angeles County Museum of Art.

Chagall, Marc. p. 188. Russian. 1877–. Born in Vitebsk, Chagall failed the entrance exams for the St. Petersburg School of Arts and Crafts. He "washed his eyes" in Paris and, fortified by fauvism and cubism, went on to record his private vision of a joyous and fantastic world whose people and objects he exempts from the laws of gravity.

...The Artists Represented in This Book

You can see his works at the Achenbach Foundation and the Santa Barbara Museum of Art.

Chirico, Giorgio de. p. 184. Italian. 1888–. After academic training in Athens and Munich, Chirico went to Paris in 1911 where his architectonic metaphysical art caused the French poet Apollinaire to proclaim him the most astonishing painter of his time. His best work juxtaposes objects and beings in unexpected relationships, creates a magic universe of space. Excellent examples in San Francisco Museum of Art and Honolulu Academy of Arts.

Constable, John. p. 102. English. 1776–1837. Reacted against ideal landscapes of his academic training and sought inspiration by painting scenes of his native Suffolk on the spot outdoors. Works in Huntington Art Gallery.

Copley, John Singleton. pp. 90, 204. American. 1738–1815. Boston born and practically self-taught, Copley became a portrait painter of great skill and psychological insight, as his works in the California Palace of the Legion of Honor and Santa Barbara Museum of Art attest. He left America in 1774, became a member of the Royal Academy.

Corot, Jean Baptiste Camille. p. 212. French. 1796–1875. Was one of the most popular and prolific painters of the 19th century. He was in Rome from 1825 to 1827 and there developed the sensitive treatment of light and space manifest in our reproduction from the California Palace of the Legion of Honor.

Cranach, Lucas. p. 152. German. 1472–1553. Was court painter of the Electors of Saxony and a personal friend of Martin Luther, for whom he designed woodcuts. Works in the California Palace of the Legion of Honor and the M.H. De Young Memorial Museum.

Credi, Lorenzo di. p. 56. Italian. *c.* 1459–1537. Was a fellow pupil of Leonardo da Vinci in the Florentine shop of Verrocchio. A superb technician, he was far less inventive and subtle than Leonardo, many of whose lost early works he is said to have copied. Examples in J. Paul Getty Museum and Los Angeles County Museum of Art.

Crivelli, Carlo. p. 131. Italian. *c.* 1430–1494. Was a Venetian painter noted for his altarpieces and especially for his pious and tender portrayals of the Madonna and Child. Work in Fine Arts Gallery of San Diego.

Dahlgren, Marius. p. 164. Danish-American. 1878–1910. Arrived in California from Copenhagen in 1878, lived in Oakland, had studio in San Francisco. You will see his paintings in the Oakland Art Museum. There are also frescoes in St. Augustine's Cathedral in Tucson, Arizona, where the artist spent his last years.

Dali, Salvador. p. 274. Spanish. 1904–. Born in Figueras, Catalonia, Dali is the most publicized of the surrealist painters, though he has been disowned by André Breton and the other surrealists as an academic reactionary. Works in Phoenix Art Museum and Mills College Art Gallery.

Daubigny, Charles François. p. 212. French. 1817–1878. Sensitive painter of the Barbizon school, he worked outdoors on the banks of the Seine and the Oise, producing evocative pictures like the *River Scene* in the California Palace of the Legion of Honor.

Daumier, Honoré. p. 159. French. 1808–1879. Leading caricaturist of the 19th century, Daumier made thousands of lithographs which remain as models of mordant political and social satire. Prints in Achenbach Foundation for Graphic Arts.

David, Jacques Louis. p. 275. French. 1748–1825. Was leading neoclassical painter of France, official artist at the court of Napoleon I, whose imperial exploits he celebrated in huge canvases like *The Emperor Distributing Eagles on the Field of Mars*, a sketch for which may be seen at the Phoenix Art Museum.

Davis, Lew. p. 276. American. 1910–. Born in Jerome, Arizona, and active in Arizona, his realistic paintings, tinged with social criticism, are a rich record of contemporary American Southwest. See his *Paradise Valley, The City, Little Boy Lives in a Copper Camp:* Phoenix Art Museum.

Degas, Edgar. pp. 74, 75, 182. French. 1834–1917. A wealthy Parisian, he studied at the Beaux-Arts, broke away from academic tradition, exhibited with the impressionists, but did not share their enthusiasm for the great outdoors. Works in Portland Art Museum, Los Angeles County Museum of Art.

Delacroix, Eugene. p. 112. French. 1798–1863. Reacted against neoclassicism of David and became leading painter of French romantic movement. Works in Santa Barbara Museum of Art, Phoenix Art Museum.

Demetrios, Aristides. p. 170. American. 1932–. After three years in U.S. Navy, attended father George Demetrios' Sculpture School, is widely recognized by critics for his sculptural equivalents of wind, water, flame. See his *Gold Rush Fountain* in Sacramento; *White Memorial Fountain* (1964) on campus of Stanford University.

Diebenkorn, Richard. p. 180. American. 1922–. Born in Portland, Oregon, Diebenkorn now teaches at UCLA. His work in both abstract and figurative forms has made him one of the foremost Western artists of his generation. He was appointed in 1965 to the National Council on the Arts. His paintings are in private and public collections from coast to coast. In the West they may be seen at Oakland Art Museum, San Francisco Museum of Art, Pasadena Art Museum, Phoenix Art Museum, and the Art Gallery of University of Arizona.

Dixon, Maynard. p. 197. American. 1875–1946. Born in Fresno, California, Dixon began his art career as an illustrator, was one of first painters to become interested in the Southwest as subject matter for art. Paintings in Oakland Art Museum, Mills College Art Gallery.

Dürer, Albrecht. pp. 47, 68, 223. German. 1471–1528. One of the greatest masters of the Renaissance and a link between Italy and northern Europe, Dürer has been called the German Leonardo da Vinci. He perfected the techniques of woodcut and engraving, left examples of graphic art that are unequalled for expressiveness, technical refinement, masterly draftsmanship. See woodcut portrait of his patron, Emperor Maximilian I, in Portland Art Museum; also works in Crocker Art Gallery, Achenbach Foundation.

Eakins, Thomas. p. 126. American. 1844–1916. Outstanding realistic painter of 19th century, left native Philadelphia in 1866, responded to realism of Manet, returned to America in 1870. See *Wrestlers* in Los Angeles County Museum of Art. Other works in Charles and Emma Frye Museum, Santa Barbara Museum of Art.

Ernst, Max. p. 189. German. 1881–. A leader of the dada movement in 1919, became a surrealist in 1924, extended the techniques of modern art with collages (pastings) and frottages (rubbings). After a long sojourn in Arizona, he now lives and works in France where his "magnificent haunted brain," to quote André Breton, still thinks up new and witty ideas. See his work in Achenbach Foundation.

Falkenstein, Claire. p. 59. American. Born in Oregon in undisclosed year of 20th century, she now lives and works in Venice, California, after a period of work in Paris. Miss Falkenstein has developed a striking individual style of sculpture in metal and fused glass. Her work may be seen at the Phoenix Art Museum, California State College at Long Beach, and on Wilshire Boulevard in Los Angeles.

Feininger, Lyonel. p. 137. American. 1871–1956. Born in New York, studied art in Hamburg, Berlin, and Paris, where he learned about cubism, a style he transformed into a geometric and poetic idiom of his own. Many paintings and drawings in Pasadena Art Museum.

Fitzgerald, James. p. 243. American. 1910–. Born in Seattle, where he has created sculpture of bronze and copper, mostly fountains, for the public embellishment of the Seattle Center. His work is also in Ogden, Utah, and other civic-minded communities.

Flandes, Juan de. p. 80. Flemish. 1496–1519. A perceptive and expressive artist, John of Flanders was employed in the service of Isabella of Castile from 1496 to her death in 1504, during which period he painted the portrait of the queen's mad daughter, Juana la Loca, which is now in the Sedgwick Collection at the University of California at Santa Barbara. During the last decade of his life, the artist painted handsome altarpieces for the University and the Cathedral of Salamanca and for the Church of San Lazaro in Valencia.

Fragonard, Jean Honoré. pp. 160, 186. French. 1732–1806. He painted the elegance and frivolity of Louis XV's court, including a series of light-hearted idylls for Madame du Barry. Painting and prints are in California Palace of the Legion of Honor. See also his *Rape of the Sabines* (after Rubens) at Dixon Art Center, UCLA.

Gainsborough, Thomas. p. 20. English. 1727–1788. A leading 18th-century painter of landscapes and portraits, Gainsborough was one of the original members of the Royal Academy founded by George III in 1768. See Gainsborough's pictures at the Huntington Gallery. There are also examples in the California Palace of the Legion of Honor, M.H. De Young Memorial Museum, and the Fisher Gallery, University of Southern California.

Gauguin, Paul. p. 278. French. 1848–1903. Born in Paris, this prototype of the genius in revolt against convention, rejected impressionism in 1887, developed a bold new art of flat colors, shadowless drawing, and massive, simplified forms, ideal for the depiction of the primitive life of Tahiti, where he sought refuge from the artificiality of Europe in 1891. Works in Honolulu Academy of Arts, Haggin Gallery, Achenbach Foundation for Graphic Arts.

Ghirlandaio, Ridolfo. p. 35. Italian. 1483–1561. Son of the famous fresco painter, Domenico Ghirlandaio, Ridolfo was a friend of Raphael, specialized in portraits. His posthumous portrait of Dante is a rare item to be seen in the Fine Arts Gallery of San Diego.

Gorky, Arshile. p. 206. American. 1904–1948. Born in Armenia, Gorky came to America at the age of 16, became one of the first abstract expressionists of the New York school, exerted strong influence on the movement from his studio in Union Square, committed suicide at 44. His work can be seen at San Francisco Museum of Art.

Goya, Francisco, de, Y Lucientes. pp. 34, 91. Spanish. 1746–1828. Born in Saragossa, he fled his home town and toured Italy with a band of itinerant bull fighters. Returning to Madrid, he soon became famous. See his work in Fine Arts Gallery of San Diego.

Graves, Morris. p. 260. American. 1910–. Born in Seattle, Graves is one of the best known of Pacific Northwest artists. The Seattle Art Museum has the best collection of his paintings in the West. See also the Portland Art Museum and the University of Oregon.

Greco, El. p. 129. Spanish. 1548–1614. Born in Crete, "the Greek's" real name was Domenico Teotocopulos. He went to Venice at an early age, was a pupil of Titian, and was enormously influenced by Tintoretto, whose religious mannerism and elongated figures and faces he adopted in his own work. The last 37 years of his life were spent in Toledo, where his own mysticism and passionate ecstatic style found their counterpart in the fanatical religious atmosphere of Spain. Works in Fine Arts Gallery of San Diego, M.H. De Young Memorial Museum.

Gros, Baron Antoine Jean. p. 41. French. 1771–1835. Favorite pupil, close friend, and fervent admirer of David, Gros painted Napoleonic battle scenes in the neoclassical manner, but a stronger use of color and a tinge of melancholy in his work foreshadow the romantic movement and had a strong influence on the painting of Gericault and Delacroix. The example of his work in the Los Angeles County Museum of Art is exceptionally fine.

Guardi, Francesco. p. 30. Italian. 1712–1793. A Venetian painter who did hundreds of portraits of his native city, Guardi was fascinated by the luminous effects of sun-drenched houses reflected in the glistening water of the canals. See works in Fine Arts Gallery of San Diego and California Palace of the Legion of Honor.

Gwathmey, Robert. p. 107. American. 1903–. Born in Virginia, Gwathmey is currently an instructor at Cooper Union Art School in New York. Example in Fine Arts Gallery of San Diego.

Hahn, William. p. 235. American. 1829–1887. A native of Saxony, Hahn's specialty was figures and animals. After his arrival in California in 1867, Hahn depicted scenes, typical of California, several of which can be seen in the Oakland Art Museum, and M. H. De Young Memorial Museum.

Hansen, James Lee. p. 261. American. 1925–. Born in Tacoma, Washington, Hansen is one of the most talented of Pacific Northwest sculptors. His abstract work in metal reflects the influence of Chinese bronzes and totemic Indian sculpture. He has his own foundry next to his studio in

...The Artists Represented in This Book

Vancouver, Washington, and casts his large bronzes by means of an improved lost wax process. They may be seen on the Civic Mall of Fresno, in the Seattle Art Museum, and in most of the major art museums of the West.

Hill, Thomas. pp. 219, 234. 1829–1913. American. Born in England, he came to Massachusetts with his family as a youth and began his career there as a coach painter. Works in Oakland Art Museum, State Capitol of California at Sacramento.

Hofmann, Hans. p. 168. American. 1880–1965. Born in Germany, he studied in Munich and Paris, taught at the University of California, Berkeley, and Chouinard Art Institute, Los Angeles, in 1930-31. A large ensemble of his work may be seen at the University of California Art Museum, Berkeley.

Hokusai, Katsushika. p. 241. Japanese. 1760–1849. One of the most popular and versatile of Japanese painters and printmakers, famed for his frequently reproduced *Wave* and his *Views Along the Tokkaido Road*. Original painting in Seattle Art Museum; color woodblock prints in Portland Art Museum and Honolulu Academy of Arts.

Homer, Winslow. p. 193. American. 1836–1910. A self-taught master of realism, Homer worked as a newspaper illustrator during the Civil War, developed keen sense of observation, evident in his American landscapes, seascapes, and portraits. Works in Henry Gallery, University of Washington, Charles and Emma Frye Museum, Mills College Gallery, Los Angeles County Museum of Art.

Hord, Donal. p. 37. American. 1902–1966. Born in Wisconsin, he moved to San Diego, attended Santa Barbara School of Arts from 1926-28, studied pre-Columbian art in Mexico 1928-29. Works at La Jolla, Los Angeles County Courts Building, and Los Angeles County Museum of Art.

Horiuchi, Paul. p. 244. American. 1906–. Born in Japan, now resident in Seattle, this artist uses ancient Oriental technique of rice paper collage to obtain lyrical effects in sensitive abstract compositions. He has been influenced by Mark Tobey. See his free-standing mural in Seattle Center; smaller works in Seattle Art Museum, University of Oregon Art Museum.

Houdon, Jean Antoine. p. 83. French. 1741–1828. Famous sculptor of the 18th-century. Works in the Huntington Art Gallery.

Jamieson, Mitchell. p. 255. American. 1915–. Born in Maryland, this artist is building an increasingly solid reputation in his adopted region, the Pacific Northwest. Work in Henry Gallery, University of Washington.

Jawlensky, Alexei von. p. 137. Russian. 1864–1942. Gave up career as officer in the Russian Imperial Guard to become a painter. Studied in Munich where he met Kandinsky, settled in Wiesbaden in 1921, formed the Blue Four group with Kandinsky, Klee, and Feininger in 1924. Works in Pasadena Art Museum.

Kandinsky, Wassilj. pp. 125, 136. Russian. 1866–1944. Born in Moscow, trained in Munich, Kandinsky abandoned a law career to devote himself to painting. In 1910 he painted his first nonrepresentational work, thus becoming a founder of abstract art. Works in Los Angeles County Museum of Art, Pasadena Art Museum, Seattle Art Museum.

Keith, William. p. 165. American. 1838–1911. Born in Scotland, he was brought to New York as a child, established himself as an apprentice wood engraver in San Francisco in the 1860's. Works in Oakland Art Museum, Keith Gallery of Oakland Library, St. Mary's College at Moraga, California.

Klee, Paul. pp. 53, 73, 136. Swiss. 1879–1940. One of the inventive of modern artists, Klee was also a musician and brought a sense of musical improvisation to his paintings. One of the Blue Four, whose work you will find in Pasadena Art Museum.

Largillière, Nicolas de. p. 155. French. 1656–1746. Born in Paris, grew up in Antwerp, where he must have seen many paintings by Rubens. Superlative example in California Palace of the Legion of Honor.

Laurencin, Marie. p. 177. French. 1885–1956. Born in Paris, she attended the Lycée Lamartine, where her drawing teacher told her, "You would be better off learning to play the mandolin." You can see a good example of her work in Haggin Art Galleries.

Lawrence, Sir Thomas. pp. 134, 135, 205. English. 1769–1830. Son of a Bristol innkeeper, Lawrence was a precocious artist who began doing crayon portraits at the age of 10. At the age of 19 he had already exhibited at the Royal Academy; at 23, on the death of Sir Joshua Reynolds, he was appointed Painter to the King. His work may be seen in the Huntington Art Gallery, California Palace of the Legion of Honor, Vancouver Art Gallery.

Lebrun, Rico. pp. 46, 87. American. 1900–. Born in Naples, Italy, emigrated to U.S. in 1924, he has taught at UCLA summer session, was artist in residence at Santa Barbara Museum of Art. Works in M.H. De Young Memorial Museum, Los Angeles County Museum of Art, Mills College Art Gallery, Santa Barbara Museum of Art.

Léger, Fernand. p. 207. French. 1881–1955. Son of a Normandy farmer, he went to Paris at age of 19, met Picasso and Braque in 1910, evolved own style of curvilinear cubism after first World War. Works in Mills College Art Gallery, San Francisco Museum of Art, University of Arizona.

Le Nain, Louis. p. 144. French. 1593–1648. He shared a common signature with his brothers, Antoine and Mathieu. Born in Laon, they worked in Paris, depicted the rude but dignified life of peasants and artisans. Louis is considered the best artist of the trio; his virile, matter-of-fact view of French peasants (in the California Palace of the Legion of Honor) is typical.

Leutze, Emanuel. p. 179. American. 1816–1868. Celebrated U.S. historical painter, brought to Philadelphia as child from his native Germany. In 1860 he was commissioned to decorate stairway in national capitol with *Westward the Star of Empire Takes Its Way*. His best known work, reproduced in hundreds of engravings, is in the Metropolitan Museum of Art, *Washington Crossing the Delaware*. Even grander is *Washington Rallying the Troops at Monmouth*, in University of California Art Museum at Berkeley.

Lorraine, Claude. p. 253. French. 1600–1682. Born in Alsace, he traveled to Rome where he made idealized sketches of scenes recalling the golden age of classical antiquity. *Goatsherd*, one of his few etchings, can be seen in the Art Gallery of Greater Victoria.

Luks, George. p. 127. American. 1867–1933. Known as Lusty Luks, because of his swashbuckling behavior, Luks was one of "The Eight." (The other seven were Robert Henri, William Glackens, John Sloan, Everett Shinn, Arthur B. Davies, Maurice Prendergast, Ernest Lawson.) See *Bleeker Street Kid* at Scripps College.

Magnasco, Alessandro. p. 210. Italian. 1677–1749. Enjoyed great popularity with his theatrically lighted, melodramatic genre paintings *(Soldiers Feasting:* M.H. De Young Memorial Museum) and his tempestuous landscapes, an 18th century prelude to romantic and expressionist art.

Mainardi, Sebastiano. p. 96. Italian. 1450–1513. A contemporary of Leonardo da Vinci, this Florentine painter was a master of portraits, noted for their sensitivity, simplicity, and style. There are three very good examples of his work in the Huntington Art Gallery.

Makowski, Konstantin. p. 186. Russian. 1839–1915. A genre painter whose vision was influenced by Russian folklore. Work in the M.H. De Young Memorial Museum.

Manet, Edouard. p. 183. French. 1832–1883. Scion of a wealthy bourgeois Parisian family, Manet became one of the important pioneers of modern art. A major work in the California Palace of the Legion of Honor.

Marin, John. pp. 2, 106. American. 1870–1953. Born in New Jersey, Marin began his career as an architect, turned to painting in 1899. Works in Arizona State University, Santa Barbara Museum of Art.

Martinez, Ricardo. p. 276. Mexican. 1918–. He was born in Mexico City, studied law at the University of Mexico. Mainly self-taught, he was influenced by Indianism and his brother's sculpture. He is active in Mexico City. Work in Phoenix Art Museum.

Mathews, Arthur F. p. 235. American. 1860–1945. Born in Wisconsin, Mathews came West as a boy and apprenticed as an architectural draftsman in Oakland, California. His notable painting *Discovery of San Francisco Bay* can be seen at the Oakland Art Museum.

Matisse, Henri. pp. 146, 229. French. 1869–1954. Leader of the "fauves" or wild beasts, he liberated color by applying it in pure pigments without reference to subject matter (if he felt like painting a body blue, he did so), created a new concept of space by juxtaposing planes of color without breaking surface unity of picture. His works are in San Francisco Museum of Art, Pomona College Art Gallery, UCLA Art Gallery, Honolulu Academy of Arts.

Memling, Hans. p. 97. Flemish. *c.* 1430–1495. A pupil of Roger Van der Weyden, he spent most of his life in Bruges where his beautifully painted pictures, calm as the canals of that city, earned him so much money that he was one of the town's biggest tax payers. His portraits are characterized by great dignity and piety, as in the *Young Man With Folded Hands* from the Fine Arts Gallery of San Diego.

Miró, Joan. p. 188. Spanish. 1893–. A leading surrealist, he evolved his own neoprimitive style in the 1940's by adopting signs and symbols of early Eskimo, Indian, and Catalonian art, adding his own witty hieroglyphics, and expressing his pictorial concepts with the uninhibited impulse of a child in strong primary colors. Lithograph in the Achenbach Foundation for Graphic Arts.

Mondrian, Piet. p. 64. Dutch. 1872–1944. He began as a painter of realistic landscapes, went to Paris in 1911, did abstract series of trees under the egis of cubism, then developed neoplasticism, the most rigorous form of geometric abstraction. His formal style, based on vertical and horizontal lines in primary colors and harmonious balance against a pure white background, has had a strong influence on modern architecture and design. Example in Los Angeles County Museum of Art.

Monet, Claude. p. 248. French. 1840–1926. Born in Paris, this most impressionist of the impressionists exhibited in 1874 a picture entitled *Impression, Sunrise*. It not only provided a name for a movement in painting; it sounded a new note: the idea that the artist's personal feeling or reaction to a landscape was more important than an objective representation of nature. See his work in the Portland Art Museum, Honolulu Academy of Arts.

Moore, Henry. p. 45. English. 1898–. The foremost living British sculptor. His semiabstract figures, both tactile and spatial in concept, indicate his aim to open up the sculptural mass. Example in Sculpture Court of Los Angeles County Museum of Art.

Munch, Edvard. p. 43. Norwegian. 1863–1944. A forerunner of expressionism, Munch subordinated plastic problems to the requirements of expressing his own hypersensitive and neurotic vision of the world, a world haunted by phantoms of anxiety and death. His graphic work is especially powerful, as indicated by the woodcut reproduced from the Los Angeles County Museum of Art.

Nahl, Charles Christian. p. 190. American. 1818–1878. Born in Germany, he came to California to seek his fortune in the gold rush. After a brief fling in the mines, he settled down as a painter and photographer in San Francisco, where his gold rush pictures were in great demand. He was also a master of anecdotal-historical painting and a very good portraitist. His works are in the Crocker Art Gallery, the Oakland Art Museum, and the M.H. De Young Memorial Museum.

Orozco, José Clemente. pp. 86, 274. Mexican. 1883–1949. Born in Zapatlan, Orozco was a pioneer of modern Mexican painting. Close to the Aztec tradition, his work owes little to European influence, much to the indigenous color and light of his native land where his works are.

Panini, Giovanni. p. 185. Italian. 1695–1768. The first artist to specialize in ruins, Panini found abundant subject matter in Rome. His architectonic drawings and paintings of abandoned temples and deserted arcades were much sought after by 18th-century tourists as souvenirs of their classical tours. He influenced Piranesi, Hubert Robert, and Canaletto. Example in Crocker Art Gallery.

...The Artists Represented in This Book

Park, David. p. 181. American. 1911–1960. Born in Boston, he came to California in 1928, studied at Otis Art Institute, Los Angeles, taught at Berkeley and California School of Fine Arts. He painted abstractly until 1950, then destroyed most of his abstract work and returned to the figure. Works in Oakland Art Museum, San Francisco Museum of Art.

Pennell, Joseph. p. 218. American. 1857–1926. A follower of James Whistler, Pennell was a great American illustrator, etcher, and lithographer. His works can be seen at Arizona State University, Tempe.

Peterson, Margaret. p. 176. American. 1903–. Born in Seattle, this gifted modern artist was an influential teacher for many years at the University of California in Berkeley. Her sophisticated cubism has been modified and strengthened in recent years by familiarity with the Indian art of the Pacific Northwest where she now lives (British Columbia). Works in Oakland Art Museum, Art Gallery of Greater Victoria, Seattle Art Museum.

Peto, John F. p. 89. American. 1854–1907. He painted the appurtenances of everyday life with affectionate attention to detail, achieved effects of realism that were matched only by his contemporary Michael Hartnett. The Santa Barbara Museum of Art has a major example of his work.

Picabia, Francis. p. 256. French. 1879–1954. By turns impressionist, cubist, dadaist, surrealist, figurative, and abstract, this Paris painter of Spanish origin was, to quote sculptor Hans Arp, "the Christopher Columbus of art, sailing without a compass." An independent spirit who exerted great influence on fellow artists, he was like yeast in the ferment of 20th-century art. Work in San Francisco Museum of Art.

Picasso, Pablo. pp. 108, 109, 207. Spanish. 1881–. Born in Malaga, he came to Paris in 1900, admired the work of Van Gogh and Toulouse-Lautrec, established himself at the Bateau Lavoir in Montmartre, and embarked on one of the longest, most fecund, and most successful careers in the history of art. Works in San Francisco Museum of Art, Portland Art Museum, UCLA Art Gallery, Fine Arts Gallery of San Diego, Art Gallery of Greater Victoria, Honolulu Academy of Arts, Achenbach Foundation for Graphic Arts.

Price, C.S. p. 258. American. 1874–1950. Born in Bedford, Iowa, went to St. Louis School of Fine Arts in 1905–1906, worked as illustrator in Portland, Oregon, 1909–10, as a cook in Canada, 1910–1914. Works in Portland Art Museum, University of Oregon Art Museum, Seattle Art Museum.

Rembrandt van Rijn. pp. 12, 46, 128, 130, 203. Dutch. 1606–1669. Born in Leyden, he was highly regarded as a painter when he settled in Amsterdam in 1631, became favorite portrait painter of wealthy burghers of the town. Works in Los Angeles County Museum of Art, Timken Gallery, California Palace of the Legion of Honor, Achenbach Foundation for Graphic Arts, Grunewald Collection at UCLA.

Renoir, Auguste. pp. 17, 182. French. 1841–1919. He began his artistic career at age of 13 as a painter on porcelain in a china factory, made frequent visits to the Louvre, where his favorite painters were Rubens, Watteau, Boucher, and Fragonard, which helps explain his affection for the pink, red, and pearly flesh tones which dominate his late pictures. Paintings in California Palace of the Legion of Honor, Haggin Art Galleries; drawing in Honolulu Academy of Arts.

Renzi, Clement. p. 215. American. An artist from Fresno, he studied in New York at the Sculptors' Workshop, was commissioned to do major work, *The Visit*, for the Fresno Civic Mall in 1964.

Reynolds, Sir Joshua. p. 101. English. 1723–1792. Dean of 18th-century British portrait painters, Reynolds, the well-educated friend of Dr. Johnson, Oliver Goldsmith, and Edmund Burke, raised art in England to the status of literature. Best examples of his work in the U.S. are at the Henry E. Huntington Art Gallery.

Ribera, José. p. 129. Spanish. 1588–1652. He worked in Italy where he was court painter to the Spanish Viceroy of Naples. From Caravaggio he adopted the use of side lights to add drama to his portraits and religious paintings. He combined realism with intense religious feeling and a certain Spanish austerity, as in the great portrait of Galileo in the Timken Gallery.

Rigaud, Hyacinthe. p. 145. French. 1659–1743. Official painter at the court of Louis XIV, specialized in grandiose state portraits of sumptuously dressed, aristocratic sitters. He ran a busy studio, turned out more than 2,000 portraits in the course of a 62-year career. Few of them are exclusively by his own hand; there were assistants to fill in the draperies and costumes. The portrait of Louis XIV in the J. Paul Getty Museum is typical.

Rivera, Diego. p. 167. Mexican. 1886–1957. Influenced by ancient art of Mayas and Aztecs, Rivera rejected his Paris training to create a revolutionary new school of Mexican painting, expressed in huge frescoes depicting the social and political history of Mexico, especially the episodes of popular revolt. Rivera's colors and subject matter were chosen with deliberate intent to appeal to the masses, to enable them to identify with a new folk image, but his style never degenerated to the insipid level of socialist realism. Frescoes at San Francisco Art Institute and City College of San Francisco.

Rodin, Auguste. pp. 174, 175. French. 1840–1917. The most famous sculptor of the late 19th century, Rodin was strongly influenced by Michelangelo, but brought certain techniques of impressionism to his vigorous, expressive, and sensitive work, notably a concern with the play of shadow and light on bronze. Work in California Palace of the Legion of Honor; drawings in Maryhill Museum of Fine Art.

Romney, George. p. 92. English. 1734–1802. A contemporary of Reynolds and Gainsborough, Romney specialized in portraits of English ladies. Work in the Huntington Art Gallery.

Rosenthal, Toby. p. 187. American. 1848–1916. A popular master of the kind of richly detailed anecdotal painting that developed from Dutch genre and the post-Revolution moralizing of Greuze, and persisted throughout the 19th century. California Palace of the Legion of Honor.

BIOGRAPHICAL NOTES

Rouault, Georges. pp. 81, 252. French. 1871–1958. This highly individual French expressionist was apprenticed in youth to a stained-glass window maker, used heavy black contours in his mature work to enclose areas of brilliant gem-like color. Works in Henry Gallery, La Jolla Museum, San Francisco Museum of Art.

Rowlandson, Thomas. p. 100. English. 1756–1827. A lusty, high-living man, Rowlandson studied art in Paris at the age of 16, went through a fortune left him by his French aunt, earned his living subsequently in London with reams of robust and sometimes ribald caricatures and lively illustrations for such books as Fielding's *Tom Jones*. Works in Huntington Art Gallery, Achenbach Foundation for Graphic Arts.

Rubens, Peter Paul. pp. 220, 233. Flemish. 1577–1640. Born in Westphalia, educated in Antwerp, Rubens became court painter to the Duke of Mantua, then to the Spanish Viceroys of the Netherlands. Works in M.H. De Young Memorial Museum, Crocker Art Gallery, Seattle Art Museum, Fisher Gallery, University of Southern California.

Schwitters, Kurt. p. 125. German. 1887–1948. Drafted into the German army in World War I, he was put in charge of hunting down deserters, scrambled the office files so effectively that no trace of the fugitives was ever found. From this antiestablishment activity it was just a step to dadism; Schwitters became leader of the movement in Germany, a master of ludicrous, calculated nonsense, but a genius when it came to collage. See work in Los Angeles County Museum of Art.

Sesto, Cesare da. p. 226. Italian. 1477–1523. A leading Renaissance painter, it is thought that he studied under Leonardo da Vinci. Works in M.H. De Young Museum.

Shahn, Ben. p. 131. American. 1898–. Born in Lithuania, he came to America at the age of 8, went to night school in Brooklyn (1913–17), worked by day as lithographer's apprentice. Work in Santa Barbara Museum of Art.

Siqueiros, David Alfaro. p. 277. Mexican. 1898–. One of the most gifted artists of the modern Mexican Renaissance, Siqueiros has spent more time in political agitation than in painting, more days in jail than in the studio. His realistic pictures vibrate with social indignation and emotional expressiveness. Work in Arizona State University Art Gallery.

Taddeo di Bartolo. p. 262. Italian. 1362–1422. A Sienese master, Taddeo was one of the early Italian humanists who liberated painting from the hieratic stiffness of Byzantine iconography. His altarpieces are in Perugia and Siena; his *Coronation of the Virgin* is a treasure of the Kress Collection in the University of Arizona.

Tamayo, Rufino. p. 157. Mexican. 1899–. Born in Oaxaca of a Zapotecan family, Tamayo studied briefly at San Carlos Academy in Mexico City, left because he found the instruction academic and sterile, immersed himself in the archeology of his native land and in modern French painting. His own art owes something to both. It has the brilliant color of folk art, is devoid of the social propagandizing of most Mexican painting, a fact that has caused Tamayo to be denounced by his more chauvinistic countrymen. Works in Crocker Art Gallery, Arizona State University.

Tennent, Madge. p. 288. American. 1889–. Born in South Africa, she was taken as a child prodigy of 13 to study at the Academie Julien in Paris, where her instructor was Bouguereau. Her real mentors were Gauguin and Renoir, from whom she learned the lessons of pure color, lyric line, and voluminous form which characterize her celebrated portraits of the Polynesian race, which she has painted with increasing authority during a 40-year residence in Hawaii. Works in Honolulu Academy of Arts and Tennent Art Foundation, Honolulu.

Tiepolo, Giovanni Battista. p. 202. Italian. 1696–1770. Last of the great Venetian decorative painters, he summed up the baroque in splendid altarpieces and operatic ceiling frescoes, one of which you will find transferred to canvas and installed in the Kress Collection of the Seattle Art Museum. See also the *Triumph of Flora* in M.H. De Young Memorial Museum, and drawings in Achenbach Foundation for Graphic Arts.

Tintoretto, Il. p. 38. Italian. 1518–1594. His real name was Jacopo Robusti (Il Tintoretto means the Dyer). Born in Venice, he sought to emulate Titian, painted great religious canvases suffused with a visionary light and peopled with elongated mannerist personages that anticipate El Greco. The influence of his magic lighting effects extends further, to Rembrandt and all the way to the impressionists. Work in J. Paul Getty Museum.

Tobey, Mark. p. 259. American. 1890–. Born in Wisconsin, worked as commercial artist in Chicago from age of 17, taught at Cornish School, Seattle, in 1922–23, was introduced to Chinese brushwork at Seattle Art Museum and by Chinese student at University of Washington. Work in

DURER

COROT

DEGAS

REMBRANDT

...The Artists Represented in This Book

Seattle Art Museum, San Francisco Museum of Art, Henry Art Gallery, Portland Art Museum, Santa Barbara Museum of Art, Art Gallery of Greater Victoria, Washington State Capitol at Olympia.

Tomme, Luca di. p. 202. Italian. 1330–1389. Influenced by Simone Martini, this Sienese painter achieved an emotional breakthrough in art by humanizing the cold and rigid figures of Byzantine religious painting. The *Crucifixion*, from the Kress Collection at M.H. De Young Memorial Museum, is a good example of his work.

Turner, Joseph Mallord William. p. 77. English. 1775–1851. Born in London, the son of a barber, Turner was a precocious youth, was admitted to the Royal Academy school at the age of 14, exhibited at the Royal Academy two years later. One of his Venetian views is in the Huntington Art Gallery.

Van Goyen, Jan. p. 213. Dutch. 1595–1656. One of the first and best of the 17th-century landscape painters, he captured the silvery light, vast sky, and transparent air of the Netherlands, depicted his sea-hemmed native land in all of nature's moods. *The Thunderstorm* in M.H. De Young Memorial Museum is characteristic.

Van Gogh, Vincent. p. 42. Dutch. 1853–1890. Son of a Calvinist pastor, this expressionist painter spent the most productive years of his short and emotionally turbulent life in France, where his devoted brother Theo directed an art gallery devoted to modern painting. Works in Honolulu Academy of Arts, Los Angeles County Museum of Art.

Van Dyck, Anthony. p. 93. Flemish. 1599–1641. Born in Antwerp he was the most gifted of Rubens' pupils, made his reputation as a portraitist in England where, from 1632, he was court painter to Charles I. His portraits of the English aristocracy set a model which would be followed throughout the 18th-century. Works in Los Angeles County Museum of Art, Fisher Gallery, University of Southern California.

Van der Weyden, Roger. p. 32. Flemish. 1399–1464. Religious piety, warm human sympathy invest the work of this major 15th-century artist who was born in Tournai and prospered in Brussels, where, from 1436 he was the official painter of the city. His deep feeling and flawless technique are both evident in the Huntington Art Gallery's *Madonna and Child*.

Velasquez, Diego Rodriguez de Silva y. p. 29. Spanish. 1599–1660. Born in Seville of Portuguese ancestry, became official painter to the Spanish court in Madrid, painted his sitters with perceptive understanding of their character. Work in Fine Arts Gallery of San Diego.

Veronese, Paolo. p. 67. Italian. 1528–1588. Called Il Veronese because he was born in Verona (his real name was Paolo Cagliari), he made his career in Venice, where he painted the pomp and pageantry of an imperial city, peopled by men and women in sumptuous costumes. The Inquisition took him to task for including too many secular details in his religious pictures. Works in Timken Gallery.

Warshaw, Howard. p. 114. American. 1920–. Artist in residence at the University of California at Santa Barbara, he has done a number of notable murals, often experiments with new plastic media. Major work in UCSB.

West, Benjamin. p. 90. American. 1738–1820. Son of Quaker pioneers, West was born in Pennsylvania, became interested in art as a child when Indians showed him how they mixed pigments to paint their faces. Works in Santa Barbara Museum of Art and Stanford Art Museum.

Wood, Thomas Waterman. p. 173. American. 1823–1903. Born in Montpelier, Vermont, he made reputation as a portrait and genre painter in Quebec, Washington, D.C., Baltimore, and New York. See *Moses the Baltimore News Vendor*, at California Palace of the Legion of Honor.

Wyeth, Andrew. p. 266. American. 1917–. Born in Chadds Ford, Pennsylvania, he was trained by his father, the well known painter and illustrator, N. C. Wyeth, and had his first one-man show in New York at the age of 20. Works in Arizona State University Collection of American Art, Charles and Emma Frye Museum, Los Angeles County Museum of Art.

Zuniga, Francisco. p. 277. Mexican. 1914–. Born in Costa Rica, where he was an apprentice to his father, a religious stone carver, Zuniga has become one of the outstanding contemporary sculptors of Mexico. His work is strongly influenced by native Indian culture and pre-Columbian sculpture. Work in Phoenix Art Museum.

Zurbaran, Francisco de. pp. 110-111. Spanish. 1598–1664. Born in Estramadura, Zurbaran was the purest, most ascetic, and most austere of the Spanish baroque painters. Monastic orders were his chief patrons; he painted many solitary portraits of monks in silent contemplation, pictures that combine realism with mysticism and communicate an intense feeling of religious devotion. Works in Santa Barbara Museum of Art, Fine Arts Gallery of San Diego.

DAVID   GOYA   TINTORETTO   MONET

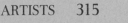

SELECTED READINGS

This selected list of readings is designed for those who seek a general introduction to art as well as those who wish more specialized references. Most of the works listed are available at good bookstores and libraries. You should also check museum bookshops for illustrated handbooks and catalogs of permanent collections and current exhibitions.

The following are among the Western museums publishing catalogs or handbooks of their collections: Arizona State College; Art Gallery of Greater Victoria; California Palace of the Legion of Honor; Crocker Art Gallery; Charles and Emma Frye Museum; Fine Arts Gallery of San Diego; Haggin Art Gallery; Honolulu Academy of Arts; Henry E. Huntington Art Gallery; J. Paul Getty Museum; Los Angeles County Museum of Art; M. H. De Young Memorial Museum; Pasadena Art Museum; Phoenix Art Museum; Read Mullen Gallery of Western Art (Phoenix, Arizona); Santa Barbara Museum of Art; Seattle Art Museum; Sedgwick Collection in the University of California at Santa Barbara; Sigmund Morgenroth Collection in the University of California at Santa Barbara; Leland Stanford Junior Museum; University of Arizona Art Department; University of Oregon Art Museum; Utah Museum of Fine Arts.

Ames, Van Meter. *Zen and American Thought*. Honolulu: University of Hawaii Press, 1962.

Baldinger, Wallace S. *The Visual Arts*. New York: Holt, Rinehart and Winston, 1960.

Behrman, S. N. *Duveen*. New York: Vintage Books, 1952.

Belloni, Gian Guido. *Prehistoric to Classical Painting* (in *Art of the Western World*). New York: Golden Press, 1962.

Bradius, A., ed. *The Paintings of Rembrandt*. Vienna: The Phaidon Press; New York: Oxford University Press.

Brown, Milton. *American Painting from the Armory Show to the Depression*. Princeton: Princeton University Press, 1955.

Carli, Enzo. *Florentine Painting* (in *Art of the Western World*). New York: Golden Press, 1963.

Cheney, Sheldon. *A World History of Art*. New York: The Viking Press, 1937.

Clarke, Eleanor P. *Designs on Prehistoric Pottery of Arizona*. Tucson: University of Arizona Press, 1933.

Davis, Robert Tyler. *Native Arts of the Pacific Northwest* (from the Rasmussen Collection of the Portland Art Museum). Stanford, California: Stanford University Press, 1949.

Dorra, Henri. *The American Muse*. New York: The Viking Press, 1961.

Drucker, Philip. *Cultures of the North Pacific Coast*. San Francisco: Chandler Publishing Co., 1965.

Ecke, Gustav. *Chinese Painting in Hawaii: In the Honolulu Academy of Arts and in Private Collections*. Honolulu: University of Hawaii Press, 1966.

Flanner, Janet. *Men and Monuments*. New York: Harper, 1957.

Frankenstein, Alfred, and Norman Carlson. *Angels Over The Altar: Christian Folk Art in Hawaii and the South Seas*. Honolulu: University of Hawaii Press, 1961.

———. *After the Hunt; William Harnett and other American Still Life Painters*. Berkeley: University of California Press, 1953.

Gardner, Helen. *Art Through the Ages*. New York: Harcourt, Brace & Co., 1936.

Gassner, John, and Sidney Thomas, eds. *The Nature of Art*. New York: Crown Publishers, 1964.

Geldzahler, Henry. *American Painting in the 20th Century*. New York: The Metropolitan Museum of Art, 1965.

Getty, J. Paul. *The Joys of Collecting*. New York: Hawthorn Books, 1965.

Gifford, James. *Archaeological Explorations in Caves of the Point of Pines Region, Arizona*. Tucson: University of Arizona Press, 1965.

Gladwin, Harold, with Emil W. Haury, E. B. Sayles, and Nora Gladwin. *Excavations at Snaketown: Material Culture*. Tucson: University of Arizona Press, 1965.

Goldscheider, Cecile. *Rodin*. Paris: Les Productions de Paris, 1962.

Goldwater, Robert, and Marco Treves, eds. *Artists on Art*. New York: Pantheon Books, 1945.

Goodrich, Lloyd, and Edward Bryant. *American Art of Our Century*. New York: Praeger, 1962.

Grant, Campbell. *The Rock Paintings of the Chumash*. Berkeley: University of California Press, 1965.

Gudiol, José. *The Arts of Spain*. New York: Doubleday & Co., 1964.

Gunn, S. W. A. *A Complete Guide to the Totem Poles in Stanley Park*. Vancouver: W. E. G. Macdonald, 1965.

Harrison, G. B. *The Bible for Students of Literature and Art*. New York: Doubleday & Co., 1964.

Haskell, Francis. *Patrons and Painters*. New York: Alfred A. Knopf, 1963.

Hawthorn, Audrey. *People of the Potlatch*. Vancouver: Vancouver Art Gallery with the University of British Columbia, 1956.

Heizer, Robert F., and Martin A. Baumhoff. *Prehistoric Rock Art of Nevada and Eastern California*. Berkeley: University of California Press, 1962.

Holm, Bill. *Northwest Coast Indian Art: An Analysis of Form*. Seattle: University of Washington Press, 1965.

Huth, Hans. *Nature and the American: Three Centuries of Changing Attitudes*. Berkeley: University of California Press, 1957.

Inverarity, Robert Bruce. *Art of the Northwest Coast Indians*. Berkeley: University of California Press, 1950.

Janson, H. W., and Dora Jane Janson. *The Story of Painting for Young People from Cave Painting to Modern Times*. New York: Harry N. Abrams, 1952.

———. *History of Art*. New York: Prentice-Hall, 1962.

Kandinsky, Wassily. *Concerning the Spiritual in Art*. New York: George Wittenborn (Speed-o-Lite Offset Edition), 1965.

Kitson, Michael, and Alexandra Wedgwood. *English Painting* (in *Art of the Western World*). New York: Golden Press, 1964.

Klee, Paul. *The Diaries of Paul Klee, 1898-1918*. Berkeley: University of California Press, 1964.

Kramrisch, Stella. *The Art of Nepal*. New York: Asia House Gallery, 1964.

Kuh, Katharine. *The Artist's Voice* (Talks with Seventeen Artists). New York: Harper and Row, 1960.

Larkin, Oliver W. *Art and Life in America*. New York: Holt Rinehart & Winston, 1960.

Lassaigne, Jacques. *Spanish Painting from the Catalan Frescoes to El Greco, Spanish Painting from Velasquez to Picasso*. Geneva: Editions Albert Skira, 1952.

Lebrun, Rico. *Rico Lebrun Drawings*. Berkeley: University of California Press, 1961.

...Publications on World Art

Lee, Sherman E. *History of Far Eastern Art.* New York: Harry N. Abrams, Inc., 1964.

Levey, Michael. *A Concise History of Painting from Giotto to Cézanne.* New York: Frederick A. Praeger, 1962.

Lipman, Jean, ed. *What is American in American Art.* New York: McGraw-Hill, 1963.

Martin, Gregory. *Flemish Painting* (in *Art of the Western World*). New York: Golden Press, 1964.

Mendelowitz, Daniel M. *A History of American Art.* New York: Holt, Rinehart and Winston, 1960.

Morley, Grace L. McCann. *Abstract Art on the Pacific Coast* (in *The World of Abstract Art* edited by The American Abstract Artists). New York: George Wittenborn Inc., 1957.

Murray, Peter and Linda. *A Dictionary of Art and Artists.* Harmondsworth, England: Penguin Books, 1959.

Myers, Bernard S. *Understanding the Arts.* New York: Henry Holt, 1958.

———. *Modern Art in the Making.* New York: McGraw-Hill, 1959.

Pearson, Ralph M. *The Modern Renaissance in American Art* (Work and Philosophy of 54 Distinguished Artists). New York: Harper and Row, 1954.

Quinn, Robert M. *Fernando Gallego and the Retablo of Ciudad Rodrigo.* Tucson: University of Arizona Press, 1961.

Raynal, Maurice, and Jean Leymarie. *History of Modern Painting* (2 vols). Geneva: Editions Albert Skira, 1949.

Read, Herbert. *A Concise History of Modern Painting.* New York: Frederick A. Praeger, 1964.

Reitlinger, Gerald. *The Economics of Taste: The Rise and Fall of the Picture Market, 1760-1960.* San Francisco and New York: Holt, Rinehart and Winston, 1961.

Remington, Frederic. *Pony Tracks* (in *Western Frontier Library*, illustrated by author). Norman: University of Oklahoma Press, 1964.

Rewald, John. *The History of Impressionism.* New York: The Museum of Modern Art, 1961.

Richardson, Edgar Preston. *American Painting, the Story of 450 Years.* New York: Thomas Y. Crowell.

Robb, David M., and J. J. Garrison. *Art in the Western World.* Third edition. New York: Harper and Brothers, 1953.

Rodman, Selden. *The Insiders.* Louisiana State University Press, 1960.

Rosenberg, Harold. *The Anxious Object: Art Today and Its Audience.* New York: Horizon Press, 1964.

Rosenthal, Erwin. *The Changing Concept of Reality in Art.* New York: Wittenborn, 1962.

Rothschild, Lincoln. *Sculpture Through the Ages.* New York: McGraw-Hill, 1942.

Rublowsky, John. *Pop Art: Images of the American Dream.* London: Thomas Nelson and Sons, 1965.

Schmeckebier, Laurence E. *Modern Mexican Art.* Minneapolis: University of Minnesota Press, 1939.

Seitz, William C. *The Art of Assemblage.* New York: The Museum of Modern Art in Collaboration with the San Francisco Museum of Art, 1961.

Seligman, Germain. *Oh! Fickle Taste.* Cambridge, Mass.: Bond Wheelright, 1952.

———. *Merchants of Art: 1880-1960.* New York: Appleton-Century-Crofts, 1961.

Selz, Peter. *German Expressionist Painting.* Berkeley: University of California Press, 1957.

Seuphor, Michel. *A Dictionary of Abstract Painting.* London: Methuen & Co., 1958.

Shoolman, Regina, with Charles Slatkin. *The Story of Art, The Lives and Times of the Great Masters.* New York: Halcyon House, 1940.

Sickman, Laurence, and Alexander Soper. *The Art and Architecture of China.* Harmondsworth, England: Penguin Books, 1956.

Simon, Charlie May. *Art in the New Land, Stories of American Artists and Their Work.* New York: E. P. Dutton & Co., 1945.

Spaeth, Eloise. *American Art Museums and Galleries, an Introduction to Looking.* New York: Harper and Row, 1960.

Spicer, Edward H. *Cycles of Conquest: The Impact of Spain, Mexico, and the United States on Indians of the Southwest, 1533-1960.* Tucson: University of Arizona Press, 1962.

Stock, Chester. *Rancho La Brea.* Los Angeles: Los Angeles County Museum, sixth edition, 1956.

Sullivan, Michael. *An Introduction to Chinese Art.* Berkeley: University of California Press, 1960.

———. *The Birth of Landscape Painting in China.* Berkeley: University of California Press, 1962.

Sunset Book Editors. *The California Missions, A Pictorial History.* Menlo Park: Lane Book Company, 1964.

Swann, Peter. *Art of China, Korea, and Japan.* New York: Frederick A. Praeger, 1963.

Sypher, Wylie. *Rococo to Cubism in Art and Literature.* New York: Random House, 1960.

Taft, Robert. *Artists and Illustrators of the Old West, 1850-1900.* New York: Scribner's, 1953.

Taylor, Joshua C. *Learning to Look, A Handbook for the Visual Arts.* Chicago: University of Chicago Press, 1957.

Toffler, Alvin. *The Culture Consumers: A Study of Art and Affluence in America.* New York: St. Martin's Press, 1964.

Tseng Yu-ho. *Some Contemporary Elements in Classical Chinese Art.* Honolulu: University of Hawaii Press, 1963.

Ulanov, Barry. *The Two Worlds of American Art.* New York: The Macmillan Company, 1965.

Venturi, Lionello. *Italian Painting: The Creators of the Renaissance.* Geneva: Editions Albert Skira, 1950.

PINCE-NEZ AND MAGNIFYING GLASS are employed to good effect in Connoisseurs of Prints. Humorous 1905 etching is by John Sloan (Achenbach Foundation for Graphic Arts).

...Works Illustrated in the Book

Photographs not listed below were provided by the museum noted with the picture. William Aplin: 23; 49; 50; 55. Peter Balestrero: 274 left.
F. W. Barnes: 253. Beinlich: 274 right. Jim Bishop: 231. Leo Bukzin: 12; 67. Century 21 Center, Inc.: 45 lower. Glenn Christiansen: 11; 24.
Homer Dana: 37. Alice Erving: 110. Robert C. Frampton: 86. G. H. Freyermuth: 224 lower. Jim Healy: 225 upper and lower. Rebecca Holmes:
99 upper and lower. Johnson: 276 lower; 277 upper. Vilem Kriz: 89 lower; 143; 165; 176; 180; 181 upper and lower; 197; 234; 235 upper. Ray
Manley: 84. V. Covert Martin: 182 left. Jack McDowell: 149 left and right; 215; 230 upper, lower. Al Monner: 248,298. Moulin Studios 179.
David Muench: 9; 44; 124. Dennis Nelson: 164; 194; 235 lower. Don Normark: 242 left and right. Karl Obert: 90 left and right. Fran Ortiz
(courtesy San Francisco Examiner): 156; 224 upper. Marvin Rand: 59. Raymond M. Sato: 281. I. Serisawa: 72; 136 upper and lower; 137 upper
and lower; 277 lower. Vano-Wells-Fagliano: 140. Julian Wasser: 73. Darrow M. Watt: 132; 133. Western Ways: 269 left and right. Sam
Weston: 135. Baron Wolman: 61 upper and lower; 167. David John Zeitlin: 71. Musées Nationaux: 314; 315.

This book was printed in Menlo Park, California, and bound in San Francisco. Color and duotone pages were lithographed by Peninsula
Lithograph Company, Menlo Park, using film for two-color pages made by Balzer Shopes, San Francisco. Jacket and cover were lithographed
by Stecher-Traung Schmidt, and binding was by Cardoza Bookbinding Company, both of San Francisco. Body type is Palatino, type for
heads is Horizon, composed by Haber Typographers, Inc., New York City. Paper for body pages is Mountie Enamel furnished by Northwest
Paper Company, Cloquet, Minnesota; paper for single-color signature is Beckett Text furnished by the Beckett Paper Co., Hamilton, Ohio.

INDEX

Pages in *italic* type show the artist's works.

The Fine Arts Gallery
of San Diego

Timken Gallery

La Jolla Museum of Art

Long Beach Museum of Art

Los Angeles County
Museum of Art

J. Paul Getty Museum

Pasadena Art Museum

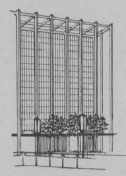

Henry E. Huntington Art Gallery

Santa Barbara Museum of Art

M. H. De Young
Memorial Museum

The California Palace of
the Legion of Honor